THE
SPECIAL CHILD
HANDBOOK

THE
SPECIAL CHILD
HANDBOOK

Joan McNamara and Bernard McNamara

An Information House Book

HAWTHORN BOOKS, INC.
Publishers / NEW YORK
A Howard & Wyndham Company

362.783
MI69s

Library of Congress Catalog Card Number: 76–41979

ISBN: 0-8015-6994-X

2 3 4 5 6 7 8 9 10

To our children,
because of the joy they bring us

Contents

7 Legal Rights of Those with Special Needs

Development of Legal Rights of Those with Special Needs • Legislation for Special Needs • The Courts and Special Needs • The Education of All Handicapped Children Act • The Legal Rights of Students • Basic Human Rights • Foster Care • Adoption • Legal Responsibilities of Parents • Legal Remedies • Directory

8 The Future of Your Child with Special Needs

The Changing Quality of Life • Education: A Basic Right • Mutual Communication • Planning a Future Through Education • Preparing for Adulthood: Independence for the Person with Special Needs • Retardation: An Example of Evolution of Perceptions • Preparing a Future • Directory

Selected, Annotated Bibliography

Index

Acknowledgments

The authors wish to thank Pat Kravik for her personal and professional help, Ron Shafer and the many parents, professionals, and people with special needs who have shared.

Information House wishes to thank Ron Shafer, Anne Brink, Beverly Savage, Dian Smith, and Buck Moffett.

THE
SPECIAL CHILD
HANDBOOK

Introduction

It is estimated that more than twenty percent of all children in the United States are handicapped in some way. The handicaps, and their causes, vary widely.

Some handicaps, such as facial deformities from a cleft palate, are usually correctable. Others, such as blindness, can be serious and permanent. Sometimes the severity of the same disease varies—one out of every ten black Americans has a sickle cell anemia trait that causes only minor problems, but one of every four hundred has the actual crippling blood disease.

Of the three million babies born in the United States each year, about one of every ten has a birth defect serious enough to require special attention. Some of these are the result of hereditary conditions; others are simply due to genetic accidents. Children with disabling conditions resulting from illnesses also require special attention. And accidents alone leave fifty thousand children permanently damaged each year.

In past centuries physical handicaps were considered works of the devil. It was thought that only families of poor moral character or inferior status had children with birth defects. A seriously handicapped or retarded child was something to be hidden away. And it was not until the nineteenth century—in 1817, when a school for the blind was opened in Hartford, Connecticut—that special education became available for disabled children in the United States.

During the early 1900s many cities began to establish special schools or special classes in public schools for handicapped children. But progress remained slow right up to the late 1960s, when a series of lawsuits brought by parents of handicapped children resulted in important court decisions extending the rights of these children to free public education. In 1975 Congress passed a law requiring the states to provide a "free, appropriate education" for all handicapped children by 1978.

Parents are also fighting for the recognition that their children are human beings with limits, rather than limited human beings. There have been many terms for problems a child may have that can limit the potential to grow and function—terms such as *handicapped, disabled,* and even *crippled.* But this book will focus on the *child who has special needs* because of a limiting physical, emotional, or mental condition.

For parents who may have children with special needs, finding help is not often easy. When we adopted a child who had had polio and needed crutches and braces to walk, we found ourselves somewhat at a loss, a bit confused, and even a little angry at our inability to meet his needs. Even though both of us had had some professional experience with children, we were unprepared for many of the practical aspects of dealing with the problems of a child with special needs.

It was one thing to read about these problems in textbooks and quite another to live with them as parents. We found ourselves overwhelmed by daily realities, by a lack of resources and services, and often by a lack of knowledge and compassion on the part of the very professionals on whom we had depended to provide guidance and help.

We had to search out on our own.

It was often difficult and frustrating, especially in the beginning. But eventually we found, demanded, or created the services and support we needed. With each of our five children with special needs we had to face different problems—hearing loss, missing limbs, paralysis, burn scars, sight loss, emotional problems, and learning disability. And each time we began anew.

We discovered along the way that perhaps because of, not in spite of, the problems we have shared, all our children are strong, independent individuals we are proud to raise.

Because of our own experiences we decided that there should be a nontechnical manual for parents of children who have special needs (and for professionals, too). Not just a listing of names and addresses of professional agencies, nor a dictionary of medical terms, nor even a comforting philosophy of life with a special-needs child —although all these aids are necessary. But a handbook based on personal, as well as professional, experience with the essential information required to get help for your child and to help you as a parent to understand and deal with your own feelings.

The purpose of this book is to guide you through the experience of raising a child with a disability, from the initial recognition of a problem to possibilities for the future. The goal is to help you ensure that your child, although handicapped, is cherished and recognized as a valued person.

1

When Special Needs Appear

Parents are often the first to know if their child has a disability, whether they fully recognize it or not. Whether they accept it or not.

Some disabilities, such as a missing limb, are obvious. But others are more subtle. Your child may have problems coping with ordinary situations. He or she may be slow to develop in certain areas. You might notice a serious lack of coordination. Or maybe you just have a gut feeling that something is not quite as it should be.

Whatever your concern, it is important to seek professional guidance regarding your observations—if for no other reason than to prove your fears are unwarranted. Some disabilities are easily correctable. In other cases children need special treatment, discipline, and education. But early detection is important if a child is to avoid some of the emotional scars children with special needs must often endure when their particular needs are unrecognized, misunderstood, or unmet.

Many children have disabilities as the result of childhood accidents or illnesses. Many others develop disabilities as the result of birth defects, some of which are quickly detected and some of which are not. Birth defects are abnormalities present at birth. Not all are disabling: Extra toes and small birthmarks are examples of birth defects that usually do not limit a child in any significant way. But other defects can cause serious disabilities, such as mental retardation or blindness, and in extreme cases, some defects can even be fatal.

Birth defects can result from a difficult pregnancy or delivery. If an expectant mother is exposed to disease or to certain drugs or toxic substances, the unborn child can be adversely affected. Tragic examples are the so-called Thalidomide children, who were born with such abnormalities as missing arms and legs after their mothers took the drug Thalidomide during pregnancy. The childhood disease rubella, commonly known as German measles, when contracted by a pregnant woman, often causes blindness, deafness, or retardation in newborn babies.

Birth defects can also be hereditary or simply the result of chance mutations.

How do you tell if your child has special needs? There are signs to watch for—and preventive actions to take—as your child grows. The search can begin even before a child is born or, in the case of parents with histories of birth defects in their families, before a child is planned. In such cases the question becomes "Will our child have special needs?" And if heredity is the major concern, there are ways to get at least an uncertain answer.

GENETIC COUNSELING

Some hereditary conditions can be predicted by genetic counseling during pregnancy or even before conception. People who have had a handicapped child born to them, or who have a personal or family background of hereditary problems, such as sickle cell anemia, a debilitating blood disease, can use counseling to determine the possibilities of such conditions recurring in their future children.

A few months before Donna and Frank Santini were married, they visited the genetic counseling center of a university hospital. Donna's younger sister, Diane, was retarded, and Donna wanted to determine if her children could also be retarded. The doctors and the researchers at the center reviewed the medical histories of both Donna's and Frank's families. They tested the couple's blood and made other studies. They especially probed the circumstances surrounding Diane's conception, birth, and subsequent diagnosis of retardation.

The center's staff concluded that Diane's retardation was not caused by hereditary factors. They were able to tell Donna and Frank, with reasonable certainty, that they would be able to plan a family with no more fear of having a retarded child than any other couple.

Genetic counseling is not always that conclusive. Often hereditary conditions cannot be pinpointed, and tests do not yet exist to determine or predict certain problems. For example, the Chou family's two-year-old daughter, Sara, was born with osteogenesis imperfecta, a condition sometimes called brittle bones. So they sought genetic guidance before planning a second child. Using current medical theories and studies, the doctors still could provide no concrete answers, no ironclad guarantees.

The Chous considered the risks involved and decided not to give birth to any more children. If they felt the need for more children in the future, they would adopt.

Genetic counseling is not for every couple. It can sometimes predict hereditary conditions, but perhaps only twenty percent of significant birth defects are genetic, or hereditary, in origin. Those hereditary conditions that can be predicted represent a small minority of the more than two thousand genetic disorders that have been defined to date.

But experts estimate that about one in five hundred couples can benefit from genetic counseling. For many couples who want to find out if they will be risking passing on hereditary disabilities to their children such counseling can predict the odds of a disability based on whatever family, personal, and scientific data are available. While it is not always possible to tell whether a particular problem will be passed on, because of scientific breakthroughs in the field of genetic research in recent years patterns of inheritance are now known for several hundred genetic disorders.

If you want to know which hereditary conditions can be predicted through genetic counseling or whether the problems you are concerned about are hereditary, your family doctor is the logical place to start. You can obtain further information on birth defects and genetic counseling from the National Foundation–March of Dimes; its address is listed in the resource directory at the end of this chapter.

Genetic counseling is best performed by a team of professionals consisting of a geneticist (a physician who specializes in genetics), researchers, laboratory technicians, and social workers. They generally operate out of hospitals or clinics. The field has expanded substantially in recent years; do some checking before you decide on a specific counseling service. The counseling staffs at some centers may lack the experience and professional training needed to deal with parents in a compassionate and positive way.

Costs vary, but you should figure on spending at least two hundred dollars, including the testing that will be required. Your medical insurance might cover part of the cost. Some states have their own genetic screening programs. New York, for example, provides some genetic testing free for residents. Check with the department of health in your state to see whether such services are available where you live.

You will probably have to visit the center several times for interviews and testing. Prospective parents must provide a complete medical and family history. This will include information on racial and ethnic backgrounds; previous pregnancies, abortions, miscarriages, or stillbirths; health information about the couple's previous children as well as about their brothers, sisters, parents, and grandparents.

The counselors will be especially interested in any diseases that are common in the families of either partner. Among the more serious hereditary diseases are Tay-Sach's disease, which is a progressive and fatal mental deterioration that affects infants; Huntington's chorea, a progressive degenerative disease whose symptoms often do not appear until middle age, when it may have been passed unknowingly to children; and dwarfism.

The couple will be given blood tests and other biochemical tests to determine if either of them is a carrier of potentially adverse hereditary traits or diseases. For example, enzyme tests can turn up possible abnormalities that cause metabolic disorders, such as the degenerative joint disease called ochronosis.

After all the interviewing and testing is done, the genetic counselors should provide guidance on what the hereditary risks are if you should decide to have children. It is not always possible to tell whether a particular problem will be passed on to future children, but counselors can usually advise about the mathematical probabilities of certain types of problems being passed on and can help you to understand what these probabilities mean.

But parents must make their own decisions. For some just knowing what the odds are is reassurance enough. They are willing to take the chance and be prepared, if necessary, to have a child with a handicap. For others even a one-in-five-hundred chance is too risky, and they decide not to bear children. For still others the prospect of a child with a disability is frightening, but they are willing to face a high risk because their wish to have children is strong.

For these couples, as well as for parents without family histories of hereditary diseases, the answer to the question "Will our child have special needs?" can be provided only after a pregnancy is actually under way.

DURING PREGNANCY

Birth defects can occur simply because an expectant mother failed to take good care of her health. Most birth defects happen during the first three months of pregnancy. Yet most women are not sure they are pregnant until after the early weeks. Defects can be caused by influences upon the mother during early pregnancy from such factors as rubella (German measles), poor nutrition, exposure to radiation, or even smoking and drinking.

Poor prenatal care can cause retardation of the unborn child. Virus infections can cause malformations. So can the use of drugs, especially narcotics and barbituates. Pregnant women should never take any drug, including aspirin, except under the advice of a physician. And even then only after she has questioned the physician vigorously about side effects. The obstetrician should also be consulted about any medication prescribed for a pregnant patient by another doctor. About five percent of all pregnant women have toxemia, a condition with symptoms that include high blood pressure, retention of fluid, and excessive weight gain. If not treated and controlled, toxemia can lead to premature births and lower intelligence of any offspring who survive.

The message is clear. If you are an expectant mother, take care of yourself. Your health can affect your unborn child.

AMNIOCENTESIS

When a pregnancy is already under way, it is sometimes possible to determine whether certain chromosomal, sex-linked, or biochemical abnormalities exist within the unborn child that could cause future medical problems. Conditions such as Down's syndrome, a type of retardation sometimes called mongolism, can be determined by a procedure called amniocentesis. Amniocentesis is a test done on a child while it is still inside its mother's uterus. It is a test primarily for diseases (both hereditary and nonhereditary) with chromosomal or biochemical bases. Genetic counselors often recommend the test to back up their own studies and conclusions. It is also used for older pregnant women. When it comes to childbirth women are considered "older" after the age of forty because the risks of having a child with some type of chromosomal abnormality dramatically increase after that age. The incidence of mongolism, for instance, is ten times greater.

An amniocentesis is done about the fourteenth week of pregnancy. Though it is a delicate and serious procedure, it requires a hospital stay of only a few hours in most cases. A local anesthetic is used, and the woman should feel only slight discomfort.

The test basically involves the insertion of a hollow needle through the wall of the expectant mother's stomach and into the uterus. Inside the uterus is a fluid, called amniotic fluid, in which the fetus, or unborn child, floats during the entire nine months of pregnancy; this fluid protects the fetus like a liquid bumper. In the test the needle is used to withdraw some of that fluid.

The fluid that is extracted contains microscopic cells from the baby. These are taken to a laboratory, where they are grown and studied to determine if there is an unusual number of chromosomes, faulty enzyme production, or other conditions that can indicate potential abnormalities.

Amniocentesis can pinpoint certain potential diseases in the unborn child. For example, Down's syndrome can be detected through examining the number of chromosomes found in the cells from the baby. Of the more than one hundred disorders with a known protein or enzyme irregularity, over sixty can be detected by amniocentesis. Such testing also can indicate Tay-Sach's disease, certain chronic lung diseases, and Marfan's syndrome, a complex series of abnormalities, including a defect of blood vessels near the heart and the eyes, and elongated limbs. Since through an amniocentesis the sex of a child can be determined, it is sometimes used for families with a history of certain sex-linked abnormalities.

But like other genetic testing amniocentesis has limitations. Many conditions cannot as yet be detected prior to birth. No test presently exists for prenatal determination of such diseases as sickle cell anemia, Huntington's chorea, dwarfism, and hemophilia (a blood disease limited to males, sometimes called bleeder's disease).

While the certainties are limited, amniocentesis can aid some prospective parents in cases when there is reason to believe that the child a woman is carrying could have a disabling condition, such as retardation. Some parents can be told in advance and with reasonable certainty that the unborn child has or does not have a specific number of conditions. Thus they are better able to consider the risks.

That was the case for the Kirks, who married in their late thirties, when both were moving ahead in their careers. They didn't begin their family until Mrs. Kirk had just turned forty. Although they felt ready for children, the Kirks did not feel prepared to care for a retarded child. And they knew that the risk of conceiving a retarded or otherwise handicapped child was many times higher for Mrs. Kirk than for an expectant mother ten years younger.

Mrs. Kirk decided to undergo amniocentesis early in her pregnancy. The analysis of the genetic makeup of the fetus she was carrying showed that their unborn baby did not have certain known chromosomal or biochemical abnormalities. This did not mean the Kirks were home free. Their child could still develop some other kind of problem or have a condition not detectable by amniocentesis. But it did clear up the possibility of a number of problems.

Four months later Mrs. Kirk gave birth to a daughter, Danyea. The baby was five weeks premature, but otherwise there were no complications. Both mother and daughter are doing fine today. Danyea is, as her father puts it, "a love." But the Kirks do not plan other pregnancies. "We don't want to push our biological luck," Mr. Kirk says.

You and your physician may decide to consider amniocentesis if you are an expectant mother whose family has a history of certain medical problems or if, like Mrs. Kirk, you are over the age of forty. Some doctors quite readily urge such patients to undergo this test. Others are more reserved about recommending it because of the dangers involved in surgical procedures with the mother and the unborn child. With amniocentesis there is a slight risk of damaging the uterus or hurting the unborn child. But when done carefully, this is unlikely to happen, and the quality of the surgical procedure is improving daily.

If amniocentesis does indicate a strong possibility that your child could have serious birth defects, the final choice of how to handle that possibility is up to you. The choices range from taking the risk and preparing for the child's potential needs to terminating the pregnancy through abortion.

You must analyze your own health, including your mental health. You must consider what the effect of having a child with special needs will be on you, your marriage, and your family. Or, if abortion is an option, you must decide whether or not you can live with that alternative—for some people the guilt about abortion might be more difficult to live with than a seriously retarded or handicapped child.

If you choose to take the risk the question of whether your child will have special needs may be answered when the baby is born, just as it is for many other new parents who may never have considered the possibility that their child could have any problems.

DETECTING PROBLEMS AT BIRTH

Some birth defects are immediately obvious at birth. They can range from clubfoot or cleft lip to missing limbs or some obvious forms of retardation. In the past, when expectant mothers were often routinely drugged at childbirth and fathers were relegated to pacing the hospital waiting room, only the doctor assisting the delivery or the hospital staff present initially knew if a baby was born with major defects. But these days more and more couples are sharing the actual moment of birth. They, too, may immediately know if there are any obvious problems, rather than hearing about it hours later from hospital personnel.

Being an eyewitness to the delivery of a baby with a deformity— especially your own child—is a jolting experience. But parents who have together experienced the birth of such a child say the immediate knowledge of the problem during a time of intense personal sharing helped them deal with it better.

Consider the experience of Leonard and Christa Burns. They had enthusiastically prepared for the birth of their second child, feeling more relaxed and confident than they had during their first venture into parenthood two years before, when their son Craig had been born. Leonard was in the hospital's labor and delivery rooms with

Christa, and he was present at the moment of birth. As their second child began to emerge, it was clear that he was another son. It was equally clear that he was missing part of an arm—his right arm, which ended just above where an elbow should have been.

"It was really a shock," Christa confides frankly. "Waiting all those months, expecting a perfectly healthy baby like Craig, and then seeing Kevin with his stump," she says, adding: "But he was our kid, from our love. It was better to know then, together, than to be told hours afterward by some stranger."

Leonard agrees. "We felt guilt and disappointment, even anger, for a good part of the first year," he recalls. But "we helped each other and worked it out for the most part. Kevin's handicap has become less of a pity and a tragedy and is just something that has to be dealt with on a continuing basis," he explains.

Today Christa concludes, "Kevin is a tough, healthy kid who happens to have an artificial limb."

Some disabilities in newborn babies can be obvious to the hospital staff but not to the parents. These can include heart conditions, certain types of mental retardation, and an abnormality known as spina bifida, where exposure of the spinal column can cause paralysis and loss of sensation and can be accompanied by other difficulties.

Other problems can be detected shortly after birth through the routine observation and testing. Among the most important tests is the APGAR test, which is now given to most babies within sixty seconds after birth. The delivery room nurse or obstetrician rates each of five vital signs of the newborn infant on a scale of zero to ten. The signs are: *A*—appearance or coloring; *P*—pulse; *G*—grimace, or reflex irritability; *A*—activity; and *R*—respiration.

The test is usually repeated five minutes after birth, and the two scores are compared for accuracy or progress. The scores predict neurological or other problems as well as chances of survival.

Newborn babies are also usually given blood tests during their hospital stay. A physical examination is done to test reflexes, movement of limbs, and functioning of vital organs, as well as to measure the size of the head. A head significantly larger or smaller than usual can mean potentially serious brain damage. A small amount of a baby's urine or a drop of blood taken from the infant's heel is also analyzed to check for a disease known as phenylketonuria, or PKU, which can lead to severe retardation. This is commonly known as the PKU test.

Early detection is important. For example, if PKU is discovered, the child can immediately be put on a strict diet that may prevent the almost inevitable retardation that would otherwise occur. Doctors say that most PKU cases can be effectively treated by diet, if diagnosed immediately after birth.

Sometimes the most obvious conditions are the least serious and the most correctable. Some birth defects that previously would have been permanent handicaps can be corrected at birth or soon after. Plastic surgery can correct physical problems, such as facial abnormalities from cleft lip. Clubfoot is another frequent deformity that can be easily corrected.

Often the conditions that, in their initial stages, are the least discernable have the most tragic consequences. An example is Tay-Sach's disease, which leads to degenerative decline and, ultimately, to death at an early age.

Indeed, many disabilities—major or minor—aren't apparent at the time of birth. So the question of whether a child has special needs sometimes can't be answered until later.

THE EARLY YEARS

Only about half of all birth defects are actually detected at birth. Many more are discovered during the early years of the baby's life, usually during the first year.

Problems are frequently spotted by the baby's pediatrician during monthly checkups. An extreme weight gain or loss, suspicious lumps, unusual head size, and slow development are among the clues that tell the doctor that there is a possibility of an abnormality. These could be slight or serious, momentary or long lasting. But they are clues that should not be ignored.

Once again, it is the parents who may be the first to detect these signs, although they may not fully understand their significance. At first Bill and Julie Fine thought it was only a matter of time before their infant son, Michael, would grab for the brightly colored mobiles they had hung over his crib, just as his older brother had. Each day Julie would give her husband a recitation of Michael's accomplishments. He laughed, he lifted his head, he rolled over.

But Michael never reached out for the gay bouncing fish. It became Bill's ritual during Michael's sixth and seventh months to ask: "Has he reached for the fish yet?" The answer was always "Not yet." Julie hung them lower in the crib, but she knew that Michael's arms only struck them by accident, just as he only seemed to look at their faces by chance. They waited until Michael was eight months old before they expressed their fears to their pediatrician.

The doctor had already been suspicious, he told them, and he referred them to an ophthalmologist, whose tests confirmed their fears: Michael was blind. He had some vision but not enough to really see, not enough to be able to discern shapes and colors. Or bouncing fish dangling from a mobile.

The ophthalmologist could not even tell the Fines why their son was blind, only that it was an irreversible condition. He referred them to a clinic at a local university, where they met with physicians, special educators and counselors, and other parents whose children were enrolled in a special program for blind children. The supportive program eventually helped the Fines to overcome their sorrow and to begin the process of helping Michael to learn to cope with his handicap.

To check for normal development, you should make sure your baby has monthly checkups during the first year and at least annual or semiannual physicals thereafter. You can also measure your child's development at home with the aid of such charts as the Denver Developmental Screening Scale or the Gesell Scale. You can find these or similar charts in books on child development, such as those listed in the directory for this chapter.

There are also tests you can do at home. You can test your baby's hearing by standing behind the child and clapping your hands loudly to see if he turns his head toward the noise. Or wave a brightly colored object around and behind your baby to see if her eyes follow its movement.

Remember that each child has his or her own rate of development, which can be slower or faster than an exact date on a chart says it should be. And slower or faster than that of any other kid on the block. Don't get caught up in comparing your child to the child of a friend or neighbor, or even to another child in the family. Each child is unique; he may be slow in walking or fast to talk. But there should be a steady progress forward.

If there seems to be an abnormal delay in the time it takes a child to reach a milestone, such as walking or talking, don't hesitate to ask your doctor about it. Often parents, who see their child daily, are most aware of what could be a potential developmental problem.

Sometimes a problem may turn out to be completely different from what it seems to be. At age two and a half Carey Anne Brown was a determined and active toddler. Although she seemed a bright child—she was able to dress herself, feed herself, and ride a tricycle—her mother, Connie, worried that there might be something wrong with Carey Anne's development. She hadn't begun to talk much; she just made a few garbled sounds. She wouldn't follow simple directions and would often throw herself on the ground screaming.

Connie's mother suggested that Carey Anne was going through a phase that she'd grow out of. Her mother-in-law told her not to worry—Carey Anne was just in the "terrible twos" and, besides, children in her family had always talked late. Even her pediatrician seemed to dismiss her concerns as those of a nervous, first-time mother. And her husband said she was spoiling the child.

Finally, without telling anyone, Connie made an appointment at a developmental clinic in a nearby city. She took Carey Anne for testing and returned two weeks later for the results. The social worker explained that while Carey Anne did not have any apparent neurological impairment, she did have a moderate hearing loss. Connie recalls a profound sense of relief that her daughter did not have brain damage or serious emotional problems. She had a problem that could be dealt with easily once it had been recognized.

Even though there can be tremendous variations in the development of different children, slow development can be an indication of possible problems. Don't panic, but be aware and watchful. For example, if your child hasn't talked by the time he is two and a half years old, don't accept excuses such as "He'll grow out of it" or "It's only a stage." Even if it is only for your own peace of mind, take your child to a doctor, including a second doctor or specialist if your family doctor or pediatrician doesn't satisfy your concerns.

If you feel that there is a problem, don't be put off by the argument that your child is too young to be tested. According to Dr. Jean Smith of Bellevue Hospital's Eye Clinic in New York City there is no magic age to test children. Dr. Smith says she has tested and fitted glasses on a one-month-old infant.

A child who has a terminal or chronic disease, such as leukemia, may display initial symptoms that could be attributed to other common and more innocent childhood problems—fatigue, occasional fevers, frequent infections—and even a good pediatrician may overlook these warning signals. When they persist, however, a cautious doctor should schedule additional routine and more complex tests or refer the child to a specialist.

Not all handicaps are diagnosed at an early age. Some children's special needs do not become evident until they start school.

ENTERING SCHOOL

It is usually during the first few grades that learning disabilities and mild hearing or sight problems are recognized. These problems are generally not serious enough to interfere with preschool activities, although they may show up in the form of disruptive behavior. In a school situation, however, the problems become magnified.

Marc was a child who always seemed to be marching with his left foot when the others in his kindergarten class were on their right foot. At naptime he was restless, and during group activities he had trouble following directions. At the first parent-teacher conference his teacher suggested sight and hearing tests for Marc. She also felt that Marc was immature for his age and advised that he repeat kindergarten the next year. Meanwhile, she suggested that his parents exert firmer discipline with him.

By the time of the second conference vision and hearing problems had been ruled out. The teacher reported that Marc was functioning at a retarded level, which possibly had an emotional basis. She referred him and his parents to the school psychologist who—after a series of tests and parent interviews—concluded that Marc's hyperactivity, poor coordination, and general immaturity indicated learning disabilities.

Learning disabilities are problems—usually organic but sometimes caused by emotional or environmental factors—that limit or inhibit a child's potential to learn and grow intellectually. Some are relatively minor, others are serious. For example, the severity of dyslexia can range from a difficulty in distinguishing between *b*'s and *d*'s, to the inability to read at all. The tragedy occurs when a learning disability, which could be helped by patience and training, is ignored and the child falls into the cycle of failure, discouragement, and increased failure.

Marc was scheduled to be passed into the regular first grade with additional tutoring for special attention to his specific difficulties. As he grows and matures, he may learn to compensate for his problem.

CHILDHOOD ILLNESSES

Many people don't seem to realize that childhood illnesses can lead to serious disabilities. Many seemingly harmless and "normal" sicknesses can cause high fever, and high fever over a prolonged period can result in damage to sight, hearing, and the general functioning of the brain and other body organs.

Because Umberto never really looked sick when he first came down with rheumatic fever, his parents had difficulty realizing the severity of the illness. In the hospital he had been restless and even troublesome to the staff. When he returned home, his family became careless about Umberto's daily medication. He had a relapse and was returned to the hospital longer than should have been necessary, emphasizing to his parents the seriousness of the results of his fever. Without continuing long-term treatment Umberto would have more relapses with a dangerous impact on his health. His condition was permanent.

These days people seldom think of childhood illness as being incapacitating. Chicken pox is an expected annoyance. But there are shots to guard against measles, and there is a vaccine for polio. One result of such immunization is a near disappearance of some formerly common diseases. But they are not gone completely. In the United States each year, for example, there are one or two isolated cases of polio, a virus disease that can cripple children and adults. Public health officials continually stress the importance of complete and current immunizations for all children and adults.

These urgings are increasingly ignored, partly because past immunization programs have been so successful that Americans have forgotten the potential dangers of childhood diseases. Federal public health officials estimate that twenty million of the fifty-two million American children under the age of fifteen are not immunized against one or more of the childhood diseases for which vaccines are available. For example, more than nineteen million are not immunized against polio, nearly twelve million lack protection against measles, and twenty-five million are unprotected against mumps.

Alarmed by public apathy about low immunization, the Carter administration in spring 1977 launched a program to immunize twenty million American children against major childhood diseases by the fall of 1979. The program also includes a permanent system to insure the immunization of the three million children born each year.

"Our national failure to protect our young from preventable diseases is a shocking disgrace," Joseph A. Califano, Jr., secretary of Health, Education, and Welfare, said in announcing the program. The goal of the program is to raise the immunization levels of American children to above 90 percent from 60 percent when the program began.

Immunization is a preventive medical measure against certain diseases that can occur only once in a person's life. There sometimes are side effects, such as a slight fever. But serious reactions are rare.

Immunizations and vaccinations should be a regular part of your child's health care. For a complete list of basic immunization needs for children by age, see the chart in the directory section of this chapter. In general, they include diphtheria, pertussis, and tetanus shots; an oral polio vaccine; a measles vaccine; a mumps vaccine; and a rubella (German measles) vaccine; plus boosters.

Just as you must protect your child against the disabling consequences of diseases, you must be on your guard for another great disabler—accidents.

ACCIDENTS

Accidents, too, take their toll on the health of children. LeRoy McCall was six years old when he ran into the road after a ball and was hit by a car traveling at a high speed. LeRoy was unconscious for two weeks. He suffered massive head injuries and a number of broken bones. When he regained consciousness, he seemed unaware of his surroundings. His doctors and parents feared his severe injuries might cause permanent retardation. After many months of therapy LeRoy was slowly able to regain speech and movement, but he remains ungainly. He attends school at a cerebral palsy center because of his continued lack of balance, for which he receives special attention.

A child weighing seventy-five pounds or less is just no match for a two-ton metal object traveling at a high speed. The results of such confrontations—if the child survives—can be brain damage, loss of sight, hearing, speech or vision; loss of movement; or the total destruction of a small child as a functioning human being. Accidental shooting, water accidents, fires, and accidental poisoning are other cripplers, especially of preschool children.

The National Research Council refers to accidents as a "neglected epidemic." Each year almost two million children are temporarily incapacitated by accidents, and another fifty thousand are permanently injured. The majority of childhood accidents involve cars; the victims are children as passengers, children as pedestrians, and children as bike riders.

All too often, the disabilities of a child-victim of an accident are painfully obvious. But in other cases they are not. If your child is involved in an accident, watch closely for the evolvement of special needs.

IF YOU FEEL SOMETHING IS WRONG

If you feel your child, for whatever reason, may have special needs, the first step—even before calling your family doctor—is to observe the child. Try to determine what it is that makes you feel there is a problem. Make a list of symptoms or problems that arise. The purpose is not to make your own diagnosis but to try to clarify what the problem may be.

The next step is to seek professional help. Your concern may be baseless, but worrying about it won't help. "I never tell parents not to worry," says one doctor. "I tell them not to worry alone." Sometimes unusual behavior is symptomatic of emotional stress or other conditions that can be altered with relative ease. But such determinations should be made by a professional. If after you observe your child, you feel something is wrong, it is time to find diagnostic assistance.

DIRECTORY

Organizations

American Foundation for Maternal and Child Health, Inc.
30 Beekman Place, New York, N.Y. 10022

Society for the Protection of the Unborn Through Nutrition
Suite 603
17 North Wabash Avenue
Chicago, Ill. 60602

Planned Parenthood—World Population Center for Family
Planning Program Development
810 Seventh Avenue
New York, N.Y. 10019

National Foundation—March of Dimes
P.O. Box 2000
White Plains, N.Y. 10602
(Information on birth defects)

Chapter References

BOOKS ON PREGNANCY

Consumer Reports. *The Consumers Union Guide to Buying for Babies.* New York: Warner Books, 1975. $1.95.
(Information on drugs during pregnancy and other safety issues.)

Hazell, Lester Dessez. *Commonsense Childbirth.* New York:
Berkley, 1976 (paperback edition). $1.95.

McCaulhey, Carole Spears. *Pregnancy After 35*. New York:
E. P. Dutton, 1976. $7.95.

McCleary, Elliot H. *New Miracles of Childbirth*. New York: Dell,
1977. $1.95.

Null, Gary and Steve, and the staff of the Nutrition Institute of
America. *Successful Pregnancy*. New York: Pyramid Books, 1975.
$1.50.

BOOKS AND PAMPHLETS
ON GENETICS AND HANDICAPS

Apgar, Virginia, M.D., and Beck, Joan. *Is My Baby Alright?*
New York: Pocket Books, 1974. $1.95. (Birth defects and
prevention of them.)

Greenblatt, Augusta. *Heredity and You*. New York: Coward,
McCann, and Geoghegan, 1974. $7.95. (Includes information
on amniocentesis.)

Harris, Maureen, ed. *Early Diagnosis of Human Genetic Defects:
Scientific and Ethical Considerations*. U.S. Department of Health,
Education, and Welfare, April 1975, publication no. (NIH) 72–75.[1]

BOOKS AND PAMPHLETS ON CHILDREN

Braga, Laurie and Joseph. *Learning and Growing: A Guide to
Child Development*. Englewood Cliffs, N.J.: Prentice-Hall, 1975.
$2.95.

Fontana, Vincent J., M.D. *A Parent's Guide to Child Safety*.
New York: Thomas Y. Crowell Co., 1973. $5.95.

Shiller, Jack G., M.D. *Childhood Illness*. New York: Stein and Day,
1974. $2.95.

Spock, Benjamin, M.D. *Baby and Child Care*. New York: Pocket
Books, 1976. $1.95.

[1] All U.S. government publications are available from the Superintendent of Documents, U.S. Government Printing Office, Washington, D.C. 20402.

U.S. Department of Health, Education, and Welfare, *Your Baby's First Year*. 1975. Publication no. (OCD) 73–15. 75¢. (Also in Spanish.)

————. *Your Child from One to Three*. 1973. Publication no. (OCD) 73–56. 35¢.

————. *Your Child from Three to Four*. 1973. Publication no. (OCD) 73–57. 45¢.

Routine Childhood Immunization Schedule

Disease	Immunization	Dates given	Boosters
"Polio" (poliomyelitis)	Sabin vaccine: TOPV (trivalent oral poliovirus vaccine)	3 doses within the first 6 months of life, at roughly 1–2 month intervals (usually at 2, 4, and 6 months of age)	18 months, 4 years
Diphtheria/ tetanus/ pertussis (whooping cough)	DPT: diphtheria and tetanus toxoids combined with pertussis vaccine	Same as polio	Same as polio, but after 6 years of age booster given every 10 years of Td, combined tetanus and diphtheria toxoids (adult); first booster given at 14–16 years
Tetanus			For "clean" wounds no tetanus booster needed if child has had DPT or Td immunization within 10 years; for "contaminated" wounds, within 5 years[1]

[1] But many doctors now prefer to use a gamma globulin preparation instead of the booster in these cases.

Routine Childhood Immunization Schedule (continued)

Disease	Immunization	Dates given	Boosters
Measles/ mumps/ rubella ("German" measles)	M/M/R: combined ("trivalent") vaccine of measles, mumps, and rubella (or measles and rubella) can be given in place of single shots of each vaccine[1]	Not before 1 year of age (unless serious epidemic)	No booster
Tuberculosis (TB)	Tuberculin test is not an immunization but an injection in the skin to test for the disease	Before (or at) time of DPT and measles vaccine	Annually if TB prevalent; annual X-ray if test remains positive

Smallpox[2]

[1] If you are a woman who has not had these vaccines yourself, or the diseases, it is important that you be vaccinated promptly. Rubella is an especially potent cause of serious birth defects. You could pass it on unsuspectingly to a woman in early pregnancy, or you could have the disease yourself without knowing it when pregnant. If you are already pregnant, you can have a blood test done to determine if you have had the disease before (many adults are just not sure), since the vaccine cannot be given to a pregnant woman.

[2] Immunization is not now given, since illness and death related to the vaccine is a greater threat than the risk of the disease itself. Exceptions are made for those traveling to known smallpox areas of the world.

2

Getting the Right Diagnosis

When you sense, or know, something is not right about your child's development, it may be difficult for you to find the right place to go for help. You may have taken a while to recognize and accept the signs of problems, but once you have, you want specific answers to your questions. Now you look for information about your child and what these signs mean. Is there something wrong after all? What is wrong? How did it happen? What can be done about the problem? What can you expect from the future? Are your fears realistic or unfounded?

WHERE TO LOOK FIRST

If you can be open enough to admit your concerns to yourselves and to share them with others to whom you turn with your questions, the first step in getting help will be less frightening. Usually, the first person people turn to for help is their family doctor.

The Family Doctor

Traditionally, people expect their general practitioner to answer all questions. They turn to their family doctor during every life crisis—from cancer to baldness, from minor first aid to complex social and moral questions. But a family doctor is not a magician. He will feel more competent, and will be more competent, answering questions in areas for which he has been trained. While a family doctor may be able to identify any general medical aspects of a situation, you cannot expect him to be all knowing, especially in the frequently specialized area of handicaps and the special physical, psychological, and educational needs of children with them.

Sometimes your doctor may be hesitant about sharing negative information with you about your child. He may indeed suspect, or know, that something is not quite as it should be. But he may be unsure about what could be done even if you are told. Sometimes, when parents press, a doctor will acknowledge that there is a basis for their fears. The doctor may actually have known the truth for some time and not shared it with them.

The answer you receive may not reassure or satisfy you: "Don't worry, it's just a stage," "Everything's fine," "Wait and see," "It's too soon to tell," or some variation on the same theme. Ask yourselves if your concerns are real, if you are seeing the symptoms clearly. If you feel that you are being honest with yourselves, then don't hesitate to ask your doctor again, or to find another source to question about your concerns. You are with your child more than anyone else, and on a more intimate level. You know your child better than any other person. Remember, too, that it sometimes is more difficult for people to accept what they see, especially if it could hurt their child or themselves.

Chances are, however, that your doctor will be understanding of your concerns. Your doctor may be able to refer you to a specialist for an expert diagnosis of the situation or for needed services. But even though he is a competent doctor, he may not always know specifically which specialist you should see, particularly when the expert you need could be a speech therapist, tutor, educational specialist, family counselor, or one of many other professionals. A survey by the American Academy of Pediatrics found that the majority of private practitioners are unable to utilize community resources effectively.

If your doctor is unfamiliar with or uncertain about the nature of your child's problem, he may be equally uncertain about where to refer you. The McGrath family took their young son, Kim, to their family doctor for guidance in dealing with the paralysis polio had caused in Kim's legs. The young doctor, who was trained after development of the preventive polio vaccines, had never even seen a case of polio. In the United States new cases of polio are rare, even though they occur quite often in the Asian country where Kim was born. The young doctor could only refer the family to a private hospital where he was affiliated because he didn't know of any other facility. It was up to the McGraths to continue the investigation after that.

Keeping all of this in mind, however, it is fair to ask your family doctor if he feels your concern is warranted or there is a need for other follow-up. Your doctor may be able to refer you to a specialist or diagnostic facility that he knows of, or you may have to do some searching on your own. But you should make certain that reports from specialists are sent back to your family doctor for follow-up if he is continuing the routine health care of your child. Often, such referral reports will be automatically sent to your family doctor, but sometimes he will have to request them, and you will have to sign a release to allow it. A specialist or clinic usually will not treat the common cold or an infected finger, so the routine, total health care of your child should be the province of one doctor, or group of doctors, that you can see on a regular basis.

Other Community Resources

There are various resources for diagnostic services in most communities. Your local hospital may be adequate for your child's special needs, particularly for standard tests, such as X rays and blood tests. A more sophisticated facility, however, such as a teaching hospital or university-affiliated hospital, will be more likely to have the advanced technology and specialists you will need for a thorough and complete diagnosis.

Today, in some places, it is possible to have tests conducted locally and then have the data sent to a specialized center elsewhere. Even if you eventually use the services of a specialized clinic or program near you, you are likely to want the "best" doctor at the "best" facility to see your child. You may end up disagreeing with the "expert" however, and perhaps you will eventually accept the original opinion of your own doctor or local service. Nonetheless, you still may feel that you need several opinions and that the doctors must be the best that you can afford (or go into debt for) before you make up your own mind about the situation. Ultimately, you will have to accept one set of test results and medical conclusions, in whole or in part, and follow the recommendations. But you may need time, more than anything else, more than any fancy testing. You may need time just to think, to get your bearings, and to adjust to your new situation before you decide on a course of action.

Even if your child's special need is strictly a medical problem, many other services may be needed outside the medical sphere. If your child has a hearing loss, for example, hearing specialists will diagnose the nature of the problem and suggest possible types of surgery, medicine, or hearing aids that the child might need. But this is not enough: Is the loss serious enough to warrant special training or special schooling? Where is this available? How can you and your child deal with the emotional factors, temporary or permanent, of the handicap? How will you pay for all of this?

Specialized Programs

You may need someone to translate medical jargon into everyday language. You may need someone to take the time just to sit down and talk to you. This is where a comprehensive program, such as a university-affiliated clinic, may have advantages for you: They can often draw upon the resources of other disciplines within their own facility, such as social workers, psychologists, speech therapists, occupational therapists, educators, and other skilled professionals. They may also have their own resources—clinics, schools, parent groups—to whom they can refer you.

Research projects are frequently part of university-affiliated programs. These have many good features: Your child can receive needed services, possibly services not available anywhere else in the area; the quality of professional and nonprofessional staff is usually high; and the information obtained through these services may benefit your child and other children.

However, there may be negative factors, too. Because of the "publish or perish" syndrome in many universities, which means a faculty member must publish articles or risk loss of status or job, some research projects are initiated because of motivations other than a desire to further knowledge in a field. It's possible for the children or others who are "subjects" of such a project to be used as "guinea pigs" and ignored as individuals. Tests and theories may be used merely because they are available or untried, rather than for their value in the situation.

Government Programs

Traditionally, government-administered programs have been downgraded by the general public. The local county or municipal government facility may have been originally designated to care for the poor, and some people, for real or imagined reasons, may question the quality of care. For example, there once was a certain social stigma attached to public hospitals. Today, most government-sponsored programs are able to provide quality services; in many cases they have superior programs. Sepcialized programs and research projects, often not adequately financed in the private sector or through medical insurance, are frequently funded through governmental sources.

Government bureaucracy is often an uncoordinated jumble. The many programs operated or financed by the government should cooperate with one another, but sometimes they are hidden from one another and from those who could benefit from them. In theory, one locally administered program should be able to refer you to the program down the hall in the county office building; in practice, they may not even know the program exists.

Your local department of health may be able to refer you to some sources of financial assistance. They may also have programs such as "well baby" clinics for regular pediatric checkups, immunization programs, or a visiting nurse service. In addition, they may administer a crippled children's program.

Every county in your state probably has a crippled children's program, which is a federal program authorized by Congress as part of the Social Security Acts in 1935. It uses federal, state, and local "matching" funds and is known in each locality by various names: Medical Rehabilitation, Bureau for the Handicapped, Crippled Children's Program, or other titles. These may be administered by state and local bureaus, such as the departments of health, education, or Social Services. See the directory to this chapter.

THE SCHOOLS

Some problems do not become apparent until a child is school-aged, and the school may be the first to notice the problem. Schools have been asked to do a multiplicity of jobs beyond teaching the traditional "three Rs," from training better drivers to seeing that all children receive immunizations. Sometimes educators are not pleased with these mandates, and many parents feel that there are too many responsibilities left to the schools instead of to the family. The new federal education laws that mandate public educational services for all children by 1978, regardless of handicapping conditions, puts an even greater responsibility on schools. Some schools and teachers will not be ready for this. Others will have already begun, with varying degrees of enthusiasm and success. In the meanwhile, schools, teachers, administrators, and parents will be struggling with new programs and ideas.

School officials must identify what special educational services a child needs, and they often assume that you, as the parents, have already taken care of any medical or other diagnosis and treatment the child requires. Regardless of the problem, your child needs regular medical checkups and may need outside diagnosis by a specialist to determine the total scope of special needs, which includes the findings of the school. The diagnoses—by outside specialists and by the school—may seem at odds with each other. This may be because each looks at the child from their own perspective, often overlooking the child as a whole in order to concentrate on the child's specific problems. Ask both sources for full explanations, and for consultations with each other if possible. It could just be two conflicting jargons with the same conclusions, or overlapping ideas, or two separate test results. You may want or need a third opinion to be able to make a judgment.

Your local school or board of education may have had experience with some of the local services you need, and it may be willing to help you get them. School boards in some areas, rather than hiring their own staff for special services, may have a contract for these services with outside facilities. These may be just what you need. On the other hand, you may be the first parent informed enough about your rights and privileges to contact them. Your education, as you "learn the ropes," may be the school's as well.

Remember that the school's mandate is to educate the child, while you, as parents, have a more complex and all-encompassing task. So while all the school may need is a psychological test to have your child placed in the proper educational setting, you may need much more; most importantly you need an understanding of what is being done and why. What a school recommends may not be best when you consider the needs of the total child—not just educational needs, but physical and emotional needs as well.

Questions About School Placement

If a school, after appropriate testing, decides that your child should be placed in a special class for retarded or learning-disabled children, for example, you need to ask many questions before you act upon this decision: What do they mean by retardation, by learning disability? What does that term mean to you? What will the placement offer your child specifically in terms of the problem the school has identified, and more generally in terms of the child's total development? Will the school reevaluate your child periodically? How often, by what means? What testing did they use to come to their conclusions? Does your child need an evaluation for possible genetic problems, or for other problems, both physical and emotional? What other alternatives have they considered, what other alternatives exist? Is your child functioning at a retarded level or displaying symptoms of a learning disability because of some other problem or multiple problems that need to be dealt with? These might include hearing or sight dysfunction; language delay or speech disorder; emotional problems; poor physical condition caused by infection, anemia, or another medical problem. Whom do you talk to about these questions that you want answered?

If the school—or other diagnostic specialists along the way—can answer all or most of your questions to your satisfaction, then you have a diagnosis you can live with—at least, for the time being. If you still have unanswered questions, you may have to do more searching, as will be discussed later in this chapter. But first, you should have some understanding of what a diagnosis is and what it can, or cannot, tell you.

WHAT IS A DIAGNOSIS?

In the simplest terms, the diagnosis defines—or should define— a problem. Sometimes the description includes the origin of the problem, which may be important for the treatment of your child or for the welfare of children that you might bear in the future. Defining a problem combines two integrated factors: testing and the tester. On the one hand, there are many different testing measurements that by themselves have little meaning. On the other hand, there are professionals who interpret the tests and who without using a systematized approach would have to depend on a more random, hit-and-miss method.

What you should look for is a professional who can utilize standardized tests and procedures in such a way that the information received can be transferred and documented by another person of equal competence—in other words, someone who can accurately use a test and pass that information on to someone else just as accurately. You should start with the premise that clinicians are not perfect and neither are all tests. But the combination of competent clinicians and sound tests should be able to provide some reasonable answers.

The Confusing Language of Testing

Compounding the problem of human error and bias and testing inadequacies is the specialized language surrounding any testing, whether for physical, emotional, mental, or educational disabilities. Each specialized jargon involves a vocabulary with unique meanings and distinct definitions whose purpose is to help a clinician in one specialty know exactly what another specialist is talking about when information is transferred.

To a parent the jargon can be incomprehensible. It often seems more like a case of using a three-syllable word when a one-syllable word would do, or of deliberately trying to confuse the parent. Sometimes the jargon can make a condition sound much worse than it is. When Gordon Harper's new teacher read his records at the start of the school year, she saw that someone had written: "Gordon has a problem of chronic ebistaxsis." This had the ring of a formidable and frightening condition or perhaps some rare syndrome. The teacher had the good sense to look up the term in a medical dictionary, where she discovered that it meant no more than that Gordon had an excessive number of nosebleeds.

The use of this selective language lends a certain aura of mystery, almost sacredness, to professionals, especially doctors. In reality the use of professional jargon is often an attempt by specialists to speak of many different problems in precise terms. It is not easy to be precise when talking of human beings, each so unique and so variable from the other. Nevertheless, if you don't understand the terms that are thrown at you by clinicians and others, ask them to explain them in plain English.

A diagnosis may range from an educated opinion based primarily on experience to a very formalized and standardized set of measurements. There are two basic questions to ask: First, does the test answer the question that you expect it to answer? Psychologists use the term *valid* to describe this qualification. Secondly, is the test reliable? This means, will it always give the same answer, or close to it, when the same person is tested under the same set of circumstances?

Why Tests Are Used

Some of the more informal tests are useful in charting the general development of children. These are tests in which the observational and scoring procedures are not as standardized as more precise tests, but they can have a high reliability when conducted by examiners with adequate training and experience. Many pediatricians, for example, use a test called the Gesell Scale to gauge normal infant and child development. Such scales help the pediatrician organize the routine information about your child's growth during regular physical examinations. The Gesell Scale, which charts the timing of events, such as when babies start to walk and talk, has a high reliability rate if used appropriately. However, parents sometimes tend to use this type of information inaccurately. When they scan the behavior charts in such child-development books as Dr. Arnold Gesell's classic *Infant and Child in the Culture of Today*, they may suffer anxiety attacks because their child does not meet the standards exactly when the charts indicate he should. For such parents a more helpful book is *Infants and Mothers: Differences in Development* by Dr. T. Berry Brazelton. Based on his long-term studies of infant development, Dr. Brazelton's book compares the development of three babies of the same age, each of whom have very different ways of reacting to their environment and different rates of growth well within the acceptable norms for their age.

Even tests that are known to have flaws can be useful. The normal height and weight scales presently used throughout the United States were developed and standardized on a specific population—white Euro-Americans in the northeastern United States—that did not include many ethnic groups that were larger, smaller, taller, or shorter than this norm. But trained clinicians who are aware of this qualification could still use this test for children from groups outside of the original norm as long as they take into consideration the range of that particular grouping and the uniqueness of the individual. A child may be measured and, in comparison to the height standards for her age, be considered exceptionally tall. If her parents are also exceptionally tall people, however, clinicians would not jump to conclusions about possible abnormal development or malfunctioning of glands. Similarly, a child at the lower end of the scale would not be rushed off for lab tests if both parents are also short in stature. What is important is the accurate but sensitive use of a test that has a good reliability and validity. These scales have now been revised with a base that covers a wider segment of the population.

Psychological Testing

One form of standardized testing that is widely discussed but also widely misunderstood is psychological testing. American folklore gives the psychologist powers beyond what the testing would ever allow. Psychological testing, such as an IQ test, is a very useful tool, but it has very definite limits. No test is considered to be even close to one hundred percent accurate.

Since an IQ test is given to children as part of a total evaluation, regardless of handicap, let's examine what an IQ, or intelligence quotient, is and what this score will reasonably predict. IQ scores are nothing more than a ratio. If we have a five-year-old child functioning like a four-year-old, the ratio would be four-fifths (80 percent) of normal, giving an IQ score of 80. We would expect that under normal circumstances this ratio would continue and the score would remain constant, so that at age ten the child would be functioning as an eight-year-old, and the ratio would still be four-fifths, giving an IQ score of 80. In contrast, a child who is functioning like a six-year-old at age five would have an IQ of 120. At age ten he should be functioning like a twelve-year-old. A child who is five years old, functioning as an average five-year-old, would have an IQ of 100. We can also give this "average" child a percentile score of 50, which means that half the population would score better than she would and half worse. IQ scores are not absolute. They could be 5 points higher or lower than the recorded score, or with less reliable tests as much as almost 10 or 15 points either way. A child with an IQ score of 90 is considered to have a score within the range of 85 to 95. The ranges, or allowances of deviation, from the recorded scores change from test to test, so that one test will use one range, a different test another. But if the child with the 90 IQ took the same test one hundred times without any change in circumstances, the scores would all fall within the range we've mentioned. The majority of the time the scores should fall within 5 points either higher or lower than the first recorded score.

The reliability and margin of error vary from test to test. There are over one thousand different psychological tests that measure various kinds of abilities and disabilities. Some are considered to be extremely reliable, and others are less reliable as general measures of intelligence, since they concentrate on a single specific task or aspect of intelligence.

Group Tests

Group tests, which most of us have seen or taken at one time or another, have some advantages over tests given individually. There is little relationship between the person taking the test and the person giving the test, which should lead to less human bias. Today, group tests are corrected by machine and given to very large populations as a way of getting standardized scores for college entrance, civil service examinations and grade-level achievement tests for children.

There are disadvantages to the impersonal group test, too. The examiner will make no allowance for the distraction of the test subject (and children, especially, are very distractible), for fatigue, or for other stresses that can lead to a lower performance on that test. With individual testing, however, a trained tester can make allowances and exceptions, or redesign the battery of tests to the specific needs of the child. A tester should use more than one type of test to give a broader scope to the evaluations.

Tests Are Not Magic

Formal IQ testing measures academic potential, and over long periods of time some tests have become correlated with performance. IQ tests, however, are far from guarantees. Even though there is more of a chance that your child will get a Ph.D. if he has a very high IQ rather than an IQ in the average range, there are many people with IQs in the near genius range who lead quiet, unassuming lives, while undoubtably some with average IQs have gone down in history as great people of their time. While IQ scores are often used to predict future performance, they are not assurances that either the predicted performance or the score will continue to remain the same. Many things can happen over the years either to raise or to lower the score, and to influence how a child uses his or her potential.

It is not possible to translate a score of 100 on one IQ test as equal to a score of 100 on another. A survey done in 1961 found that a score of 100 on one test could be as low as 91 on another and as high as 113 on still another. Thus the test scores for the same child could be dramatically different, depending upon which test is used, and this is why a statement of IQ scores is often given in combination with the test name. A trained tester would be familiar with the fluctuations and he or she would be able to indicate if a particular test score would be higher, or lower, than some other estimate of the child's potential.

Since intelligence tests have such great fluctuations, they are not as accurate an instrument as some people think; there is no magic crystal ball included in the testing equipment. An isolated IQ score should not be taken as an assurance of future success or a dire sentence of failure. What is important is what is made of the potential that the scores reveal.

Kept within perspective, IQ testing is a useful tool in helping to diagnose a child's ability, problem areas, and general potentials. The tester is not looking for an exact score—whether 22, 92, or 122—but rather the general range. Is the child's potential in the average, below average, retarded, or superior range? The tester can allow considerable fluctuation within that range and still have some idea of the child's general intelligence.

The Stanford-Binet test, a standardized test with a respected reputation, is considered by some to be the father of all IQ tests. It dates back to a 1905 scale derived by Alfred Binet and Theodore Simon; the scale was revised drastically at Stanford University in 1937 and underwent major revisions again in 1960. Because of the test's very long use, there is a large body of professional literature indicating its strong and weak points.

The normal testing procedure is to give a child several examples of the types of questions on the test, in order to familiarize him and also to give the tester some idea of where the child's abilities lie. The tester attempts to give the child a few initial questions that he can answer with confidence but that will not bore or annoy him because of their simplicity. When the child can answer a series of questions correctly, that point in the testing is established as a starting point of the test, giving the tester what is called a basal age. The testing continues until the child reaches a point where he consistently fails to answer a series of questions correctly. This upper limit is referred to as the ceiling age.

The reliability of the Stanford-Binet test increases with the age of the child. The test is also considered to be more accurate for predicting mental retardation in young children than it is in determining above-average ability.

The Prejudice of Tests

IQ tests can be useful as an indicator of potential, including potential problems, but they have their shortcomings. For example, one controversy over the Stanford-Binet test is the contention that it is culturally biased because it is designed for the majority culture in the United States, with little consideration, if any, of minority cultures. It could still be considered accurate, since success in society is usually measured by the norms and standards of the majority culture. But the tests can be misleading about the intelligence quotients of both minority-culture and handicapped children.

For example, if a child doesn't speak English and is given an IQ test with a heavy emphasis on verbal ability, he would do very poorly, indicating a potential for difficulty in an English-speaking school. But this would give very little indication of his true abilities, even though at the moment it would be an accurate indication of his academic functioning.

The same might hold true for a child with other difficulties, such as hearing or vision disabilities, emotional problems, or poor motor skills. If the test includes sections in which the child is deficient, the test results could give a poor indication of actual intelligence, even though it might correctly indicate academic problems. Unless the test is designed so that it can point out these areas of need in order to work with them, the test might have little value.

If a child, after having mastered English or corrected some other problem, were retested, a dramatic increase could be anticipated in the score, as well as in her ability to do well at schoolwork. Unless something as dramatic as this takes place, however, it would be very unusual that her IQ score would jump radically. The deviations would be too extreme to explain in a logical manner, for example, if a child with an IQ of 50 later scored a 100 without perceptible changes in her life.

It was originally thought that any change in the diagnosis or the child's functioning was due to some weakness in the test used to measure the child. However, studies have shown that there can be improvement or decrease in scores primarily related to environmental factors to which the child is exposed. It can be presumed based on these studies, that a child whose environment provides enriching experiences will gain slightly more than the same child placed in an impoverished environment. Put another way, if you stimulate a child, he can more easily reach his potential; if you deprive him, you can stunt his development of that potential.

A child who does poorly on an IQ test and in his school performance is already faced with disadvantages. If this child is unable to learn coping skills, unable to deal with academic pressures and demands because of innate inability or because of outside problems or disabilities, his low score will most likely remain constant or may even decrease. We should also remind ourselves of how difficult it is for a child who is doing poorly at school to be able to increase his motivation to learn and to deal with the frustrations of school and the problem-solving processes. A child who does well is often rewarded by his own successes, whereas a child who does poorly is reminded of, or "punished" by, his failures. The negative reinforcement that the unsuccessful child will receive just from his lack of progress will not be an incentive to try harder. Unless this child receives the intervention of extra help and encouragement, and experiences some success, he may be too discouraged to try at all. Unless the child from the minority culture learns how to maneuver in the larger society, with or without outside help, she usually cannot hope to compete successfully in that larger sphere.

It makes sense to expect that a child from the United States (excluding Alaska) would fail miserably on a survival test for Eskimo children in the Yukon. Truly this child would be considered below average in his new environment at the Arctic Circle. If the child had good native ability, and perhaps an aptitude for outdoor skills, his score would probably increase over time if he survived long enough. For the same reason it can be expected that a transplanted Eskimo child would increase his score after a period of successful adjustment to life in the suburbs of the United States. For the most part, however, your children will not have such dramatic changes in their environment or their test scores. To a great extent, they have already made their adaptation, poorly or well, to their surroundings.

The Special Child and Testing

We have primarily discussed testing the average child, but how is a child tested who is not considered to be average—a child who is visually handicapped, non–English speaking, or hard of hearing, or with other physical or emotional handicaps—without penalizing that child for belonging to a different cultural group or for having a disability?

Attempts have been made to develop tests that are less dependent upon language, motor skills, an overwhelming amount of cultural assumptions, and other stumbling blocks for certain segments of the population. Several tests have been developed that will not additionally handicap a person as much as previous intelligence tests have done.

One example of such a test is the Columbia Scale of Mental Maturity, which was originally developed for children with cerebral palsy. Children who have motor problems can take the test without being penalized in any way for their lack of coordination or dexterity. For example, a child being tested does not have to move her hands to manipulate blocks or other objects; she can just nod or point at the correct answer.

Another test is the Leither International Performance Scale, which was initially used with diverse ethnic groups in Hawaii and in several foreign countries. As with the Stanford-Binet, the test begins with a very easy task of the type the child will encounter throughout the test, but the distinctive feature of the Leither is that it does not have any verbal instructions.

The Importance of Multiple Testing

Diagnosis by one single discipline is usually not adequate to answer all needs. Even if the primary problem were only a physical one, testing by a multidisciplinary team at a diagnostic clinic can be useful for the many other facets of development not covered by the primary discipline.

When Mari Febro was diagnosed at birth as having spina bifida, a defect in the spinal column that can cause paralysis and other physical problems, she was carefully monitored by orthopedic specialists and other professionals at a children's hospital. As she grew older, her parents and pediatrician noticed that she was extremely slow to speak and, in fact, had very little speech at all, while other children her age were communicating well at nursery school. The hospital chalked it up to possible retardation that perhaps was undetected previously. But when Mari was scheduled to be enrolled in a preschool program for special-needs children, a complete evaluation was done, including a physical examination, and it was discovered that she had a significant hearing loss. What one service accepted at face value, another took the time to investigate through several kinds of tests. With additional training and hearing aids, Mari will be able to communicate, to learn and to participate in the world around her.

Some of the problems we have mentioned in relation to testing can be avoided by the use of multiple testing. Testing a child with several different kinds of tests, including the standard tests of routine physical examinations, can help indicate specific disabilities. One score that does not fit in with scores from other tests could indicate a problem area, or merely a test where the child was tired or confused. The tester has the option of excluding that one test score or of following up with further testing, depending upon what the tester feels is needed.

Multidisciplinary testing is also very helpful because it expands the number of professional and personal approaches to your child's assessment. This should help lessen any personal bias that could be detrimental to the child; it tends to avoid "blind spots" that we all (including professionals) may have in certain areas. More importantly, the whole child and the entire problem can be viewed at one time.

Depending upon the disability, your child may be seen by a variety of professionals, who can help in getting a complete picture of the child's development. The professionals you may meet can range from doctors of many different specialities to psychologists, social workers, and psychiatrists, as well as speech therapists, physical therapists, occupational therapists, inhalation therapists, nurses, and possibly a whole range of medically based technicians whom you may never see, such as nutritionists, lab technicians, and endocrinologists. Each member of the diagnostic team you encounter should be able to bring a unique body of knowledge helpful in diagnosing your child's needs. Frequently the professionals may overlap one another in training or experience. For example, the nutritionist and pediatrician may both be quite capable of arranging a diet for your child, even though they might occasionally have difficulty agreeing on which theory of nutrition would be most appropriate.

Each professional on the team usually has a role that is well defined by his or her profession. Depending upon interests and personality, a particular team member may also be competent to discuss other areas as well. For example, if an educator is not part of the team, another specialist may make it their responsibility to be familiar with the community resources in education.

Many times the diagnosis is a combined effort of two or more team members, frequently the whole team, exchanging information and then arriving at a total picture of the child. The child is not just an orthopedic problem or a neurological case but a whole, total person who has needs in many areas that must be met if any one problem is dealt with. This is the main advantage of a team approach over the work of an isolated specialist.

PREPARING A CHILD
FOR THE DIAGNOSTIC PROCESS

The feelings and fears of the child should not be forgotten in the testing process. You should be ready to prepare your child for any of the diagnostic procedures, and if need be, you should ask for suggestions on how this can be done. Some professionals will ignore the need for this kind of communication, but others can provide useful guidelines. Some of this will include careful explanations, in detail, of what steps will occur and what reactions, or side effects, to be prepared for. You do not want to overprepare a child or create anxiety when none need exist. You can take your understanding of all of this information and translate it to your child simply, without minimizing pain, difficulty, or fears the child might have.

Fears are not vanquished by ignoring them but by recognizing them, dealing with them, and then moving on to other things. Fear of the unknown can be especially debilitating, which is one reason you should explain things to the child in a clear, calm manner. You should never say, "Don't be afraid, it won't hurt." Instead, if it indeed will hurt, you should say so. You can explain that the pain will be momentary, of a long duration, or whatever is the case. Remember that a child's sense of time is different from yours. If you say he'll just be in the hospital for a short time for a test, the child may envision this as only an hour or so (or even shorter if the child is very young) when it actually may be a day or so. It may help to compare the length of time with the time it took for some other experience the child remembers.

Even though you want to explain everything carefully, don't barrage your child with too much potentially frightening information at once. Small steps, with time in between to digest each step, works better. You may need to explain why Mommy and Daddy are letting strange people poke and prod, and also that the procedure won't be an instant cure.

Children often confuse diagnosis with correction and don't understand why they have to go through all of this nonsense if the problem, which they may not fully understand or even recognize, won't disappear as a direct and instant result.

A child who is going into the hospital for extensive diagnostic tests should be aware, to the best of his or her ability, of what will happen, how long it will take, and how he or she will feel during the process. To prepare a child adequately, you may have to corner the doctor, nurse, or other specialists to find out for yourselves what will happen. All too often, a competent professional's time is so limited that it may be difficult to catch him or her long enough to ask these questions.

Another practical reason to explain what is happening to the child is to elicit their cooperation as much as possible. For example, the child who wiggles and squirms in fear or restlessness in the X-ray lab makes it extremely difficult, if not impossible, for the X rays to be taken. Some children have to be strapped down, causing even more fear. The same holds true in testing situations for vision, hearing, IQ, muscles, or other tests. An uncooperative or frightened child cannot help but prejudice the test results in a negative manner. A child who doesn't respond to oral cues, or who doesn't understand what is being asked for, and why, may score lower than he or she should on a hearing test, for example, if the tester isn't aware and responsive to this problem.

As parents, you have a right and obligation to know about any procedures before they are undertaken with your children. You should understand what you are agreeing to and the reasons they are necessary. You should have an idea of what the results are expected to be and what side effects are possible.

When their son Bobby was to be admitted into the hospital for extensive testing, Robert and Millie Rosa felt tremendous guilt, fear, and anxiety. But they also felt that their son should be spared some of this fear and anxiety, if possible. The tests were complex, and some of the side effects unpleasant, so they felt is was important that he be prepared for what he would have to undergo; if he knew what was happening, and some of the reasons for it, he could probably deal with it better.

The Rosas asked the hospital social worker to help them. He contacted the various specialists who would be involved with Bobby's workup—doctors, nurses, technicians, and others—and got as much information on the procedures as he could. Then both he and the Rosas talked with Bobby on several occasions about this upcoming hospital experiences. They gave as much information as they thought he could handle at his age.

As it turned out, Bobby was much more aware of the seriousness of his condition, and much more mature, than either his parents or the social worker had given him credit for. As adults so often do, they had underrated his capacity to understand and cope with negative or uncertain information. Even though it is not vocalized, children have a way of getting to the heart of matters in ways that can be disconcerting to protective adults; native intelligence combined with capacity to pick up the emotional undertones of situations make children hard to fool for long.

The confirmation of his own suppositions about his condition seemed almost to be more comforting than worrisome to Bobby. Perhaps this was because he could finally know the truth and affirm his own perceptions of reality. At any rate, his energies could now be directed more constructively than would have been the case had he been wondering about what was happening around him and to him.

Trying to prepare a child for psychological testing by cramming her with information the night before is not only ineffective but potentially damaging. You can frighten her more than she might have been by putting too much emphasis on the testing, by over-preparing her. A child anxious to succeed, or one who anticipates the bad parts or pain rather than concentrating on what is happening, can freeze and become as terrified or uncooperative as a child who is totally unprepared. Rather than helping the child to do better, overpreparation can either falsify the result to the extent that he may fail to live up to the potential arrived at, or more likely, overpreparation can create such anxiety for him that he will perform worse than he would have under normal circumstances.

THE RESULTS OF THE DIAGNOSTIC PROCESS

Out of all the testing your child must undergo, you should get a diagnosis geared to a definition of your child's problem. The diagnosis should include strengths as well as weaknesses. No child should be all negatives; almost all children, including those with severe disabilities, have positive points. By looking at both sides you will learn what is lacking, but you will also learn what exists to be worked with and nurtured. A child with an IQ of 60, for example, is classified as a moderately retarded child, with significant intellectual impairment; you would anticipate only limited academic achievement. On the other hand, with an IQ as *high* as 60 the child will be able to learn many things, things that can make the child feel satisfaction and perhaps provide a limited potential for a constructive life that can contribute to society.

There are many factors that make for contented, successful adults.

For many success depends less upon material things—money, power, status—and more on the intangibles of good health, personality, and the ability to relate with compassion to others. The child with the 60 IQ may be more successful in obtaining a job and living a happy life than the genius who is unable or unwilling to relate to others. You should remember that handicaps come in many forms. Your focus as parents should be on the whole child. To use an old phrase, you need to think of a "well-rounded individual." If one or more areas are limited, you can probably find other areas of independence and compensation.

What You Should Be Looking For

When you consider the "whole child" in relation to a diagnosis, there are some basics you will want to know: Is your child in basically good health (excluding the medical disabilities indicated)? What can be expected about school performance? How does your child feel about the problem? What specifically can be done about the handicapping condition? All of these and other questions are basically concerned with what is the problem? How will it be managed? And how will your child adapt to his surroundings?

The diagnostician has a responsibility to give you a clear understanding of what the diagnostic tests mean. The raw data have very little use for you and could be misleading, so you should ask the diagnostician not only to perform the testing but to provide explanations and translations from his or her special language and field.

You may find some who are very reluctant to give you formal testing data. These reports are usually intended to be read by other professionals and often are confusing to those outside the field. But without reviewing the content of these documents, how will you be able to judge derogatory, inaccurate, or misleading statements made concerning you or your child?

Due to the misuses of such information in the past, Congress passed the Freedom of Information Act that has opened up once confidential (but exclusionary to the individual it concerned) sources, such as credit, insurance, and school records. As a result of this law increasing numbers of facilities are willing to write a report or summary that outlines the main points and supporting data of a diagnosis in terms easily understood by the lay person, including the origin or reasons for potential problems (if known) and any recommendations for future treatment or special planning.

If You Are Unsatisfied

The problem of confidentiality and accuracy may need to be handled with discretion by the parent. In order to give a diagnostician a better understanding of your child you might be willing to discuss some intimate personal details of family life and strife. You might be less than willing to have this information forwarded to other agencies. Sometimes agencies are quite willing to give the total report to the parents or to forward it on to other agencies in its complete form. It used to be commonplace for agencies to forward great masses of personal and diagnostic information to other agencies without permission but to refuse adamantly to show this material to parents or child. This type of treatment eventually led many parents to question these actions, especially in terms of school records. Parents began to assert their rights to know and to keep information confidential.

If you disagree or are not totally pleased with the way your agency does things, ask them to explain their practices. They may have reasons you might not have thought of before. Then again, they may have no reason at all; they may operate as they do just because "it's policy," because no one ever did it differently, or because no one ever asked them to do it any other way. Perhaps if you could raise some valid points to consider about your viewpoint, the agency might make a shift in policy. Perhaps not, but it's worth trying.

Before you disagree, you should make certain you know what it is you are disagreeing with. And this is where full disclosure and explanation of all material is essential. If you feel you understand what is said but find it unacceptable, you do not have to allow the agency, in most cases, to share its conclusions with others unless a court or the law mandates it. Most programs have a policy of "informed consent," that is, information concerning you or your child cannot be viewed by others without your permission (after the reasons for the disclosure are explained to you). While the reports will remain at the agency, they will not be released.

If you are aware of certain inaccurate information, it may not be difficult to make changes if they involve basic factual data, such as birth dates, telephone numbers, or a misrecording of data that you personally related to the agency. However, a clinician usually will not change his or her clinical impression merely because you do not agree with it; even if you can back up your opinion with factual data, it still may not change. In the end, if you feel that you are still unable to resolve conflicts and you strongly feel that the diagnosis inaccurately reflects your child, then the option remains for you of not consenting to have the material released and of going elsewhere for services.

On the other hand, you may have a diagnosis that you are at least somewhat satisfied with. If so, the next step is to develop a plan for dealing with your child's special needs.

Frequently, you will be faced with the fact that the diagnosis, in defining the needs of the child, can be much more sophisticated than the services available to meet the needs. We are probably most aware of this within the educational system. It would be difficult if not impossible to take each and every child into account when setting up a school program, so the individual needs of each child are often not adequately met. Even the "normal" average child within the educational system can face a difficult time; some school authorities make great efforts to draw up a curriculum of sufficient breadth and depth to meet the needs of most children, but this is not always the case. We hear about the above-average child who is denied the specialized curriculum necessary for her continued accelerated progress. It is even more difficult for the child with special needs. While the average or above-average child has to deal with a curriculum that is not ideal, she will usually have the ability to satisfy her interests elsewhere, perhaps at home or in the community. But the child with special needs will have a more difficult time meeting his needs. This is partly because of discrimination and partly because of the complex nature of some of the resources required. Parents become increasingly dependent upon the available, if imperfect, services.

When you cannot get services geared to a child's specific needs, you must often make difficult choices. The child with learning disabilities could presumably go either into a regular classroom with tutors or into a specialized classroom, if both are available. Should he compete with average children in the regular classroom or with children who have similar problems? Should he remain in the mainstream or should he take advantage of the smaller class size of the specialized program?

The child who needs crutches and orthopedic braces may face different opinions about the amount of therapy, surgery, and bracing she should have. Should you accept the conservative approach and brace the child the maximum amount? Or should you follow the more liberal interpretation and brace the child minimally?

With the first option, if you accept the premise that the diagnosis should not remain constant and that it should be periodically reviewed, the child may develop confidence to progress toward less dependence upon the appliances. But there is also the possibility of severely limiting the child's mobility and chances for full exercise of her limbs. With the second choice, if you have been too optimistic, you may be overextending the child's ability and endurance, forcing her to retreat to former levels of activity and appliances in the face of unrealistic expectations. A setback can be psychologically traumatic as well as physically damaging. Many variables can intervene to change the ability of a child to function, especially in the area of academics. The child's attitude toward himself and—for a child with special needs—toward the handicapping condition is possibly the most important indicator of positive growth. The child with a physical or mental handicap is not necessarily severely disabled, but a child with very low self-esteem, even if not otherwise disabled, is most definitely handicapped.

Richard Smith was considered hyperactive, disruptive, and a poor student. He often got into trouble at school. Since his handicap was an "invisible" one, that is, a handicap that was not readily seen, it took both the school and his parents time to recognize that he really did have a handicapping condition that was affecting his behavior and development in other areas as well. A diagnosis showed that Richard was not retarded but that his intelligence was below average and he had some specific learning disabilities.

Initially it was hard to distinguish if Richard's hyperactivity was due to these factors or to environmental pressures, or whether a combination of the two created a vicious unending circle. Richard's family was recovering from the effects of a divorce, and in trying to refocus their lives they found themselves under increasing stress. His mother, Evelyn, wanted to return to school, which she had put aside when she started to raise a family. She was also in desperate need of a job so that she could support the family. But because of Richard's frequent school problems and disruptions, she was called into school so often that the excessive absenses threatened the part-time job she did manage to get.

Even though she initially expressed doubts about being able to handle her son's behavior, Evelyn was willing to cooperate with the social worker on developing different techniques of discipline for her son, and on changing her parenting patterns for all of her children. The diagnosis helped Evelyn to understand her son's problems, and she was offered reassurance that she really would be able to cope with it all.

Both Richard and Evelyn had been responding to each other in a very negative way; Evelyn had never had adequate preparation or support to parent a handicapped child, and Richard had never been accepted as he was, a young boy with a handicapping condition. Instead, at home and in school, he was recognized primarily because of his deficiencies, his deviations from the expected normal pattern. While Evelyn was being assured of her abilities to parent a child with special needs, Richard too was given assurances: He was shown that he could accomplish things, and he was given new responsibilities along with more appropriate expectations. When he was able to accept that his mother's desire to return to school and that her need to work were not rejections of him, but instead beneficial to the family of which he was an important member, his behavior started to improve.

Richard's main academic problem was a reading disability. His strong desire to read had been masked by his misbehavior. When he no longer was expected to achieve impossible goals, and when he became aware that he was appreciated as a person, even though he had some problems, he began to try to achieve. His academic work remained a challenge, achievement was difficult, and progress tenuous, but since the original expectations for him were now significantly modified, he was able to experience some success.

Over time Richard was no longer considered to be such a problem child; he became a more easygoing person who could be outgoing and friendly. Instead of being told the trouble Richard had gotten into that day, Evelyn was more likely to hear about some accomplishment. Richard's activities were channeled into more constructive outlets, and his mother was no longer afraid to work with him at home to keep his behavior within acceptable limits. Problems did not disappear, but they were dealt with in ways that could lead to acceptable progress within certain, and, more realistic, limits.

THE USE AND MISUSE OF LABELS

In your efforts to find services for your child's special needs and evaluate the diagnosis of those needs, you will probably run into the problem of labeling. A label is a method of trying to fit round pegs into square holes; when people find the pegs don't fit the holes, they decide there is something wrong with the pegs. Thus, children who don't seem to fit society's ideas about what is "normal" are tagged with labels that often represent a misuse of terminology that might be appropriate in other situations. How frequently have you heard the phrases "Can't you hear me? What's the matter, are you deaf?" or "Stop acting like a retard"? It is appropriate to use the terms *deaf* to describe a child who cannot hear well in order to obtain special services for that child. But it is inappropriate to use the term as a means of denying the child her civil rights and an opportunity for an active, full life.

The labels can make it difficult to match the special needs of your child with the services that are available. In our present educational system, for example, it has always been difficult to develop services for the uniqueness of the individual, especially when he or she has special needs that change with time and experience. A child can develop beyond the services of a specialized setting, but the system may not allow enough flexibility for all his needs. For instance, a blind child may benefit from the rich diversity offered by a public school that is not available from his special school, but the public school may not be able to adjust to his special limits.

Some children may carry multiple labels because they have a combination of handicaps. Sometimes these labels are applied to define the child rather than the problem. But a child is a person, not a label. Carey Anne, for example, is a child who is deaf, not a deaf child. She is not defined by her handicap, even though it may significantly limit her, but by her humanness first and above all. A child who is blind may have an IQ ranging from severely retarded to genius; he may be fat or skinny, well adjusted or not so well adjusted. Although there are programs that try to fit the round pegs into square holes, your area probably does not have a program specifically designed for children who are overweight, blind, and are fascinated with music. But perhaps your area's program can be adjusted to meet the needs of all children—whether they are fat or skinny, whether they have sight or are blind. The child with special needs should be given a full and complete education that will allow her to explore personal interests, such as music, while she develops other skills necessary for coping with the outside world.

Sometimes, the public's aversions to the labels associated with handicapping conditions, even if the label (diagnosis) is inaccurately used, can hamper the development of services to deal with those conditions. The public seems to respond more easily to some handicaps than it does to others. For example, federally funded services for the blind and deaf were developed in the United States in the nineteenth century, but services for crippled children were not provided on a wide scale until passage of the Crippled Children's Act in the 1930s. Services for developmentally disabled children are of even more recent origin. Even today, it seems that society can accept an "old established" handicap such as blindness more rapidly than retardation or mental illness. The opening of a school for the deaf in a community is likely to stir little response, but propose to open a school for retarded children and an uproar may result.

Labels As Flexible, Functional Tools

Labels are convenient tools, not absolute truths. For example, many children who are considered to be retarded at a young age move out of that technical classification as they grow older. Many individuals who are labeled as "borderline" or minimally retarded are able to shed the label once they are able to hold down simple jobs and blend into the rest of society. One study found that twenty percent of children who as a result of tests were determined to have retarded mental development were retested at a later age and no longer scored in the retarded range. The question remains whether they were misdiagnosed in the first place or whether they benefited from some type of services to the extent that they could improve their academic functioning enough to score higher on the follow-up tests.

The parents in these cases faced the strange dilemma of having children who were no longer eligible for specialized services for the retarded but who at the same time were not ready, or not able, to enter into the mainstream of the general school population.

One of the most distressing situations for parents is when their child with special needs doesn't quite fit the established criteria for obtaining services for these needs. This would include, for example, the child whose IQ is just slightly above the acceptable school limit for specialized services, or the child whose vision is slightly too good to be accepted into the sight-saving program but whose needs make regular school programs inadequate. Such children may actually find their educational needs frustrated for lack of a proper label. Sometimes, program criteria are so rigid that they exclude many of the children whom the program was originally designed to serve.

Deliberate Mislabeling

In such cases there is sometimes a temptation for a clinician to label a child as mentally or physically disabled so that she may obtain the specialized services. One purpose of a diagnosis is to provide a label that will be used as a flexible tool to provide service to a child, not as a stigma that could unnecessarily brand and stigmatize her for life. But sometimes the label itself can be more harmful in the long run than the lack of certain available services. At this point, a more flexible diagnosis might be helpful. But both parents and professionals should determine that the specialized services in question are really worth the risks of possible mislabeling.

Mislabeling Because of Inaccuracy

Mislabeling can also result from an incomplete diagnosis. If the diagnosis does not fit the needs of the child (which may be very different from what the parent might want), it can cause serious problems. A common example of this is the formal psychological testing of children from minority cultures, which we have mentioned before. Children scoring rather low might be placed in a setting for children with retarded mental development, even though they are not really retarded, thereby depriving them of the appropriate specialized services that are needed. If we assume that an intelligence test measures ability to perform in an academic setting, then in this case the diagnosis may be accurate in that it will strongly predict poor school performance. But such a diagnosis is extremely incomplete because it does not consider the underlying causation or problem. It also does not meet the child's needs realistically, or offer remedies to the situation. It may be very true that the child may have difficulty competing in a class geared to the mainstream culture, but he may be very capable in his own environment.

What such a child probably needs is some kind of "bridge class" that would allow him to learn the new culture and its language and prepare him to compete. But by placing the child in a class so totally inappropriate for his needs, the diagnosis may become the prognosis: The child may readily adapt to fit the norms and limited academic expectations for a child with retarded mental development, adopting behavior that readily fits the label.

The Effects of Prejudice

Prejudice and politics have a dramatic effect upon the diagnosis, which is often demonstrated by the stigma that our society places upon handicaps. For example, *retardation* is frequently conceived as a very strong negative word and may be very reluctantly used, even where it is clearly appropriate. Part of the reason for this lies in the poor definition of the word. If we use the word to mean only those who in adult life will need constant adult supervision, leading completely dependent meaningless lives, we would really be speaking about only one half of one percent of the population. But if we use the IQ score of 70 as the upper limit—that is, those able to work at supervised jobs—we would mean three percent of the population. And if we include very mildly retarded individuals and those referred to as borderline—that is, able to hold unskilled routine jobs as independent citizens—we would be speaking of up to sixteen percent of the population. Obviously, there are great differences in these various segments of the population and their abilities. Yet, the term *retardation* is often used without explanation of what the speaker means by the word.

There is a growing controversy among professionals who use psychological testing among various interest groups about the capacity of traditional psychological tests to test many of the subcultures and other subgroups of our society accurately, including both minority children and handicapped children. Unfortunately, such children are often losers when the controversy swings to either extreme. On the one hand, some children from these groups are denied certain needed services because of a blanket rejection of the validity of the testing instruments. On the other hand, some testers who have very little understanding or sympathy with some of these groups may be mislabeling children with average intelligence as having problems. The latter would be true only if the criteria for normality were defined as the ability to earn a doctorate. But in relative terms, many of these children would place well within the educational abilities of seventy percent of the population.

"Hyperactivity"—A Common Label

An example of the way a label can get tossed around by both the general public and by professionals in many fields is frequent misuse of the term *hyperactivity*. Hyperactive children do exist, and they do have a special need that requires special attention. But because there isn't a clear definition of hyperactivity, a child may be incorrectly diagnosed, or labeled as hyperactive when he is merely a bit rambunctious or when he has other special needs that are being overlooked.

After a long hard day with children, most parents would be quite willing to label their children as hyperactive. Children as a group, if we compare them with adults, appear to be hyperactive. In reality, the hyperactive child isn't any more physically active than any other child, according to tests using an instrument that counts the total number of miles walked while the machine is worn. In the test, children who were labeled hyperactive and those labeled normal had no significant difference in the amount of movement recorded during a day. The term *hyperactive* may be more applicable for the child with the shorter attention span or who has a low frustration tolerance.

The cause of hyperactivity is more important than the description. The treatment for a neurologically impaired child who has poor impulse control, and is thus labeled hyperactive, is dramatically different from the treatment for the child who may be labeled hyperactive but whose behavior stems from emotional problems. This can be very hard to decipher. The neurologically impaired child's difficulty in school-based learning may also cause extreme frustration and emotional strain for the child, as was the case with Richard Smith. The child who is labeled hyperactive at school but who can sit and watch three or four straight hours of television without ever moving is probably mislabeled.

Again, in dealing with such problems of labels and what they mean or do not mean, a diagnosis that brings in many disciplines can be more useful than a single diagnostic test by any one specialist. All aspects of the child's development and functioning need to be examined by a battery of tests and testers, including social workers, physicians, and others.

Special Help for Your Child

All of this should help the professionals design an individual treatment plan specific to your child's special needs. This plan could include several different aspects or approaches to problem areas that do not impinge upon development in other areas. For example, a physical therapy program would take into account the psychological needs of the child and attempt to direct some of the exercises in the form of "normal" activities, such as bicycle riding and swimming.

It is all too easy for professionals to forget how limited a parent's time can be. If the time spent in waiting rooms is counted, you may find that an enormous amount of time that could have been spent more constructively with your child or the rest of the family has been wasted. If a combined treatment plan does nothing more than stop five different specialists from requesting that you be in five different places at the same time doing five overlapping tasks, you have made a tremendous gain.

YOUR ESSENTIAL ROLE IN THE PROCESS

It is important that any diagnostic and treatment plans include the parents. As parents you must not forget that you are the only ones who are with the child twenty-four hours a day, seven days a week, and you probably have a better understanding of the child's strengths and weaknesses than anyone else. Most likely, you are the first ones to identify a problem, even though you may also be the last ones to be able to come to terms with the situation. You may hope against hope that the problem will just quietly go away. But none of us would be involved in a diagnostic process unless there were questions that we wanted answered.

You, as parents, should be the most important members of the diagnostic team; your feelings and observations should be taken into account in making the final diagnosis. The final decision of what should be done rests with you. This is why it is so important that you speak openly about what you have seen and what you are worried about, and that you ask questions.

If You Are Having Difficulty

If you feel that you have a problem getting answers to your questions about the diagnosis and treatment of your child's special needs, or if you have reason not to accept the diagnosis, then you may have to consider seeking help elsewhere. The services may not meet your needs, or you may need additional help with your own ability to communicate your needs. If you have difficulty developing a trusting relationship with a diagnostic service, then more than likely you will have trouble obtaining a diagnosis and treatment that is going to be useful to you and your child. Again, this could be the result of problems on your part, on the part of the professionals, or a combination of factors. But if you still have unanswered questions, you must find a way to get them answered—for your own sake as well as for your child.

When you feel that the answers you need are not given by the diagnostic source—doctor, school, clinic, or specialist—you may need a second, or even a third or fourth, opinion to make certain that a disappointing or unsatisfactory diagnosis is correct or incorrect. Or you may merely want to double-check whatever opinion you get. Sometimes, you may be confused, especially when you receive conflicting data that doesn't appear to make any sense at all.

Ellen Schwartz was told by local public school authorities, after a prekindergarten screening session, that her five-year-old son, Adam, was retarded. This came as a shocking revelation to her, and she could not believe it. So she sought a second opinion at a diagnostic clinic that was part of her local hospital. The clinic tested Adam and concluded that he had a significant language delay.

Ellen was confused by the differing diagnoses and recommendations that the school and the clinic made. To her, *retardation* was a strong word; it meant a child who would be totally dependent for life. But language delay seemed like just a childhood phase to pass out of.

The truth lay somewhere between these two stereotyped views. Each of the diagnoses was somewhat correct but imperfect. One problem was Ellen's views of retardation. She heard the word and immediately applied a stereotype of severe retardation, which she knew did not fit Adam, who was so near to normal in most areas. Although she could agree that he acted younger than his age and could not speak as well as other children his age, she knew he could run and jump and do so many other things. He was immature, not retarded, she asserted.

Ellen subsequently learned that professionals have a language of their own and that both diagnoses were actually describing the same child in different terms. Each pointed out similar problems in Adam's development, but each had used different perspectives and had therefore reached different conclusions.

Adam was five years old and not yet in school. His language ability was about that of a three-year-old, and his mother felt he acted more like his four-year-old sister than like other children his own age. As part of their screening program the school had given Adam a psychological test that required extensive language skills, and on this test he had scored as a mildly retarded child. The clinic, on the other hand, had used a test originally designed for deaf children, which therefore did not depend upon language skills; the test is sometimes accused of giving a high estimate of IQ scores, but it can give a clearer picture of what a child can do in areas outside of the area of language. They also used several other kinds of tests in order to get a more balanced picture of Adam's development and where his major disabilities, if any, existed.

The differences between the two sets of test results were not all that large. Each indicated that Adam would probably have difficulty with academic work and would need special help in school. But each clearly indicated that Adam had the potential to be a self-sufficient, independent adult. One problem that was resolved for Ellen was interpretation of these results—that is, she was given an understanding of what the complex jargon of the testing would mean when translated into daily realities.

These explanations made sense to Ellen. She could agree that Adam's development was slow, since she could readily compare it to the development of her other two children and of other children in the neighborhood. She could accept the fact that college might not be in Adam's future. She had not been worried about this, but about his ability to be a reasonably satisfied, self-supporting adult.

The social worker at the clinic helped Ellen to see ways in which she could help Adam to fulfill his potential now and in the future by recognizing his abilities rather than focusing upon his disabilities. Adam was enrolled in a school that had a specialized program to meet his needs.

The Pilgrimage

Like Ellen Schwartz, you may have to get more than one opinion before you can determine, understand, and accept answers about your child's special needs. The danger, however, is that your search to find answers may become a pilgrimage to find the answer you want to hear or to find the nonexistent cure to wipe away the problem. The DuBoises' family doctor referred them to a local hospital clinic, which diagnosed their infant daughter, Lisa, as having cerebral palsy. But the clinic gave them no idea of what this would mean: Would she walk? Talk? Could exercises, surgery, or medicine change the outlook? What schooling would she need?

When they could not find satisfactory answers at the clinic, they tried other doctors—neurologists, orthopedists, physiatrists—and each gave them slightly different answers, based on their differing approaches to the problem. Finally, the family talked to another parent who had gone the same route and was able to share some of their feelings of frustration and anxiety and their desire to find an expert who would make it all go away. They began to realize that in part they were looking for the doctor who would tell them that it was all a mistake, or give them a prescription like a cold cure. The DuBoises were able to find a more receptive clinic, whose social workers could help them deal with all of the information that the other professionals on the diagnostic team provided. But the DuBoises may not have been able to accept this had they not begun to look at their own hopes and reactions. Until then they could not deal with or make sense out of any of it.

A difficult situation arises when you stop looking for information to understand your child's special needs and what to do about them, when you begin a "pilgrimage." You may not even be aware that you are doing this, you may feel dissatisfied with what the majority of professionals have to say about your child and continue searching for a better diagnosis.

The search for better news or a miraculous cure is more than just costly in dollars and time. It is also costly in your ability to help and work with your child and in the strain it puts upon your whole family. The more time spent searching for the "right" answer, the one most promising of optimum development, the less time other children and your marriage receive in proportion. Sometimes the search is a way to avoid the fears you may have. This is why it is important to be able to talk about these fears, perhaps "exorcise" them from your approach to the problem.

Keeping an Equilibrium

The welfare of one child in the family needs to be kept in perspective: That child is just *one* part of a total family that usually includes two marriage partners and perhaps other children who have equally important needs. When the child with special needs is made the central focus of concern and activity for a prolonged period of time, the entire family often suffers. The child himself may develop a sense of importance or dependence that is out of bounds and ultimately destructive to healthy emotional development. You should make sure that you do not give your children the added handicap of a crippled spirit, a twisted sense of self-esteem.

During the months that the DuBois family searched for answers, their two older children were often unintentionally ignored: The conversation at the dinner table or elsewhere focused on Lisa; Eric and Marie were left more often with baby-sitters; and much of the DuBoises' free time and money that formerly was spent on family leisure activities were invested with Lisa's problems. Marie's schoolwork began to suffer, and her teacher complained that she was inattentive and moody. Eric's nursery school reported that he was having frequent accidents during the day, and he began to wet the bed at night as well, even though he had been dry for a year or two previously. Lisa, too, was becoming difficult to manage. She demanded attention, she was cranky, and she threw tantrums when she couldn't have her way.

After the DuBoises started to work seriously with a clinic program, some of their family life began to return to a more normal pattern. As things began to be seen in perspective by their parents, all of the children gradually received more attention and more discipline, and the situation, once recognized and dealt with, slowly improved.

This is not to say that programs and treatments should not be chosen and reviewed carefully, or that all family problems will disappear once a program is begun. But a search that becomes compulsive and never-ending will waste valuable time in your child's too-short childhood and puts excessive strain on family life. It becomes an "acting out" of your desire for the "perfect" normal child, when you could better realize your time by valuing the child as he or she is at the moment and working with professionals to help reach the potential that exists.

HELP FROM OTHER SOURCES: PARENT GROUPS

Frequently, when you are looking for answers, the best people to turn to are parents of other children with handicapping conditions. There are numerous state and local organizations, many of them started by parents searching as you are, that can help you find ways to get these answers. It may seem at times that you are charting new territory, with an isolated and singular concern, but many, many others have been there before you and have experienced the same difficulties and emotional turmoil. You may be able to profit from these experiences, both the successes and the mistakes, although you may have to make the same mistakes yourselves before you fully understand. It's all part of the learning process.

Such parent groups vary tremendously. At a basic level, it's helpful and supportive to share experiences—the successes and mistakes of others. These may shorten your road to services and lighten your burdens. But because one group specializes in one area, you cannot expect that it will always be so. The same group may have chapters with varying interests and levels of organization. One organization may have tightly knit programs, another loose contacts between members. Don't give up on parent groups because of one unsatisfactory experience.

Most national organizations started off at the local parents level. Some remain closely in touch and supportive of the initiating parent groups, others are more remote. Don't automatically assume that because an organization has a national title, large budget, and perhaps even a prestigious reputation, that you have found nirvana. Some of the organizations have such specialized purposes—pure research, for example—that they are of little use to parents. Others are as cumbersome to deal with as any government bureaucracy, and still others—a very few—are wasteful to the point that their honesty is questionable. Thankfully, this last situation is not the case for the overwhelming majority of parent groups and other organizations. If you have questions along this line, you might find revealing information in a group's financial data and other annual reports or other published material. Compare how much is spent on administration and fund raising with how much is actually spent on direct services to the concern the organization is dedicated to. Check with your local Better Business Bureau. Groups should also be listed with the Internal Revenue Service as tax-exempt nonprofit organizations.

The main focus of most national parent organizations is to help establish and support local groups and to stimulate better services and attitudes toward citizens with special needs, generally through legislation and public education. An advantage of a national organization in our mobile society is that if you move to another area, you may still be able to find a local branch of a support group.

The national organization may know less about the current situation in your community than you do, but it should be able to refer you to the local group or chapter that does know your community or can help you learn more about existing resources and potentials. Again, like professional organizations, not all national parent-initiated or -organized groups provide the same services. Some limit themselves to specific tasks, such as legislation or community education; some chapters may coordinate complete service programs with schools, camps, and fancy equipment, while others may hold small struggling meetings of parents who may urgently need your help in their attempt to get something moving in your community. Even if you contact the wrong group, a group that cannot help you with your specific need, they may still be able to redirect you. It's worth a thirteen-cent stamp and ten minutes of your time writing a letter or making a call. Keep writing, keep calling, keep asking questions, and you will probably find out where the answers are.

Marc was diagnosed by his school's testing program as having a learning disability, and he was scheduled to receive special help in his first-grade classroom. His parents wanted to learn more about what learning disabilities really meant, particularly what they would mean to their son, so they joined a local chapter of a national group concerned with children with learning disabilities. They found, however, that the large group meetings tended to be focused on areas that they probably would not be concerned with for several years: legislation, junior high school adjustments and programs, setting up fund-raising plans for the chapter. They were pleased to find, though, that the local chapter had taken on the responsibility for organizing several less formal "living room" meetings for parents who needed to share experiences. They attended such a meeting for parents of primary-school-age children and found it quite helpful. This was the type of emotional and practical support they had been looking for.

At the end of Chapter 5 there is a partial list of parent groups and other national organizations concerned with children who have special needs. If there is no local parent group listed for your area that shares your interests, or if you find that a local group listed no longer exists, don't despair. The national headquarters of the group or even another chapter within the same state may be able to tell you of the chapter you need. If not, they may be willing to lend their support to start a new or rejuvenated chapter in your area.

Starting a Parent Support Group

If you are totally on your own and want to start a local support group, you might try contacting the local resources—schools, clinics, and hospitals, that deal on a professional level with your concern. They may be willing to sponsor the group. Their sponsorship may mean financial help, assistance in contacting other parents, and donation of meeting space and professional guidance. Or perhaps they will merely lend their name and public approval to your endeavor.

You should have some ideas about what you want the group to accomplish, both immediately and in the future. Your short-range goals need to be limited and realistic; it's better to plan simple projects and have them succeed than elaborate ones that never quite make it. You may have to alter your plans as time goes on and as your needs change.

Your local newspapers, television and radio stations, and church school and civic bulletins may be willing to publicize an organizational meeting. Be sure to give your name and telephone number as well as the place, date, and time of the meeting. Some people may need directions or more information. Others may not be able to attend but want to be involved with the group. Tack up notices in local stores, libraries, places of worship, schools, transportation centers, and other gathering places.

At the first meeting you can introduce yourselves and your needs and ideas and ask for response from the audience. If the group is reluctant to speak up, ask them to jot down ideas on a pad you can pass around. If the group is small enough, you can set up chairs in a circle, then each person in turn around the group introduces himself and tells why he's attending the meeting. You should be the people to start this off.

One way to get started is to schedule another meeting in two or three weeks with an experienced speaker from a field related to your concern. It should be someone that can speak or lead a discussion on an area that the group has previously expressed a strong concern about. It may take several "programmed" meetings before people are comfortable enough to have any kind of real sharing of problems. On the other hand, it may come about spontaneously at the first or subsequent meetings, either during the program or over coffee afterwards.

Don't hesitate to contact any of the groups listed that you feel might be helpful. Even if you find that you don't always agree with some of their programs or approaches, they may be able to provide useful information that can save you time and effort. The more informal information you can discover through these contacts can also be revealing: It can be reassuring when your specialist, school, or program is highly recommended, disturbing when that's not the case. You then have to interpret this feedback in light of what you know about the source. For example, they could be prejudiced in favor of their own philosophy or program, with or without justification.

Sometimes new chapters or groups need additional support to function. This help may come from the parent organization at a national or state level, from a neighboring group, or occasionally from a different type of organization, such as an agency, hospital, or another kind of parent group.

A group of parents whose children attended a newly founded program for autistic preschoolers joined together to form a parent group. Their school was unable to provide much guidance, and they lacked both funds and experience, so their group was not an immediate success. Along the way, a local chapter of a parent group for retarded children invited them to join them as a kind of special committee, since they shared some common problems, such as schooling and development. The parent group did this until they were able to start off on their own a year or so later. That year with the established parent group taught the parents something about the skills needed to organize a group during a period when their membership and goals were very fluid. At the end of their "apprenticeship" they had a better idea of what they wanted and how to get it.

When There Is No Support Group

Sometimes when a parent group does not exist it may not be possible to start one: There may not be anyone willing to sponsor a new group or enough interest in your area to gather members for your group. This may be particularly true if you live in a rural area or if your child's special needs are very specialized indeed, such as an unusual disease or condition. You may have to settle for correspondence or newsletters to share with other parents with similar experiences.

Susan Lewis wanted to talk to other parents whose children had experienced accidental injury. She had difficulty dealing with the reactions of others to her daughter Cathy's burns, and she also had difficulty resolving her own feelings about her responsibility for the injuries Cathy received after tipping over a hot pot of water on the stove. Even though she read many articles on the frequency of young children reaching for hot pots on the stove as her daughter had, and she had discussed things with the social worker at the local hospital where Cathy had been treated, Susan still wasn't satisfied. She felt that talking to others could help. But there did not seem to be any organization or group she could join, within her own community or elsewhere, and there didn't seem to be enough parents with similar experiences in her small town whom she could urge to form a group. Even if there were, they were probably as uncomfortable as she with their own circumstances and, thus, weren't very accessible.

Eventually Susan met another young mother when Cathy returned to the hospital for additional surgery. After noticing that the other mother's child was being treated for burns, she overcame her usual reserve to make conversation with this total stranger. Over coffee at the hospital cafeteria and during the many months of treatment their children underwent, the two women discussed some of the problems that appeared to be bothering both of them at various times. This informal, infrequent contact was valuable to Susan and to the other mother, and it filled a need that other resources were not able to meet.

Aware and concerned parents of children with special needs, whether individually or in parent groups, have made many significant changes in the practice of social service agencies, government regulations, school policies, and community attitudes involving the handicapped. As a result of new legislative and government directives, the handicapped and their advocates must often be included in the planning for the services that are available to them. However, in some cases such consumers have been frightened of the agencies and other groups that are supposed to serve them and have been reluctant to seek an active role in the decision-making process.

Today, a growing number of people with handicaps, and their advocates, are seeking out and demanding services as a right, not as a charitable privilege. In some ways this new mood is reminiscent of the surge of unionism in the 1930s or the civil rights movement of the 1960s. There is a very strong militancy and a consistent, and insistent, demand for rights in many areas of their daily lives—jobs, education, access to public buildings, and basic dignity as human beings.

Those are goals you eventually may well want to look forward to out of concern for the future of your child with special needs. But meanwhile, whether through the help of other parents or other resources, your first goal is to obtain the proper diagnosis of and treatment for your child's needs. As you proceed toward that goal, you will find that the most far-reaching effects of your situation are the emotional aspects, your feelings toward your child and all that is involved with raising that child.

DIRECTORY

Also see: Chapter 5 Directory for parent group information

Some Tests Commonly Used in Diagnosis

Auditory Discrimination Test (ages 5–8), language oriented

Bender Visual-Motor Gestalt Test for Children (ages 7–11), psychological

California Test of Personality (ages 5 and over), psychological

CAT: Children's Apperception Test (ages 3–10) emotional

Durrell Analysis of Reading Difficulty (ages 6–12), reading

Marianne Frostig Developmental Test of Visual Perception (ages 3–8), visually oriented IQ

Illinois Test of Psycholinguistic Abilities (ages 2–9), language oriented

Leither International Performance Scale (ages 3 and over), non-language-oriented IQ

Lincoln-Oseretsky Motor Development Scale (ages 6–14), motor skills

Memory-for-Designs Test (ages 8 and over), visually oriented IQ

PAR: Preschool Attainment Record (ages: preschool), general development

Parsons Language Sample (no age range), language

Peabody Picture Vocabulary Test (ages 2.5–18), language

Stanford-Binet Intelligence Scale (ages 2 and over), IQ
Vineland Social Maturity Scale (ages birth to adult), social
    development, IQ
Wechsler Preschool and Primary Scale of Intelligence (ages 4–6), IQ
WISC: Wechsler Intelligence Scale for Children (ages 5–15), IQ
WRAT: Wide Range Achievement Test (ages 5 and above),
    scholastic

Chapter References

Attshuler, Anne. *Books That Help Children with a Hospital
    Experience.* U.S., Department of Health, Education, and
    Welfare, 1974, publication no. (HSA) 74–5402.[1]
Brazelton, T. Berry. *Infants and Mothers: Differences in
    Development.* New York: Dell, 1969.
————. *Toddlers and Parents: A Declaration of Independence.*
    New York: Delacorte Press, 1974.
Weiner, Florence. *Help for the Handicapped Child.* New York:
    McGraw-Hill, 1973.

State Agencies for Crippled Children's Services

ALABAMA
    State Department of Education
    Crippled Children's Services
    Montgomery 36104

ALASKA
    State Department of Health and Social Services
    Maternal and Child Health and Crippled Children's Services
    Juneau 99801

ARIZONA
    State of Arizona Crippled Children's Services
    1825 East Garfield Street
    Phoenix 85006

---

[1] All U.S. government publications are available from the Superintendent of Documents, U.S. Government Printing Office, Washington, D.C. 20402.

ARKANSAS
State Department of Social and Rehabilitative Services
Crippled Children's Services
Little Rock 72201

CALIFORNIA
State Department of Public Health
Crippled Children's Services
2151 Berkeley Way
Berkeley 94704

COLORADO
Colorado Department of Health
Maternal and Child Health and Crippled Children's Services
4210 East Eleventh Avenue
Denver 80220

CONNECTICUT
State Department of Health
Crippled Children's Services
79 Elm Street
Hartford 06106

DELAWARE
Department of Health and Social Services
Maternal and Child Health and Crippled Children's Services
3000 Newport Gap Pike
Wilmington 19808

DISTRICT OF COLUMBIA
D.C. Health Services Administration
Maternal and Child Health and Crippled Children's Services
1875 Connecticut Avenue
Washington 20001

FLORIDA
Department of Health and Rehabilitative Services
Crippled Children's Services
Tallahassee 32304

GEORGIA

> Department of Human Resources
> Crippled Children's Services
> Atlanta 30334

GUAM

> Department of Public Health and Social Services
> Crippled Children's Services
> Government of Guam
> P.O. Box 2816
> Agana 96910

HAWAII

> State of Hawaii Department of Health
> Crippled Children's Services
> P.O. Box 3378
> Honolulu 96801

IDAHO

> Idaho State Department of Environmental Protection and
>   Health
> Maternal and Child Health and Crippled Children's Services
> 650 West State Street
> Boise 83707

ILLINOIS

> University of Illinois
> Crippled Children's Services
> 833 South Wood Street
> Chicago 60612

INDIANA

> State Department of Public Welfare
> Crippled Children's Services
> Indianapolis 46207

IOWA

> University of Iowa
> Crippled Children's Services
> Iowa City 52241

KANSAS
Crippled Children's Commission
Crippled Children's Services
Wichita 67202

KENTUCKY
Commission for Handicapped Children
Crippled Children's Services
1405 East Burnett Avenue
Louisville 40217

LOUISIANA
State Department of Health
Crippled Children's Services
New Orleans 70160

MAINE
Department of Health and Welfare
Maternal and Child Health Services and Crippled Children's
Services
Augusta 04330

MARYLAND
State Department of Health and Mental Hygiene
Crippled Children's Services
301 West Preston Street
Baltimore 21201

MASSACHUSETTS
State Department of Public Health
Crippled Children's Services
Boston 02133

MICHIGAN
Department of Public Health
Maternal and Child Health Services and Crippled Children's
Services
Lansing 48913

MINNESOTA
    Department of Public Welfare
    Crippled Children's Services
    Centennial Building
    Saint Paul 55101

MISSISSIPPI
    State Board of Health
    Crippled Children's Services
    P.O. Box 14
    Jackson 39205

MISSOURI
    University of Missouri
    Crippled Children's Services
    Clark Hall
    705 South Fifth Street
    Columbia 65201

MONTANA
    State Department of Health
    Maternal and Child Health and Crippled Children's Services
    Helena 59601

NEBRASKA
    State Department of Public Welfare
    Crippled Children's Services
    1526 K Street
    Lincoln 68508

NEVADA
    State Department of Health
    Welfare and Rehabilitation
    Maternal and Child Health and Crippled Children's Services
    Nye Building
    201 South Fall Street
    Carson City 89701

NEW HAMPSHIRE
    State Department of Health and Welfare
    Crippled Children's Services
    Concord 03301

NEW JERSEY
    State Department of Health
    Crippled Children's Services
    P.O. Box 1540
    Trenton 08625

NEW MEXICO
    Department of Health and Social Services
    Crippled Children's Services
    Santa Fe 87501

NEW YORK
    State Department of Health
    Crippled Children's Services
    84 Holland Avenue
    Albany 12208

NORTH CAROLINA
    State Board of Health
    Crippled Children's Services
    Raleigh 27602

NORTH DAKOTA
    Special Services Board of North Dakota
    Crippled Children's Services
    Bismarck 58501

OHIO
    State Department of Public Welfare
    Crippled Children's Services
    Columbus 43215

OKLAHOMA
>   Department of Institutions
>   Social and Rehabilitation Services
>   Crippled Children's Services
>   Oklahoma City 73105

OREGON
>   University of Oregon Medical School
>   Crippled Children's Services
>   3181 Southwest Sam Jackson Park Road
>   Portland 97201

PENNSYLVANIA
>   Department of Health
>   Maternal and Child Health and Crippled Children's Services
>   P.O. Box 90
>   Harrisburg 17120

PUERTO RICO
>   Department of Health
>   Maternal and Child Health and Crippled Children's Services
>   San Juan 00908

RHODE ISLAND
>   Department of Health
>   Maternal and Child Health and Crippled Children's Services
>   Providence 02903

SOUTH CAROLINA
>   State Board of Health
>   Maternal and Child Health and Crippled Children's Services
>   Columbia 27201

SOUTH DAKOTA
>   State Department of Health
>   Maternal and Child Health and Crippled Children's Services
>   Pierre 57501

TENNESSEE
Department of Public Health
Crippled Children's Services
Nashville 37219

TEXAS
State Department of Health
Crippled Children's Services
Austin 78756

UTAH
State Department of Social Services
Maternal and Child Health and Crippled Children's Services
44 Medical Drive
Salt Lake City 84113

VERMONT
Department of Health
Maternal and Child Health and Crippled Children's Services
115 Colchester Avenue
Burlington 05401

VIRGINIA
State Department of Health
Crippled Children's Services
109 Governor Street
Richmond 23219

VIRGIN ISLANDS
Department of Health
Crippled Children's Services
Charlotte Amalie
Saint Thomas 00802

WASHINGTON
Department of Social and Health Services
Crippled Children's Services
Public Health Building
Olympia 98502

WEST VIRGINIA
Department of Welfare
Crippled Children's Services
State Office Building B
1900 Washington Street East
Charleston 25305

WISCONSIN
State Department of Public Instruction
Crippled Children's Services
Madison 53702

WYOMING
State Department of Public Health
Maternal and Child Health and Crippled Children's Services
Cheyenne 82001

There are many types of diagnostic clinics. This listing is of some that are affiliated with universities.

Association of University Affiliated Facilities

The following developmental diagnostic centers belong to the Association of University Affiliated Facilities. They are all concerned with the emotional, psychological, and physical problems that interfere with a child's growth. Since they are all affiliated with major universities, they can take advantage of those institutions' varied and valuable services. Contact the facility nearest you for further information.

ALABAMA
University of Alabama at Birmingham
Andrew E. Lorinz, M.D., Director
Center for Developmental and Learning Disorders
1720 Seventh Avenue
South Birmingham 35223
Phone: (205) 934-5467

University of Alabama at Tuscaloosa
Joseph W. Gallagher, Ph.D., Associate Director
Center for Developmental and Learning Disorders
P.O. Box 6302
University 35486
Phone: (205) 348-5086

CALIFORNIA

University of California at Irvine
Kenneth W. Dumars, Jr., M.D., Director
Division of Clinical Genetics and Developmental Disabilities
Department of Pediatrics
California College of Medicine
Irvine 92664
Phone: (714) 633-9393, Ext. 677

University of California at Los Angeles
George Tarjan, M.D., Director
The Neuropsychiatric Institute
Mental Retardation Program
760 Westwood Plaza
Los Angeles 90024
Phone: (213) 825-0121

University of Southern California
Wylda Hammond, M.D., Director
University Affiliated Program
Children's Hospital of Los Angeles
4650 Sunset Boulevard
Los Angeles 90027
Phone: (213) 663-3341, Ext. 788

COLORADO

University of Colorado Medical Center
John H. Meier, Ph.D., Director
John F. Kennedy Child Development Center
4200 East Ninth Avenue
Denver 80220
Phone: (303) 394-7224

DISTRICT OF COLUMBIA
Georgetown University Medical Center
Phyllis Magrab, Ph.D., Director
University Affiliated Center for Child Development
3800 Reservoir Road Northwest
Washington 20007
Phone: (202) 625-7138

FLORIDA
University of Miami
Robert Stempfel, M.D., Director
Mailman Center for Child Development
Box 6—Biscayne Annex
Miami 33152
Phone: (305) 350-6631

GEORGIA
Georgia Retardation Center
James Clements, M.D., Director
4770 North Peachtree Road
Atlanta 30341
Phone: (404) 485-5111

Athens Unit
James Clements, M.D., Director
Georgia Retardation Center
850 College Station Road
Athens 30601
Phone: (404) 549-6423

ILLINOIS
Illinois Institute for Developmental Disabilities
Herbert J. Grossman, M.D., Director
1640 West Roosevelt Road
Chicago 60608
Phone: (312) 431-8000

INDIANA

Indiana University Medical Center
Arthur L. Drew, M.D., Director
Riley Child Development Center
1100 West Michigan Street
Indianapolis 46202
Phone: (317) 635-8431

University of Indiana
Henry J. Schroeder, Ed.D., Director
Development Training Center
2853 East Tenth Street
Bloomington 47401
Phone: (812) 337-6500

IOWA

University of Iowa
Raymond Rembolt, M.D., Director
University Hospital School for Handicapped Children
Iowa City 52242
Phone: (319) 353-5847

KANSAS

Kansas UAF Central Office
Richard L. Schiefelcusch, Ph.D., Director
Ross H. Copeland, Ph.D., Associate Director
Bureau of Child Research
224 Haworth Street
Lawrence 66045
Phone: (913) 864-4295

Parsons State Hospital and Training Center
Sidney L. DeBriere, M.D., Director
2601 Gabriel
Parsons 67357
Phone: (316) 421-6550

University of Kansas
William L. Hopkins, Ph.D., Director
James F. Bidde, Associate Director
John T. Stewart Children's Center
352 New Haworth Hall
Lawrence 66045
Phone: (913) 864-4950

University of Kansas Medical Center
John Spaulding, M.D., Director
Herbert C. Miller Clinic
Rainbow City 66103
Phone: (913) 831-5744

KENTUCKY
University of Kentucky Medical Center
Vernon L. James, M.D., Director
Center for the Handicapped
763 Rose Street, Annex 3
Lexington 40506
Phone: (606) 233-6318

MARYLAND
Johns Hopkins University
Matthew Debuskey, M.D., Director
The John F. Kennedy Institute
707 North Broadway
Baltimore 21205
Phone: (301) 955-4001

MASSACHUSETTS
Children's Hospital Medical Center
Allen C. Crocker, M.D., Director
Developmental Evaluation Clinic
300 Longwood Avenue
Boston 02115
Phone: (617) 734-6000, Ext. 2116

Walter E. Fernald State School
Raymond Adams, M.D., Director
Eunice Kennedy Shriver Center
200 Trapelo Road
Waltham 02154
Phone: (617) 899-8135

MICHIGAN
University of Michigan
William Cruickshank, Ph.D., Director
Institute for Study of Mental Retardation and Related
  Disabilities
130 South First Street
Ann Arbor 48108
Phone: (313) 763-3171

MISSOURI
Saint Louis University
Allan Barclay, Ph.D., Director
Child Development Clinic
1401 South Grand Boulevard
Saint Louis 63104
Phone: (314) 772-7990

University of Missouri at Columbia
Eleanor Chaheen, M.D., Director
University Affiliated Facility
University of Missouri Medical Center
TD-4 West, Room 127
Columbia 65201
Phone: (314) 882-6957

NEBRASKA
University of Nebraska
Paul Pearson, M.D., Director
Meyer Children's Rehabilitation Institute
444 South 44th Street
Omaha 68131
Phone: (402) 541-4730

NEW JERSEY
    Kean College of New Jersey
    Arthur Jonas, Ed.D., Director
    Institute of Child Study
    Union 07083
    Phone: (201) 527-2326

NEW YORK
    Albert Einstein College of Medicine of Yeshiva University
    Gerald Golden, M.D., Director
    Rose F. Kennedy Center
    1410 Pelham Parkway South
    Bronx 10461
    Phone: (212) 430-2400

    New York Medical College—Mental Retardation Institute
    Westchester County Medical Center
    Margaret J. Gianini, M.D., Director
    Division for Disorders of Development and Learning
    Valhalla 10595
    Phone: (914) 347-5300

    New York Medical College—Mental Retardation Institute
    105 East 106th Street
    New York 10029
    Phone: (212) 876-5500

NORTH CAROLINA
    Box 523
    North Carolina Memorial Hospital
    Chapel Hill 27514
    Phone: (919) 966-4417

OHIO
    Ohio State University
    William M. Gibson, M.D., Director
    The Nisonger Center
    1580 Cannon Drive
    Columbus 43210
    Phone: (614) 422-8365

Ohio University
Elsie Helse, Ph.D., Director
Center for Human Development
Athens 45701
Phone: (614) 594-8962

University of Cincinnati
Jack H. Rubenstein, M.D., Director
University Affiliated Cincinnati Center for
  Developmental Disorders
Pavilion Building
3300 Elland Avenue
Cincinnati 45229
Phone: (513) 559-4621

OREGON

University of Oregon
Robert H. Schwarz, Ph.D., Director
Center on Human Development
Eugene 97403
Phone: (503) 686-3111

University of Oregon Medical School
Victor D. Menashe, M.D., Director
Crippled Children's Division
3181 Southwest Sam Jackson Park Road
Portland 97201
Phone: (503) 225-8362

PENNSYLVANIA

Temple University and Saint Christopher's Hospital
Edward Newman, Ph.D., Director
Developmental Disabilities Center-UAF
Ritter Hall Addition
Temple University
Philadelphia 19122
Phone: (215) 787-1356

TENNESSEE

University of Tennessee
Robert G. Jordan, M.D., Director
Child Development Center
711 Jefferson Avenue
Memphis 38105
Phone: (901) 528-6500

UTAH

Utah State University
Marvin F. Fifield, Ph.D., Director
Exceptional Child Center
Logan 84321
Phone: (801) 752-4100

WASHINGTON

University of Washington
Irvin Emanuel, M.D., Director
Child Development and Mental Retardation Center
University of Washington, WJ-10
Seattle 98105
Phone: (206) 543-3224

WISCONSIN

University of Wisconsin
F. Rick Heber, Ph.D., Director
Waisman Center on Mental Retardation and
    Human Development
2605 Marsh Lane
Madison 53706
Phone: (608) 262-1728

3

Your Feelings and Your Child's

Throughout history societies have had contrasting attitudes about people with handicaps. A few ancient cultures considered mentally retarded people to be sacred because their affliction set them apart from others. In the Roman Empire part of the popularity of Julius Caesar might have been attributable to the fact that he had epilepsy, which was thought to be possession by the gods.

SOCIETY'S VIEW

In most past societies, however, people with handicapping conditions were shunned or rejected. In many cultures a child born with a deformity was viewed as an evil omen or as a sign of the moral corruptness of the parents. In medieval Europe the retarded and mentally ill were sometimes burned to death as witches or agents of the devil. Even in more recent times individuals with handicaps were considered to be victims of a cruel twist of fate, but persons to be avoided nevertheless. Families with children with special needs were looked upon as struggling martyrs, people to be admired for their virtuous submission to the suffering of their tragic offspring.

Just being different can be dangerous in any society. People have often been persecuted for having different religious or political beliefs. But individuals with handicapping conditions, with special needs, did not choose to be different. They have no righteous cause to fall back on for strength. People with handicaps are different from the norm in some ways, but not in all ways, not in essential ways that make them less worthy or less important.

Giving birth to a child with special needs is no longer considered to be a punishment by God. But handicaps still make some people uncomfortable, because of either the vestiges of superstition or their ignorance about handicapping conditions. Plastic surgery to correct a facial deformity such as a harelip does not change the basic worth of a person, but often the physical change makes it easier for others to recognize and accept that person's worth. Some people have difficulty seeing the person; they focus on the handicap. Some react to handicaps with uncertainty, discomfort, or even revulsion. Parents need to make their child with special needs aware of these reactions and to show him ways in which to deal with such reactions, while emphasizing that his value as a person has nothing to do with his handicap.

Developing public awareness and understanding about handicapping conditions has been a slow process. Up until the beginning of the twentieth century handicaps and poverty were often linked in the public mind. It was commonly believed that to be handicapped or mentally ill meant to be poor. Indeed, America's first insane asylums were almshouses and hospitals for the poor. Poverty was widely thought to be synonymous with lazyness; the only reason a person could not support himself in such a land of opportunity, it was said, was a lack of desire or an unwillingness to work.

Slowly, a distinction between poverty and selected handicaps began to emerge. Some handicaps, such as blindness or deafness, began to be considered as acceptable reasons for being poor, and the government began providing some public support for these afflictions. Because blindness and deafness were so common in mid-nineteenth century America, they became more easily understood and ceased to evoke such great fear.

Gallaudet College, a land-grant college exclusively for the deaf, is a legacy to a growing public concern over deafness in the late 1800s led by social reformers such as Doreathea Dix. Established in 1864, Gallaudet College today continues to be one of the only schools in the world that provides specialized instructions for deaf students at a college level. Although the students may have hearing limitations, there are no limitations on their intellectual abilities. One newly hired professor who was teaching students who were deaf for the first time expected to find a group of handicapped and, therefore, limited or dull pupils. He was amazed at the number of geniuses in his class. The level of intellect among students is high at Gallaudet because it represents one of the few opportunities for people who are deaf to get a college education. As a result competition is keen, and the college can accept only a limited number of students from among the best applicants. Only about one-tenth of children who are deaf go on to college, compared with one-third of children with hearing.

Gradual Changes in Public Awareness

Eventually, other handicapping conditions began to get public attention and support. In the mid-1930s, Congress passed the Crippled Children Act, which authorized state and local government agencies to reimburse individuals with orthopedic handicaps, or their families, for certain expenses, such as the cost of leg braces. President Franklin D. Roosevelt, who was partially paralyzed as the result of polio, undoubtedly gave a large political and psychological boost to the legislation. Americans could accept a president who was handicapped as long as they did not have to be visually reminded of it. There are few pictures of President Roosevelt that would make people aware that he was unable to walk. To succeed, he had to appear as "normal" as possible. In point of fact, his physical handicap did not seriously impair his functioning as president of the United States.

Since the thirties the crippled children's program has been expanded in most states to include other handicapping conditions, such as heart and respiratory problems. As a result of this program many people with orthopedic and other handicaps have been provided with opportunities that would have been denied them previously, and their families have been spared the tremendous burden of financing their children's care completely on their own.

Developmental disabilities, ranging from learning disabilities to retardation, were among the last handicapping conditions to receive public attention. Again, a sympathetic president helped to create an atmosphere that led to legislation providing those with developmental handicaps both the opportunities and the acceptance that were so sorely needed. When President John F. Kennedy could talk freely, and with loving concern, about his mentally retarded sister, and when he urged the public to accept increased responsibility for such persons, the individual with retarded mental development took another step closer to the civil and human rights that for so long had been denied them.

When Jimmy Carter became president in 1977, there were early signs of renewed presidential awareness of the needs and abilities of persons with handicapping conditions. To most people who saw President Carter's dramatic walk down Pennsylvania Avenue after his inaugural speech the new president was only aimlessly waving to the crowds. But persons who are deaf, and who saw the president's walk in person or on television, knew that some of his hand gestures were the unmistakable sign language for the words *I love you.* Among his first appointments, President Carter named Max Cleland, a triple amputee, to head the Veteran's Administration.

What is more important, however, is that persons with handicapping conditions no longer need depend on a sympathetic president to obtain their rights. For the 1970s also brought new laws to guarantee those rights. One large step forward came in 1973, when Congress passed the Vocational Rehabilitation Act, prohibiting discrimination against the handicapped by any organization that received federal funds. That was followed by the 1975 law requiring states to start providing free education for all handicapped children by 1978. But whether these rights will become a universal and accepted reality still remains to be seen.

The Handicapped: A New and Strong Minority

The new laws are evidence of the growing awareness among people with handicaps about their rights as individuals and of their increasing demands to be guaranteed those rights. In the past, efforts to aid people with handicaps were led by professionals who work with the handicapped rather than by the handicapped themselves. Today, the leadership role of these veteran advocates for the handicapped is being usurped and challenged by those who are handicapped. Indeed, sometimes these traditional advocates have even been viewed as part of the oppressive system by those who are handicapped.

Individuals who have handicaps are coming out of the closets, and their friends and families are coming with them. There are few people who do not either know a handicapped person or have a family member who has a handicap. As more people who know persons with handicaps become aware of the need to obtain equal opportunities for such persons, the potential for change becomes greater.

The growing militancy of persons with handicapping conditions was demonstrated in April 1977, when hundreds of disabled persons staged a protest march and sit-in at the Department of Health, Education, and Welfare in Washington, D.C., to object to the failure of the federal government to issue regulations carrying out the 1973 law banning discrimination against the handicapped. The protest was reminiscent of the civil rights marches and sit-ins of the 1960s. Indeed, one protester who is blind told a reporter: "I marched for my civil rights as a black man in the sixties. I never thought I'd see this day when handicapped people would rise up and demand their rights. We've been begging for a long time. Now we're demanding our rights."

HEW Secretary Joseph A. Califano, Jr., promised the demonstrators that his department would issue the regulations promptly.

YOUR FEELINGS ABOUT PARENTING A CHILD WITH SPECIAL NEEDS

While many of you may have known a person with a handicapping condition, you were probably unaware of their needs until you became personally involved with them. Frequently, people's first involvement may come when they become parents of a child with special needs. Although you may have a friend, an acquaintance, or a relative who has a handicap, your role as parent is different and your responses unique.

Even under the best of conditions, parenthood itself can be a rude awakening for which you haven't been fully prepared. But most parents adjust and even actually enjoy their role as parent. Living with a handicapped child can be a little more difficult. You had probably never dreamed that a child of yours could be anything but perfect: the ideal baby, Little League champion, and Ph.D. scholar. Suddenly, you face a new and unexpected event that is frequently presented to you in negative terms: Your child can't ——, doesn't——, isn't——. It's like the television news: The news is most often about what went wrong in the world, seldom about what is right.

When the Burnses' first son was born, they were typical new parents. They worried when the child cried and when he didn't cry. They read all the current books on child care and development, and then they anxiously watched for signs of normal progress as defined by the experts. They were certain that their baby was the most advanced and most beautiful baby on their block, if not in their whole town.

By the time their second child was expected, they felt more comfortable and realistic about their roles as parents. More self-confident, they felt they had met and succeeded at many tests of parenthood. But the discovery that their second son was handicapped by a missing forearm was more than an unexpected shock. They were not ready for this type of parenthood; it was beyond their realm of expectations. They experienced a whole new set of adjustments and a series of emotional upheavals before they could feel nearly as comfortable in parenting their younger son as they had with their older son.

The typical responses of parents when they discover their child has special needs have been studied extensively, and they are generally well understood by the helping professionals. Their initial reactions are often similar to mourning the death of a loved one. Perhaps that is exactly what you have to do: Mourn for the loss of the perfect child you had dreamed and hoped for, so that you then can learn to live with and love the child you do have. If your child was unexpectedly born with handicapping conditions, you were forced to make these difficult adjustments almost overnight. But if you discovered that your older child had special needs or if you anticipated disabilities at birth, you may have been aware of the possibilities before a final pronouncement was made to you. This, however, did not make the realization of your fears much easier to deal with.

Denial

Your first reaction to difficult news may be to pull away, to try to find time and a sheltered place to think. This is called denial by the professionals. It's as though you were trying to avoid reality. In truth, you need time to digest all the information and its ramifications and to prepare for the future. You may try to shut it out of your minds with such reactions as "No, it can't be" or "I can't believe it." You know it *can* be, but you have great difficulty understanding why. You may be worried about so many factors: your abilities to meet the child's needs; the child's future; your own reactions to the child now that your expectations have been shattered; the lack of answers to your questions; your lack of preparation for parenting a child with special needs; your not knowing what to expect. Responsibilities and obligations weigh heavily upon you, and you worry about your capacity to meet them.

While denial is a normal part of the process of adjustment, it is probably the most difficult stage for the child, especially the child who is beyond toddlerhood. He is being denied attention to his needs, particularly the need to be accepted by those around him. This can lead him to falsely conclude that you do not care for him anymore, that in your eyes he is the negative image of his handicap and nothing more. In trying to deny the more unpleasant realities of a handicap, you may also be doing your child a disservice by failing to help him deal with the condition and, even worse, by placing on him the difficult burden of going along with your denial in order to protect you.

Nor should you ignore a handicapping condition in an effort to protect your child from reality. Can you imagine, for example, how difficult it is for a child who has seizures to be told there is nothing wrong, nothing to worry about? She, too, may wish there were nothing wrong, but she knows that something strange, and often frightening, is happening to her.

Children with "invisible" or subtle handicaps can experience more problems than children with obvious conditions. For example, a child with a learning disability may be ridiculed by friends and punished by parents and teachers because, for no visible reason, she is unable to achieve what is expected of her. In fact, she is being asked to achieve something that is just as impossible as expecting one of us to single-handedly block the charging defensive of the Oakland Raiders football team.

Guilt and Anger

The denial stage is frequently followed by one of guilt. As parents of a child with a handicapping condition, you may begin to feel guilty about everything: guilty that you are not brave; guilty that you resent the child; each of you guilty that you have failed the other in some way; guilty that you have failed your child. You may retreat from your normal behavior, becoming your own judge, jury, and executioner. You may set out to punish yourselves, or, worse, you may try to "make it up" to your child through overindulgence.

You may experience guilt feelings even though you know that you have no reason to feel guilty. One of you may also have guilt feelings for some unrealistic reason, perhaps feeling that the other is holding him or her responsible for the child's handicap. Frequently, guilt builds into frustration and then vents itself in anger. You may direct your anger at the most convenient target: each other. But even in the unlikely event that there is some direct parental responsibility for a handicapping condition, recriminations are not going to help the child or the family. This is the time you, as husband and wife, will have to communicate and work together as you probably never have before. And, usually you can come out of the experience with a stronger, fuller relationship.

A danger is that guilt and anger will continue to consume your energies when you should be adjusting to the reality of dealing with the special needs of your child. Sometimes, anger is turned toward those outside the family; the family doctor is a common target. People tend to assume that doctors have godlike powers, and they can become disillusioned when they discover they can't cure every condition. There may be times when you will have justification for being angry, but unfocused anger because of unrealistic hopes or imagined wrongs will at best be ignored by professionals and will often be met by hostility. What is worse, the uncontrolled anger will make your problems of adjusting even greater for you and your child with special needs.

That was the case with the Coles after they discovered that their daughter Lara had a disabling disease. The Coles had been using Dr. Middleton as their family pediatrician for years. They thought highly of him, and they had recommended him to friends. Their four children looked forward to their annual examinations by the doctor, or his infrequent visits when they were ill, because he was a gentle man who truly had a way with children. But Lara Cole's visits in between her usual checkups seemed to increase as she started to acquire an unusual number of respiratory problems. At first Dr.

Middleton was not overly concerned, but he became worried enough finally to refer the Coles to a specialist for a consultation. The Coles had also been worried but had not dared to ask the doctor about their fears, and he in turn had found it difficult to speak with them about what he feared would be bad news.

Lara's parents went to the consultation very worried and unsure of why they were going. The new doctor was even more difficult to talk to because the Coles did not know him and were somewhat awed by his plush office and the air of importance that seemed to surround his practice. As usual with a consultation, the specialist did not share his findings about Lara with her parents but sent them back to their family doctor, who had requested the consultation.

Dr. Middleton explained to the family that Lara had cystic fibrosis, a hereditary disease that affects a child's lungs and pancreas. They listened quietly, even politely, but he was surprised that they asked few questions.

The old adage about the messenger of bad news being the person who loses his head often applies in the case of a diagnosis about a handicapped child, the professional giving the news is often angrily rejected by the parents. The Coles developed a growing anger toward Dr. Middleton for not telling them sooner about Lara's condition and for not curing their child. They were even more angry with the consulting doctor, whom they felt didn't care at all about their daughter.

The Coles subsequently found it difficult to go to Dr. Middleton's office because they were always on the verge of anger; so they started to avoid him. Dr. Middleton, in turn, began to feel very uncomfortable around the Coles. He could feel their anger but didn't know how to deal with it. He was quite worried and concerned about Lara's illness but found it impossible to share this with the family. He began to dread appointments with the Coles as much as the Coles did.

When the Coles had sought Dr. Middleton's aid before, he had always been able to deal with the problems quickly and successfully. But now they saw their doctor being unsure, worried, and unable to offer the same type of ready cure. They were shocked to discover a problem that he could not cure. They were unaware that part of the breakdown in communication between them and the doctor was their reluctance to have their own fears confirmed. Dr. Middleton, even though he was a highly trained professional, was also reluctant to believe his own suspicions and to share with the parents his concern that their child could have a serious, and possibly terminal, illness. Furthermore, much had happened in the field since Dr. Middleton's medical school training, when cystic fibrosis had been discussed only briefly as a relatively rare condition.

It would be helpful if, as part of their medical training, doctors could gain insight into the emotional needs of their patients. In many professions programs are being developed to help professionals understand the process that patients and their families go through. Rather than only reacting to negative feelings, professionals need to be able to work with the feelings that may be directed at them. In this case, the Coles and Dr. Middleton could possibly have eased their situation by seeking to reestablish their old relationship on the common ground of trying to accept and deal with the special needs of Lara.

If the parents are not able to control their angry feelings, the problem becomes greater. Professionals become wary about working with them, and friends find it difficult to socialize with them. Then the hostility increases in response to these reactions. If you find yourselves caught in this kind of vicious circle, ask yourselves why you are doing this and how this type of behavior will help you and your child. You might think that it makes you feel better to have someone to blame, but in the long run it is very self-destructive.

When you are still searching for causes of an unexplained handicapping condition you may tend to look in a negative way. You may blame yourselves and others, and you may get angry at other, "less worthy" parents who still have healthy children. You are angry because you feel that no one understands or cares what you are going through or what you are feeling. You may feel isolated from your former routine way of life. You may have many needs, yet you are afraid to ask for help, and you are angry that no one offers help. But you might also resent the offer of help as an intrusion.

Your guilt and hostility may be turned inward in an attempt to punish yourselves for supposed wrongs. Of course, this can be as self-destructive as anger that is turned outward. Susan Lewis blamed herself for her daughter Cathy's burns on her arm, face, and neck after she reached for a pot of hot water on the kitchen stove and accidently spilled the water on herself. After the initial recovery period Cathy was well enough to leave the hospital, although she would have to return for some skin grafting. In the meantime both the doctor and the hospital therapist wanted Cathy's mother to do some simple exercises with her daughter at home to maintain the mobility in Cathy's arm, neck, and lower jaw.

Susan, who already had been helping with her daughter's treatments at the hospital, agreed to the home therapy, since traveling back and forth to the hospital was not practical. Once home, however, Susan found that she was becoming resentful of the request. She felt she really didn't know what to do, and she was afraid because the exercises seemed to cause Cathy pain. This increased her guilt feelings over not being more vigilant about safety in the kitchen. She began avoiding many of her friends, believing that they too felt that Cathy's accident was her fault. Above all, the inability to help her child increased Susan's unspoken anger toward Cathy for placing her in this situation, anger that made her afraid she would deliberately hurt her daughter.

At times like this, when guilt piles on guilt, you have to break out of the walls you've built and ask for help. Asking for help seems difficult, and you may confuse asking with begging. Eventually, Susan contacted the hospital and explained that she was having difficulty maintaining the therapy. At the hospital's suggestion she was able to find a private therapist for Cathy in their community. Susan began to realize that she didn't have to compound her guilt by forcing herself to do what she was not ready for. She began to reconcile her guilt feelings. After all, she could be replaced as a therapist but not as a mother. She is still the one to whom Cathy will turn for security, love, and all the other essentials that she will need to grow up to become a well-adjusted adult.

Moving Toward Adjustment

When you feel yourselves becoming isolated, it is time for you to break out. To your surprise, your relatives, neighbors, and friends may have wanted to support and help you but didn't know how. They may be willing to give rides to the hospital, baby-sit, or lend a sympathetic ear if you would just ask. You also need people with whom you can relax. Like cars, you don't run without fuel, and fuel to you may be opportunities to get away from the pressing realities, such as dinner out, a movie, or a few friends in for coffee. Without some means of restoring yourselves, it becomes difficult to give all that you must to your child with special needs.

Parents set the tone for their children's reactions. Guilt is a normal reaction, so don't be surprised if your child also feels guilty for being handicapped. Feeling guilty because your child feels guilty will start you off on another vicious circle, so avoid that and instead try to help your child over these feelings by looking toward the future. For you to continue wallowing in feelings of guilt and anger is to leave your family without a parent. Your handicapped child needs a giving parent. A parent who is overburdened with guilt and remorse has little time left for anything else.

Failure to overcome reactions of denial, guilt, and anger after a reasonable time can threaten the emotional and psychological stability of the child with special needs and of the family itself. The Simon family seemed unable to accept the fact that their young son, Andrew, had cerebral palsy. They were still involved with denial and anger, and many months after the initial diagnoses they still had not been able to help him deal with his condition. Like the DuBois family, the Simons had contacted many doctors in their search for answers. But whereas the DuBoises finally settled on an approach to their Lisa's needs, the Simons were unable to do this and continued their search for "help." They had been to several major hospitals in their part of the country, but they never stayed with any of the programs and rarely followed advice. They refused to accept the diagnoses that were given, and they ignored most of the recommendations.

Mr. Simon complained that the doctors didn't know what they were talking about and that they were trying to "rip him off." He refused to accept his son's limitations, expecting that he would some day follow in his own footsteps as a football coach. His wife babied Andrew and was afraid to allow him out of their house or yard. Andrew became a behavior problem and couldn't relate to children his own age; he spent his time by himself or with his baby sister. Andrew felt that his parents didn't like him. He could feel the tension in the house, he could see his parent's marriage falling apart, and he felt it was all his fault.

THE NEED TO SHARE

One of the most difficult parts of dealing with your feelings about a handicap and what effect it has on your family is being able to share your feelings and to work them out as a family. Husbands and wives can go through the stages at differing speeds and in different ways. If you are able to help each other, you will probably end up with a better adjustment than if you are at odds with each other. This is especially important in the earlier stages, when there is a natural tendency to isolate oneself. The family avoids friends and relatives because they feel uncomfortable, anguished, and perhaps guilty.

People spend differing lengths of time in adjusting, and each of you may be working through different feelings from your spouse. For example, one of you may already be trying to find the special resources your child needs, but your spouse may take longer to recover from the initial shock and denial. You can make your spouse feel guilty for being "unaware" and for denying your child help if you fail to understand that he or she may simply need more time than you to accept the reality. But by the same token, you can prolong the guilt your partner may feel by avoiding discussion of the problem. One way to defuse guilt and anger is to discuss these feelings openly.

If you can help your partner understand that a handicapped child is nothing to feel guilty about, you may be able to help him or her over the hurdle that is blocking the way to eventual adjustment. But if the response remains hostile, or your spouse continues to be guiltridden, pushing may be futile or counterproductive. It may take more time, or it may be time for you to seek professional help. Family members often need professional advice in order to help one another, so don't be afraid to ask for such assistance and to use it. The directory in the back of Chapter 5 lists some resources to tap.

Often, fathers are more distressed than mothers at the unexpected news that their child has a handicapping condition, probably because of the obligations that the man of the family traditionally has been expected to shoulder. In addition to the personal shock, men, even in today's growing climate of shared family responsibility, often worry about their financial burdens and, sometimes, even about their virility. Some men erroneously presume that the entire family's survival rests completely on their shoulders. They cannot allow failure, doubts, or fears to show or to be shared by other family members. This antiquated, stoic approach to fatherhood can be more foolish than brave. And both parents must realize that by sharing their doubts, fears, and problems, they can help each other to unburden their worries.

Mothers usually acquire a different perspective because they usually spend more time with the child. Even when both parents work, mothers are often automatically delegated most of the child-raising responsibilities. Since she is more likely to be involved with the minute-by-minute needs of the children, a mother may be the first to become worried about some problem of development in a child, and she may have difficulty communicating this concern effectively to her husband. If he is resistant to the idea that his child has a serious problem, she may even seek professional advice about the child without her husband's knowledge or full understanding. In doing so, she will be moving further and further ahead of her husband in adjusting to any problem.

The less involved a father is with the care of his children, the harder it is for him to accept the idea that his child has a handicapping condition. A father misses the little growing signs of problems that mount daily in the mother's view. Eventually he gets hit all at once, without any warning signals or preparation. A father in this case may try to retreat from the situation. Since the mother may be further along in the adjustment, it may be difficult for the parents to work together.

The first thing a father should do in such a situation is to try to find out exactly what his child's condition is and what can be done to deal with it. A father is sometimes reluctant to be present when his child is seen by a doctor or other professional; he tends to leave this task to his wife. But to understand the special needs of your child, you, as a father, should be there when those needs, and the reasons for them, are being diagnosed. If you feel you don't understand what your wife is talking about when she mentions her concerns about one of your children, take the time to find out. In order to see what problems your child has, you may first have to figure out what is normal for other children in the same age range. If you are able to face the problem, you will make it easier for the whole family to face it.

Caring for children is an awesome responsibility under any circumstances, but caring for a child with special needs can be overwhelming. You don't have to be superparents in order to take care of a child with a handicapping condition, even though at first it may seem that way. Most handicapped children have quite ordinary parents, like yourselves, so don't sell yourselves short. More than likely you do have the ability to care for your child, especially if you are willing to help each other and to ask for outside help if it is needed. It may not be as impossible as you think.

A Child's Reactions to Special Needs

Remember, too, that your child also can have difficulty adjusting to the fact that he or she is "different." Your child cannot be protected from reality forever and will need your help in learning how to cope. Often, however, it is amazing how easily a child can solve some of the worrisome problems that parents experience.

The DuBois family had been worried about how their daughter Lisa was going to be able to handle other people's reactions to the crutches and braces that she needed in order to walk, as well as her awkward gait, as a result of cerebral palsy. Her father, Dave, especially still felt uncomfortable about the stares Lisa received from strangers when they went out, but he didn't quite know what to do about it. Dave wanted to protect his daughter from emotional harm. He sometimes felt like venting his anger at the rude people who stared at Lisa or made thoughtless comments within earshot.

One afternoon the family went to a local fast-food restaurant for lunch. Lisa was first in the door at the overcrowded restaurant, and in an instant the whole place fell silent as all eyes turned toward her. Lisa's parents were taken aback, but Lisa took charge of the situation, yelling out a friendly "Hi!" that could be heard throughout the room. Her greeting was returned by several people, and she proceeded to charge down the tightly packed aisles, like Moses dividing the Red Sea, with her family trailing behind her.

Later, when the family was back in the car, Lisa told her parents she did not like people staring at her. Dave found it easier than he had expected to talk to Lisa about the way some people react to handicaps. She had already solved the immediate problem by developing her own way of coping, but she still needed to talk about her feelings.

Parents' and Children's Feelings

One of Dave's major concerns was that Lisa would not be accepted by others. He found that as he became more relaxed about her handicap, so did those around him. He could remember his initial denial of Lisa's handicap and his anger and hostility that he directed at people around him. At first he just could not believe Lisa had cerebral palsy. The social worker described to him the five typical stages that most parents go through—denial, guilt, sadness, adaptation, and adjustment—but for him the most intense feeling was anger, anger at the whole healthy world. He was angry with his wife for giving birth to a child with a handicap, angry with the doctors, and angry with God. His angry reactions toward his wife nearly destroyed their marriage before he was able to resolve his feelings.

Dave recalls that the two big questions that haunted him were "Why me?" and "Why can't they help?" He is still not sure he has found answers to those questions, but somehow they don't seem as significant anymore. Now he feels like an old pro. Once a month he now works with a group of parents who help other parents of children with special needs over the rough spots.

Dave Dubois's reactions were not unusual. Most parents go through the five stages just described in their adjustment to the news that their child has special needs. It is normal to move through these stages at your own pace, there is no fixed time or order. The danger is becoming stuck in one of the stages prior to adjustment and not moving on.

Overreactions

Once you get past the denial and guilt stages in adjusting to a handicapping condition, you may find yourselves overreacting. You may feel like one of those electronic television tennis games, constantly bouncing off the walls of the situation, constantly moving, roaming aimlessly. A real problem develops when you can't change course and push on to find the middle ground. Some families never stop feeling angry or guilty, others drop all their old activities and former social life.

Very few parents go through an adjustment period without overreacting at some point. Most tend to test both sides of the emotional gamut, from being overconfident to totally losing confidence, before they eventually adapt to some degree. Sometimes they wonder what all the fuss was about when they have successfully gone through the adjustment period.

While you are attempting to adapt to new situations and alternatives, you may find yourselves feeling constantly tired; working through your emotions can be just as exhausting as physical labor. You may feel that you are losing control of your emotions and find yourselves crying at the oddest times or heaving deep sighs as you think of what might have been. Between all the extra demands of hospitals, doctors, teachers, traveling, therapies, money, emotional turmoil, and worry, you can become emotionally drained and worn down. You can become despondent, short-tempered, or frantic.

It may seem impossible and somewhat irresponsible to find time to relax. You may wonder, "How can we relax and enjoy ourselves when our child's whole future is at stake?" But in order to keep yourselves going, to really be of help to your children, you need to be calm and collected, not frantic.

Being more relaxed means you are more like your "old selves" and are helping to restore normal family patterns. This offers security to the child and, at the same time, tells her that it's all right to feel happy and to play, too. Children take their cues on how to behave from you. If you go out for an evening when the child does not yet have her feelings worked out, when she is not yet secure, she may complain that she is unloved and deserted. But don't limit your activities on this account. Instead, talk it over with her and help her work through her feelings.

The Need to Reevaluate

As you start to gain focus and face new realities, you may have to start all over again, returning to the original source of the diagnosis to find out what was said. The first time you were probably concerned with how to make it all go away and whom to blame. Now your questions may focus on how to live with the situation and how to help your child deal with it in emotional and physical ways. You may need a repetition of information on schools and other programs, resources, and treatments, and you may now be more ready to incorporate these recommended courses of action as part of your daily life.

A major part of Cathy Lewis's out-of-hospital therapy for her burns was encouragement to use her muscles. It was better for her to reach for her own glass of milk, even though it was messier, slower, and even painful, because this helped her return to ordinary activities, return to normal.

What is normal for your child may be difficult to establish. We would hope that he or she can attain as normal a life as possible without ignoring limitations.

You may go through a period of hoping, but, while you may never really give up these hopes, you may have to learn to balance them with present realities. You may hope that medical science will make new discoveries that will change your child's condition—that is a good and valid hope—but you do not have the luxury of time to wait for that miraculous discovery. You must be willing to utilize what is available to you now. You may hope that the new therapist will solve a problem, but you should be ready to praise both the therapist and the child for the hard work and progress they make, even though it may be far short of your secret dreams.

The goal now is to mix hope with realism and to try to get your family back on an even keel. For the most part your children, including both the child with special needs and any other children, look to you for cues on how to respond. The first step in the adjustment may be to discard your ideas about the traditional roles of husband and wife.

CHANGES IN FAMILY LIFE

Traditionally men have considered themselves the family leader in our culture. As the provider and protector, the father in his reactions helped or hindered the normal adjustment of the whole family to a crisis. But this kind of stereotype creates a heavy load for a man to carry, especially when the protector role has been threatened, if not shattered, by the "injury" one of his children has sustained. A father may feel that he has failed to protect his child against this unforeseen assailant. The role as provider is also under assault when bills, or the fear of them, begin to mount. The husband's role of un-disputed family leader is defaulted when he has no idea of how to lead, where to lead, or what to do about the handicap. His previous training has not prepared him for this.

The stereotype mother has been the nurturing, caring life giver, around whom the family revolves. This role as life giver is disturbed with the birth, or later discovery, of a child with a handicapping condition. If the handicap is a result of illness or accident, a mother may feel she has neglected her duties as guardian of the home. As a result her confidence in her ability to care and nurture may be shaken as she is faced with new demands outside her experience and ex-pectations. Even in the most open marriages, with the most mature individuals, vestiges of the past can cling like faint shadows, if perhaps only at a subconscious level.

Because of such stereotypes both parents may try to take on im-possible tasks alone. But this is the time for parents to reach out to each other, to share their doubts and fears, their love and under-standing, without worrying about their supposed roles as all-knowing family protector or family life giver. A single parent facing these problems may need to find additional resources outside the extended family. But for a couple, the first place to look for and to find help is within the family. It is important to maintain strong caring and supportive relationships that ultimately can lessen the burden.

It may be easier for you to help each other with emotional bur-dens if you are accustomed to sharing other responsibilities as well, if the family works together to deal with daily tasks. Problems such as finances and medical decisions are easier to share if you also share obligations for the care of the house and care of the children. When fathers are not locked into total responsibility for financial matters and mothers for domestic matters, mutual support and encourage-ment help make difficult decisions and difficult times more bearable and manageable.

A father who is able to go with his handicapped child to some of the specialists is better able to understand not only the diagnosis but also the feelings of his wife and child. He is better able to establish a relationship with the professionals concerned with the diagnostic process, which will make it easier for him to ask questions and to develop a trust and confidence in the professionals.

It is extremely difficult to trust the judgment of people that you never see, especially when their judgment will affect the lives of your family and the future of your child. Placing the total burden on the wife for receiving the diagnosis is not only unfair, it is dangerous to her role as wife and mother. Fathers who do not participate in the evaluation process may treat their wives like traitors, when she passes along reports that are less positive than the fathers hope to hear.

In order to work through the process successfully, it is necessary that both parents be involved. If demands of job make it totally impossible for the father to make weekday appointments, perhaps the appointments can be arranged for weekends. Or he may be able to find time in evenings or during the day to talk to the professionals directly, in person or at least by telephone. Both parents will then be able to discuss the pros and cons of difficult decisions and to help each other over the rough spots, as well as to celebrate progress.

If you are a father who was slow to get involved and now feel confused with all that is going on, it's still not too late to try to catch up. If you can't understand why your wife is having a hard time at home with your child, find a day when you can switch roles; stay at home and give your spouse a deserved day away from the house. At the end of the day full of child care, dishes, and vacuuming, multiply all these chores by 365 days and you may get an idea of what your partner faces on a day-in-day-out basis. Even if both of you work and you are already sharing tasks, it may be time to reassess who is doing which task; everything may not be as equal as you have been assuming.

You each should also make a list of where you are spending your time. If you find that, increasingly, one or both of you is spending most of your time dealing with the handicap, the school, the doctor, the parent group, fund raising, and so on, you need to stop for a minute and put everything in perspective. Not only could you be dropping old activities that were meaningful and renewing to you, but you could be neglecting the other members of your family and even the welfare of the child with the handicap, a child who needs to be considered as a whole child with many different needs beyond those of the handicap.

Mothers tend to do this more than fathers, and, as a result, fathers can feel neglected to the point of resenting the handicapped child. If the family works together, priorities can be reexamined and reorganized—time for a family outing may be just as important as a therapy visit, or the two could be coordinated to overlap. One of the other family members may be willing to take over some of the extra responsibilities associated with the handicap if that means they would have more time with the parent who had been taking on that responsibility.

A Family Perspective

It may seem that your child's special needs are paramount. Undoubtedly the handicap may focus your attention first on these needs, but the needs of the entire family and the child need to be considered first. It may seem difficult to integrate the special needs of one of your children into the family patterns, but it needs to be done.

If you neglect the family and the other important needs of your child, it can cause even more serious problems. For example, your other children can create crisis situations, consciously or unconsciously, to get some of the attention that is focused on the child with the special needs in order to remind you that they are still around and have needs themselves.

Involving the Family

It is both essential and practical to involve the other children as much as possible without burdening them with your problems. How much you tell and involve them depends on their ages and temperaments, but children do understand more than parents often give them credit for. If you, as parents—and perhaps neighbors, relatives, and older children in the family—are acting upset or strained in relation to the handicap, you will have to explain and reassure younger children. They probably sense the change in routines or feelings in the atmosphere without any words being said, and they need to have this all explained to them. It is extremely unfair to leave children in the dark.

You may be explaining, reexplaining, clarifying, and expanding for some time to come. You will be answering the same questions in slightly different ways as the children grow older and need different kinds of information. It may not be very significant to a preschool child if her brother has a handicap as long as he is a good playmate, but in adolescence, and even preadolescence, questions of social acceptance and genetics may arise. If the family has a negative feeling about the child or the handicap, or hasn't yet had time to work all their feelings through, an adolescent may be afraid to mention her sibling to her friends, much less have him around when her friends are around.

These feelings, such as resentment for being deprived attention, or being overburdened by having a sibling with special needs, may either be valid or exist only in the child's mind. But either way they deserve your serious and sympathetic attention. Responding with anger or telling the child she should be thankful she is not handicapped is not the answer. You should try to discuss with your child all of his or her conflicting feelings and how each family member can help one another. Also, you should be able to take advantage of professional help when you need it.

You may discover that you have been letting the child with special needs take advantage of family relationships. You may then realize that you have not been fair to any of the family members. A child who has never had to cope with the realities of demands and responsibilities will have a very difficult time adjusting to the outside world. Overprotection is a normal reaction, but now is the time to move on to the job of helping your child with special needs develop into an independent self-sufficient individual.

The special needs of a child with a handicapping condition may be quite different from the ordinary needs you are used to, and they may demand a great deal of extra effort. But these needs can be, and should be, made a routine part of your life. When they do become as routine as the need to put out the garbage, brush your teeth, or read a bedtime story, there will be less inconvenience to other family members—and an easier adjustment by the child with special needs.

PARENTING A CHILD WITH SPECIAL NEEDS

One group of parents in Michigan, talking about the qualities that they considered important in parenting children with special needs, agreed that the first consideration is that the child should be viewed first as a child and only second as a child with a handicap.

They felt strongly that children with handicaps should be, and need to be, treated the same as any other child—with firmness but flexibility, with love but with limits. A family may have to accept a wide range of behaviors different from those of a child without a handicapping condition. For example, a four-year-old who has motor problems or retarded mental development might not be able to cope with the same physical demands as a child without these problems. But parents should remain consistent on the guidelines for discipline they establish within their family.

Most of these parents were able to take pride in the small successes as well as the larger accomplishments that their children experienced, partly because they tended to focus on the present, the daily realities, rather than constantly worrying about an uncertain future. Most of the parents agreed that such qualities as openness, flexibility, and the ability to set realistic goals and limits were important in parenting children with special needs. But the most important factor to all was good communication among all the members of the family—parents and children alike.

As parents, you want your children with special needs to be as "normal" as possible, whatever this means to you. You are forced so many times to focus on what is lacking, the limits, that you may forget what is there and what potentials exist. (On the other hand, you may go overboard in the opposite direction and totally ignore limits, perhaps in a forced effort to make the child normal in the ways you've expected.) Depending upon the child's handicap, there will be many things the child will be able to do independently, or with minimal adaptations to the environment, if you will let them try.

Linda used a wheelchair to get around, but she wanted to attend a school dance. Her parents immediately rejected the idea as ridiculous and embarrassing. Linda was well aware of her limits, that she could not get up and dance like the other kids, but she felt she would have a good time anyway. She enjoyed listening to the music and the opportunity to talk with her friends at a social occasion. She felt her friends accepted her as she was, and as an equal, and that her parents treated her like a child.

Like any teen-ager, Linda wanted opportunities to feel free and independent. It was hard for her parents to realize that she had the normal desires and turmoil of an adolescent even though she was confined a great deal by her lack of mobility. Their overprotection annoyed Linda, and she fought them all the way in order to maintain her worth as a functioning person.

An example of her struggle to assert herself in small ways was the running battle she waged with her father over her clothes closet. Since Linda could not stand up independently, she couldn't reach the closet pole, which ran across her closet at the standard height. She always had to ask one of her sisters to help her get her clothes, which both she and they resented. But Linda's father refused to lower the pole or to help her work out some other system.

After Linda graduated from college and began earning her own money, she moved away from her parents and into an apartment. One of the first things she did was to hire a carpenter to lower the closet pole and several other fixtures in the apartment. Here, there was no one around to help her, so she had to be able to do everything for herself or do without. It was difficult, but succeeding gave her a sense of accomplishment and pride in herself.

Overprotection

In reorganizing your family life after the discovery that one of your children has a handicapping condition, you may forget what that child can or will be able to do for herself. Instead, you may make plans for others to do things for her. You are falling into the common trap of overprotection. It is easier and faster for Daddy to tie shoelaces for his four-year-old child instead of patiently waiting as the child laboriously learns to tie them on his own. So it is with a child with a handicap. You may "do for" rather than take the extra time to teach, to wait, to find out how to accommodate the environment to limitations that the child may have.

If your child wants a drink of water, a heart condition or lack of mobility is no reason why she should not get it for herself. Be creative with ways to make difficult tasks possible, and realize that they will not be without effort and an accompanying sense of accomplishment. Finding the easy way around a problem instead of working with a child to gain skills and confidence is just another way of doing it for the child, robbing her of independence. A lot more might be possible than you initially think.

Start with examining your house and how it is set up. You might need to make some minor or major changes to make it function optimally. This may mean ramps, lower shelves, an orderly place to put toys, removal of sharp edges on in-place furniture, and so on. These may increase the child's ability to cope with the environment efficiently without cushioning him severely from reality. Take the time to look at the house from your child's view and you may come up with some simple solutions to tricky problems.

You have to balance what is possible, what is a potential, and what is out of the question. A child who faces the constant frustration of an impossible task becomes discouraged, but the satisfaction of succeeding at some long-range difficult tasks can overcome discouragement and lead to an increasing sense of accomplishment. Don't take away challenges just because they are difficult, or bend over backward to make everything easy; if *necessary*, adapt the environment, but leave opportunities for growth.

You may discover that your child can adapt the handicap itself, as, for example, using a crutch to reach a light switch that is too high or, perhaps, kicking an especially aggressive classmate in the shins with an artificial leg. (While you would probably voice your disapproval of this type of behavior, you may secretly applaud your child's creativity and independence.)

As a child grows, so should her responsibilities. The difficulty at first is to find the middle ground between asking the child to do the impossible and protecting the child from doing anything. As you become more used to the handicap, more secure and relaxed in dealing with the realities it imposes, you will feel more comfortable about what you should ask, what you will have to adapt, and what will have to be avoided or deferred until a later date. You will feel freer about experimenting and making mistakes.

It is of the utmost importance for the child to be valued as a human being and to be treated as normally as possible. This helps prepare him for the demands of the larger world outside the home. Constantly to be treated as different is unnecessary, is difficult for the child to deal with, and can stunt normal development. A child with special needs will so often be treated as different by others that she needs a strong sense of self, a strong sense that she is a valued and valuable person. At the same time, this larger world will make heavy demands upon the child, which she needs to be prepared for as much as possible.

Your Child's Need for Responsibilities

You should allow and encourage all your children, regardless of special needs, to understand not only their limits but their strengths. If all the children have tasks in the house, it is unfair to exclude the child with special needs automatically. There is more than likely a task that he can do, or one that can be adapted or invented for him.

All the children in the McCall family had daily chores to do, from making their own beds and keeping their rooms neat to putting out the garbage and setting the table. After six-year-old LeRoy McCall was struck by a car and suffered injuries that impaired his sense of balance, his parents and brothers and sister tended to baby him, they were very protective toward him as he moved around the house. Gradually his parents became concerned that LeRoy was becoming spoiled and lazy from all of the extra attention and accommodations to his handicaps. Certainly, there were some tasks that were beyond him, and some that would take him twice as long, but they felt that he should at least try to relearn some of the tasks expected of all the other children.

"With five children in the house, I'd have time to be nothing more than a maid if everyone didn't pitch in and do his part." LeRoy's mother, Edna, decided. "My son may not be able to do things the way he used to, but he'll have to start learning again, because I won't be here forever to wait on him when he's a man."

Her husband agreed. The McCalls began to find ways to reintroduce LeRoy to his responsibilities as a family member. It wasn't easy at first. For example, at dinnertime, LeRoy did not have the coordination to take the plates and glasses to the table without breaking some. So, at first, his mother set him to work folding napkins.

"It took twice as long—no, maybe three times as long—as one of the other kids, and he whined and complained about it," Edna remembers. "But he did it, and soon it took him less and less time. And he began to see himself a little differently, like a boy instead of a sick baby everyone took care of."

After the napkin folding demonstrated that a little work wouldn't hurt anyone, Edna invested in some unbreakable dinnerware. Now when its LeRoy's turn to set the table, she doesn't worry about broken dishes. Her oldest son figured out a way for his brother to carry in the plates efficiently, adapting the chore to fit LeRoy's abilities at the moment. And all the children started to view LeRoy as just one of the family again, instead of as some breakable doll.

A child who is frequently on the receiving end of assistance should also have opportunities for giving. Giving and receiving, and mutual cooperation, are a normal family process. Learning to give makes it easier for the child more frequently on the receiving end to accept that help as normal. It also helps him to find ways and situations where he is able to give. There are very few children whose handicap is so severe that they are totally excluded from participating in normal family life. It may take extra time and effort, and perhaps a little creativity, but there are many ways to help your child with special needs be a functioning member of your family.

Understanding Special Needs

Although Michael Fine was blind, he was beginning to learn many things at his nursery school that would help him in achieving independence. He had learned small tasks, such as efficiently dressing and eating, that would be stepping stones toward larger ones later on. Michael's father, Bill, wanted to understand more about what Michael's life was like, what problems and feelings Michael has as a child who could not see. Bill went to school with his son one day and watched the children and their teachers and took time to talk to Michael's teacher about his son's abilities and problems. She explained that it is hard to imagine what these problems are like unless they've really been experienced. She suggested that Bill try going through some of his daily tasks blindfolded.

The Fines tried the idea by having dinner at home blindfolded. Initially apprehensive, they began to relax as they realized that no one would judge them for the mess they were making. They also realized how difficult being blind is for their son and how well he really copes with it.

Bill and Julie talked about their experiment with friends. Soon they found themselves being invited to a local public school to lead the children with sight in the experience of a "blind snack" and as a way to give them insight into what it is like to be blind. Later, a local civic group also gave a "blind dinner" as part of an education campaign to make its members aware of the needs of individuals with handicaps within their community.

Bill Fine felt that he better understood the challenges that Michael was facing. He also felt a sense of pride in Michael's accomplishments, accomplishments he had previously taken for granted or even secretly been ashamed of. It became apparent to Bill that his son was special in a positive way, because of what he could accomplish despite limits.

In many parts of the country structured programs have been set up like the Fines' informal little experiment with blind meals that demonstrate to nonhandicapped children and adults just what the experience of having limits means. Some programs sponsored by parent groups or agencies introduce a specific handicap; others try to show a range. In one school a school-sponsored health program included a session in which students wore blindfolds, heavy earphones, and lightweight poles that limited their movements in order to show them how it feels to have a handicap. In such programs students are supervised by several staff members, who after the experience lead discussions with them about their feelings and discoveries.

It is important for you to understand as much as possible what it is that your handicapped child must deal with. Parents tend, however, to project these feelings on their children without realizing that they have their own methods of coping, that they frequently adjust and adapt better than the parents would in the same situation. Every child will not take the same route in the same time with the same reactions on the way to adjustments. Children will often go through many periods of anger or despair as their understanding increases about what the handicap will mean. The problems that are monumental to a six-year-old are usually inconsequential to a fourteen-year-old, and vice versa.

Encouragement or Pushing?

When you work with your child, you need to keep in mind the differences in individuals and their methods of dealing with life. Some children are natural "go-getters" who will try anything once, while others tend to be cautious about new situations. If you set up a model of the way in which your child should handle himself, you are bound to be disappointed. This is especially true if you base your expectations on what you have seen in late-night TV movies and in novels. The classic stereotype of the "martyr," a polite, modest person with a handicap who "knows his place" is reminiscent of attitudes toward other minorities who have been expected to stay out of the mainstream of life and all its opportunities. Another stereotype, the "hero" or the brave "gusty" person with a handicap who "overcomes" it to become a celebrity, is perhaps an ideal that parents hold up in efforts to force their child into achievements that can bring them pride at whatever price. Parents may try to fit themselves into these roles as well.

As parents you need to help your child reach her full potential without trying to do the work for her or pushing her beyond what is realistically possible. You need to be available to help your child pick up the pieces when he fails, but you must be willing to stand aside when your help is not wanted. Most people learn by trial and error; if you take away the chance to try, you also take away the chance to learn; if you take away the error, you take away the experience of trying.

There is a great difference between pushing a child and encouraging. You can encourage the child in reaching his potential, but you cannot do it for him, and neither can you force it upon him. You may find it frustrating to cope with a period of despair, or the disappointing results of overoptimism, with your child. But it is probably even more frustrating to have to stand on the sideline while your child works through a difficult time by herself.

You may want to encourage your own Linda to go to a school dance and to participate in normal school activities, but you cannot force her. There is no reason why a handicapped person should be denied a social life, or forced to become a recluse, but if that person is not ready to deal with interacting with others, then pushing may only result in disaster. Your role, then, is to build or reestablish confidence in the individual as a person of value. If you criticize his lack of confidence, you only succeed in further eroding confidence.

THE REACTIONS OF OTHERS

In helping your children establish their own self-esteem, you should not allow them, or yourselves, to be treated as second-class citizens. This means you should also not feel or treat yourselves as though you were. Many people just do not know how to deal with individuals who have handicaps. Their sense of basic etiquette does not include this situation, and they feel ill at ease and uncomfortable. For example, in attempting to be gracious, they may tend to be rude. In such a situation, you can politely, but firmly, remind them that your child does have feelings and would like to be treated like everyone else. Most people will respond positively if only given the chance to understand how you—and your child—feel. The few who remain prejudiced and rude are seldom worth knowing.

Getting Children Involved

Eventually your children will have to face and solve these problems of daily living without your protection. Some children are just natural social butterflies and, with or without the handicap, would have an active life. For others the handicap only serves to accentuate their feelings of isolation. Again, there are ways in which you can intervene. For younger children you might consider spending a little extra money to build an unusually well equipped play structure that could act as a magnet for other children in the neighborhood, or you might maintain a fresh supply of cookies within the house. You may end up having to tolerate the noise created by every child in the neighborhood congregating at your house, but it may be worth it for your own child's sake.

This is not to say that you should try to "buy" company for your child. Bribes tend to backfire. You can probably remember a situation in your own childhood when you tried it, only to find that everyone deserted you as soon as the candy, or whatever treat, was gone. Everyone likes to be liked for who they are, not for what they can provide others. When your child discovers that you have in essence "bought" him friends—and he will—his self-esteem will crumble. He will think that he is so worthless that he cannot have friends on his own.

What you can do, however, is find ways for your child to become involved in the mainstream without pushing him into it headlong. For an older child, consider becoming involved with local youth programs, such as scouts. Most programs are chronically short of adult volunteers; they would be more likely to welcome your child if your services were part of the deal.

Also, most areas have at least one scout troop in which children with special needs are integrated with other children. If your area does not have such a program, ask the local council, listed in the telephone directory, to consider establishing one. Such groups do take more effort, but if you are willing to pitch in, they already have their first volunteer and resource person. If your local council officials are uncertain about such a program, you can help by showing examples from other areas. The national office listed in the Directory of Chapter 5 should be able to provide assistance.

You can help your child by providing opportunities, but then it is really up to the child. A child who has a poor self-image may still find it impossible to make friends, to interact comfortably with others. A child who has not been taught appropriate ways to deal with other people may be rejected by others; just because a child has a handicap does not mean that you can forget about teaching social graces in addition to providing special therapies. But a child who is taught such things as part of the routine growing-up process, in which he is treated as a child who happens to have special needs rather than as a "special" child, will probably have little more difficulty dealing with other children or adults than any other child.

Even when the family has established a normal role for the child with special needs, there will be periods of stress. The preschool child is usually not overly concerned that he is different, he tends to view the world as different. Playmates may accept him without reservation at this stage. It is only when children begin to become more socialized, subject to adult attitudes, that social values are placed on differences.

The first negative experiences the child will encounter usually occur during the early school years. A child who has received support from home and is secure will have difficult days, but in the long run she will be able to face them. As parents your first reaction may be to protect your child from the rough spots rather than help her deal with difficulties. She can, with help, learn to cope. By establishing herself as an individual, she can overcome prejudice and can accomplish much. She may have to explain to teachers and other adults what she can and can't do, or deal with the class bully or the random name-caller on the playground. Sometimes these are shattering experiences, but they are not so different, really, from experiences faced by other children. These challenges give a child a solid base of experience in dealing with other difficult problems related to the handicap and to life in general.

Adolescence is a period of testing, establishing an identity, and experiencing insecurity. Most people can look back and remember this as a painful, or at least tumultuous, period in their lives. The child with a handicap has an additional dimension to deal with. The child who enters adolescence prepared, using his experiences of success and failure, will not only survive, much to his surprise, but he will grow. It may take longer in some cases, and at times it may be more painful, but a child who has a handicap can arrive at adulthood as a fully developed person who may be better prepared to cope with the real problems of life.

The Reactions of Those Close to You

As you become more adjusted to your child's handicap, you will still have to deal with the reactions of others who may not be prepared to accept the condition as a matter of routine. You may be startled by comments from relatives or friends about how brave you are in such a tragic situation. What they view as tragic you are beginning to view as a matter of fact.

At times, questions from relatives and friends can aid you in clarifying your thoughts as you form your own answers. It is reassuring when your friends and relatives can work through their own feelings and accept your child as he or she is. They then can be very supportive to you. Unfortunately, this adjustment frequently takes more time for those outside the immediate family. Since the realities are part of your daily life, you are forced to make adjustments. Those outside the family may find it easier to deny the problem rather than to adapt to it. Sometimes the first such reactions you have to start dealing with are those of your own parents. Grandparents are known for their wisdom; if they managed to raise you, they are presumably able to survive anything. And indeed, they may be able to provide insight that will be helpful and comforting to you. However, as helpful as they wish to be, grandparents and others can meddle and become involved with a crisis in child raising that may be beyond their experiences.

Some relatives and friends may never make the adjustment and may continue to view your child only as a handicap instead of as an individual. Your child may then be the subject of pity, which is seldom useful to him and which is frustrating to you because you realize these people are concerned for the child.

You need to intervene before this becomes a major problem. It is unnecessary when you are trying to help your child reach realistic potentials to have to fight every step of the way with those who want to "protect" the child, just as it is unnecessary to have to apologize to others who seem to chide you because the child has not "cured" himself of his handicap.

The Lees had the problem of an overly helpful and sympathetic, but misguided, grandmother, who would visit them and try to sneak "treats" and "good wholesome food" to their son, Alex. Alex was on a strictly regulated diet, with everything balanced and measured, and these well-meaning extras from grandmother invariably made him ill. The Lees couldn't seem to convince her of the harm she was doing. She was causing emotional damage as well with her sympathy, calling Alex her "poor baby" in front of him and praying for a miraculous recovery. The Lees finally set down a difficult ultimatum. Either the snacks or the visits would have to stop, and the prayers would have to be said in private. Now that she knows that they will carry out their threat, the treats have disappeared. The prayers still continue to be audible, even though she tries to keep them private.

The Knapps, on the other hand, had one grandparent who denied the existence of their son Jonah's retardation, rationalizing that retardation was just a "phase" that Jonah would outgrow. Another grandparent rejected Jonah completely and even refused to acknowledge Jonah as his grandchild, calling him a "pitiful specimen" and totally ignoring him when they were both present in the same room. The Knapps hope that both grandparents will be able to come to grips with some of the realities of the situation, but they doubt that the adjustments will come soon or to any great degree.

As your family develops positive attitudes, you may be met with skepticism. It may take time, but your example can win over the doubters. In the meantime, you should try to avoid the well-meaning but inappropriate help offered. Sometimes, you can sidetrack some of it harmlessly, but it becomes more than just unhelpful when you are trying to cope on the one hand with your own feelings and on the other with relatives who are still deeply upset and unaccepting of a child who has a handicap. Somewhere in the middle is a child who may not initially recognize her limitations and consider herself handicapped.

A Growing Awareness of Differences

Frequently the young child with a handicap will view the condition matter-of-factly and only slowly learn that others are different. While the child is trying to figure this out, you may be worrying about the future. The child begins to realize that she is different, but it takes a while to define *different* as having limits others do not have. The child, unlike society, does not define *different* as being automatically inferior. This comes from experiences outside, which can be surprising to the child.

Children with special needs will eventually sense the reactions of others, and they, in turn, will react to those reactions. Michael Fine was three before he realized that the rest of the world could see and he could not. He had assumed that everyone had the same capacities. Children don't become really aware in differences in people until they are about three or four years old, and they may not fully understand them for several years after that. A child will usually be pre-adolescent or adolescent before he fully understands the social implications of differences in age, sex, race, and handicaps.

Children who become handicapped at an older age will usually go through stages similar to those of the adults around him. If the child has a strong sense that he is valued, and is of value, he is better prepared to handle being different without feeling inferior. There will be times when such children will test limits, they will go without medication to see if they really need it or try an impossible task beyond their capabilities. Some of this will be an attempt to deny a handicap or prove it doesn't exist in a concrete way. There will be periods of anger and frustration at being the "only one" who has to or who can't. This can be more painful if the child is denied a role in the family other than one of being served.

Sam was angry with his family, and the anger grew more intense every day. Due to a progressively degenerative illness Sam was confined to a wheelchair with very limited mobility and use of his extremities. His major complaint was not that he was so ill but that no one in the family respected him. At sixteen, he felt that he was not allowed privileges given to his younger brothers, and he was outraged that they were put in charge of him when his parents went out.

"I am older than both of them. They should listen to me but they don't," Sam complained. "I get treated like the baby of the family." He retaliated by making constant demands for service from his brothers, which they resented and which led to a more strained relationship. Sam was having serious emotional problems and was becoming increasingly more isolated.

You might assume that Sam would be overwhelmed with fears of death, but instead his first need was to be accepted as a person and a young adult. He could not cope with other problems as long as this one was unresolved and growing worse.

If constantly compared to others or put down for having limits, a child will develop a strong sense of inferiority. The same sense of inferiority can occur if the child is babied or spoiled by excess attention. Sam was old enough to try to fight this, but even young children are aware, even if you always aren't, that the treatment he gets is special. He may conclude that this is because he is unable to cope, in a negative sense. Or he may develop a false sense of self-importance and superiority, which will become an additional handicap.

It is extremely difficult for a child to find that sense of equilibrium between being dependent and independent. Part of the experience of growing up for any child is trying to achieve an awareness of who he is and what he can do. Frequently, this is a more involved process for a child with special needs. Asking for help gracefully is as difficult a skill to acquire as learning to give help gracefully, and so much harder for a child, who is simultaneously struggling to be an independent person.

Marty, a young adult in training at an occupational center for the retarded, made it his responsibility to help Richard, another student who happened to be the terror of the workshop. Most of the counselors had given up on Richard, and his outrageous behavior was making his expulsion from the program likely. But Marty felt he could reach out to Richard and help him learn how to cope.

Every day Marty would spend some time with Richard, talking or just fooling around. As they became friends, Marty was able to get Richard to control his behavior somewhat. When asked why he helped Richard, Marty said that he knew how it felt to be slow and left out and that he too sometimes felt angry like Richard did. But people had helped him understand that he was good, and he wanted to help Richard feel this too.

Marty had achieved a very firm sense of self-worth and was able to reach out past his own limitations to help another. He realized he was slow to do some things, but he didn't feel that this made him inferior. He could ask for help when he needed it, but he felt he wasn't limited to receiving; he could also give help to someone else. Marty may have been handicapped in some ways, but he showed a sense of compassion, concern, and responsibility well beyond what many "normal" people demonstrate in their everyday lives.

Just what your child with special needs can achieve may depend on the severity of the handicap. But whether or not your child can adjust to his or her limitations and develop into a self-sufficient and responsible adult may depend largely on whether you as parents can make the adjustment and provide the guidance, discipline, and love your child will need in order to grow. It won't always be easy, but millions of parents have proven that it can be done. Probably, so can you if you are willing to modify some of your initial expectations.

CHANGES IN LIFE-STYLE AND ASPIRATIONS

When your child was born, and even before, you had all sorts of dreams and hopes, some of which were originally planned for yourselves. You may have achieved some dreams, and others you have put aside, depending upon your children to take them up again. But when you discovered that your child was handicapped in some way, you may have felt that many of these dreams were destroyed, perhaps forever. Perhaps many of them were. Originally, you may have been concerned that your child would have a happy life, as defined in terms of money, power, and prestige. Of course, these do not automatically guarantee happiness or success. Having a handicap does not destroy happiness, but many people frequently think and act as if it did. You can still realistically hope that your child will lead a rich and fulfilling life, and you can help maintain that hope for your child.

You may have established a very comfortable way of life with set patterns and expectations that are suddenly changed with the introduction of a child with a handicap. A family that was very active in rugged outdoor sports may feel that a child with physical limitations, such as a heart condition, may destroy the possibility of enjoying these activities as a family. A family who expected that all of the children would go to college may feel that the future is exceedingly dim for a child who is slow at school.

You may have to reexamine your old life-styles, even question old values, and establish new priorities for your family. You may be able to meet these challenges successfully and may gain from them. A family may have to severely limit their camping, for example, but by being inventive and creatively using available resources they can find ways for everyone to enjoy the experience together. A family may have to withdraw the application to Harvard they had written up in their minds for twenty years in the future and instead become concerned with vocational training or sheltered workshops. All of this may cause stress, but if you are fortunate, you just may end up with a family that has a greater understanding of love and a sense of togetherness.

DIRECTORY

Also see: Chapter 5 Directory for parent groups and counseling services.

Chapter References

BOOKS

Ayrault, Evelyn West. *You Can Raise Your Handicapped Child.* New York: G. P. Putnam's Sons, 1964.

Blumfield, Jane; Thompson, P. E.; and Vogel, B. S. *Help Them Grow: A Practical Handbook for Parents of Handicapped Children.* Nashville, Tenn.: Abington Press, 1971.

Coffin, P. *1,2,3,4,5,6, How to Understand and Enjoy the Years That Count*. New York: Macmillan Co., 1972.

Heisler, V. *A Handicapped Child in the Family*. New York: Grune and Stratton, 1972.

Hewett, S. *The Family and the Handicapped Child*. Chicago: Aldine, 1970.

Kvaraceus, William C., and Hayes, Nelson E. *If Your Child is Handicapped*. Boston: Porter, Sargent, Inc., 1969.

McDonald, Eugene T. *Understand Those Feelings*. Englewood, N.J.: Prentice-Hall, 1964.

Wentworth, Elsie H. *Listen to Your Heart: A Message to Parents of Handicapped Children*. Boston: Houghton Mifflin, 1974.

PERIODICALS

Children Today, U.S., Department of Health, Education, and Welfare, U.S. Government Printing Office. $5/year.

Closer Look, periodical of the Bureau of Education for the Handicapped of the Office of Education, U.S., Department of Health, Education, and Welfare. (Write to : Closer Look Mailing List, Box 1492, Washington, D.C. 20013; free of cost.)

The Exceptional Parent, P.O. Box 964, Manchester, N.H. 03105. $10/year.

4

How to Find Schools
and Programs

Now you have a name for your child's condition. It has been explained in technical jargon that is difficult to absorb. But what does it all mean in emotional and practical terms? How can you use this information today to help your child meet the problems of tomorrow's world?

In the best circumstances you will have learned something about the special treatment, training, therapy, education, or other services that your child needs. These services may substantially reduce or even eliminate the problems. At the very least they should help you and your child adjust to the realities of the situation and learn to compensate for the limitations.

But all too often your ability to take advantage of the practical guidance you have been given will be limited because the programs in your locality are inadequate. The U.S. Office of Education estimates that only about half of the approximately seven and a half million handicapped children in the United States between the ages of three and twenty-one are in adequate programs. Despite increased government spending and new federal legislation, as many as one million handicapped children are not receiving any educational services at all. The ultimate frustration is to find that a program *does* exist that can meet your child's needs but that there is a waiting list that could delay placement for a year or more.

Your objective must be to make the most of the potentials available. You want to find your child's strengths and build upon them. In order to do this, you are undoubtedly going to need outside professional help. Sometimes the frustrations of trying to get this help can seem more difficult to deal with than the problem itself.

HOME OR RESIDENCE

The decision to keep a severely handicapped child at home or to find other residential alternatives is an individual matter that is dependent on the abilities and energies of each family. There is no rule that applies to all cases. Only the family itself can decide what is right for them.

When the Knapps' son Jonah was born, their doctor knew immediately that the baby had Down's syndrome and would be retarded. Later tests only confirmed his opinion. The doctor's advice was to institutionalize the baby immediately, before the Knapps became attached to him. They decided not to follow their doctor's recommendation.

Undoubtedly, emotions played a strong role in their decision, but, because they had a neighbor whose child had the same condition, the Knapps were also aware that children with Down's syndrome *could* achieve within limits. The child had brought not only crisis into their neighbor's home but happiness as well. While the Knapps could not be sure this would be the case in their family, they did know that their son Jonah was not to be lightly rejected.

On the recommendation of their neighbor, the Knapps joined an early infant stimulation program and participated in its parent support group. Here, under the guidance of social workers, mothers and fathers with similar children could talk out their feelings and hopes. After eighteen months Jonah's mother could speak with the conviction of experience: "He has value. You can't throw away people who don't fit into your set of values, your priorities. Jonah has his own strengths, perhaps quite different from the ones we expect."

The Knapps were feeling more confident that they had made the right decision. It is easy, however, to overestimate or underestimate your own capabilities. Before making the decision to keep your child at home or to search for a suitable institutional setting, you should have a complete diagnosis and a clear understanding of the implications for your family.

If you feel unable to deal with the challenges of parenting a severely handicapped child, you may well consider institutionalization. As distasteful as this may seem at first, it could be destructive to an entire family to attempt to cope with the round-the-clock, demanding care required by a severely handicapped child. Your feelings of distaste may be products of the poor image institutions for the handicapped have received over the years. Such institutions were often considered places for undesirables who should be hidden away from the rest of society. Out of sight, out of mind. At the same time, those with the training needed to provide help for handicapped people were always concentrated in the large state institutions, while resources at a local level were almost nonexistant.

Fortunately, attitudes are changing and institutional facilities no longer must hide away children with handicaps. New philosophies and legislation have done much to improve the climate. So have court rulings, such as a federal court decision ordering that disastrous overcrowding at New York's Willowbrook School for the Retarded be eased by reducing the number of residents from 5,500 to 250. This was to be done by dispersing the residents among a variety of community-based living arrangements, including foster care, group homes, small residences, and return to their families; other resources within the community, such as recreation, schools, and training programs were made available to the returning residents.

Immediately upon the birth of your child or after getting diagnosis you may be advised to place the child in an institution before you become attached to him or her. This is usually the worst time to make such a decision, since you are still unaware of the full extent of the child's needs and your ability to handle them within your community. Frequently, the advice to institutionalize a child comes with pressure and with a stereotyped reaction to the abilities and rewards of a child with special needs. Some children may not be able to be cared for at home, some families may not be suited to taking care of a severely handicapped child, but if resources were made available many more children could be cared for within a family setting.

All children will someday leave home, including your child with special needs, if for no other reason than you will not live forever. Parents need to prepare their children for the challenges of independence in adult life as much as they can. Some children need specialized services, such as adapting their physical limitations to certain household setups or responsibilities. Other children will be less independent and need adult assistance or supervision. A very few will be totally dependent, requiring twenty-four-hour nursing care.

Large institutions often have been unable to meet the needs of children and adults with specialized needs. Today, hope is placed upon smaller living arrangements, including foster family care, where a person lives within a substitute family, and group living arrangements, such as hostels, halfway houses, and group homes. Group homes and other small familylike living alternatives should be located within the community, preferably within the community that the individual resident comes from, and should have access to vocational, educational, and other resources.

Regrettably, there are not nearly enough group homes for those who need them. States have previously invested massive amounts of money in large state institutions and neglected smaller residences. As states and local organizations move to develop homelike living arrangements, they frequently encounter a storm of protest from local community members. These people are reacting to outdated stereotypes that hold that people with physical or mental limitations will behave poorly in their neighborhoods and will become a liability to the community as a whole. Such fears are groundless when a group home is run properly with a qualified and dedicated supervisory staff. A group home can be an asset to a community and may well be the best-run home on the block.

It does not make sense to hide away people who are somehow different from the general population. There is no reason why retarded or physically handicapped children and adults cannot live in the community and make contributions as worthwhile citizens, rather than existing only as public burdens.

Much has been done to achieve this more humane and practical end by providing home nursing care and special residences in which architectural barriers have been eliminated. The United Cerebral Palsy Association has developed model housing for young adults, which allows them to work or study within the community and lead independent lives away from their families, just as other young people do.

Only time and actual experience will provide some of the answers that you will need in order to make a decision about whether to care for your child at home or to seek out institutional care, either on a full-time or part-time basis. Talking with other parents who have had to make similar decisions can help, particularly concerning the practical and emotional problems one encounters each hour of each day, although you may also need professional advice.

You may find that there are few alternatives available to you. For most families round-the-clock private institutional care is prohibitively expensive. In addition, a growing number of states, for economic and social reasons, no longer provide large institutions. The Knapps, for example, later discovered that even had they attempted to follow their doctor's recommendation to institutionalize their child, it no longer was a viable option because the department of mental hygiene in their state had decided that children with retarded mental development were better off at facilities within a community, preferably in their own homes.

Government agencies of health, public welfare, or social services may have information on local resources your child may be able to use. You also should contact the U.S. Health, Education, and Welfare Department's Office for the Handicapped for guidance, and the National Education Association's Council for Exceptional Children. Two publications that may have helpful information on institutional, educational, and diagnostic services are the *Directory for Exceptional Children*, by Porter Sargent, and the *Directory of Facilities for the Learning Disabled and Handicapped*, by Careth Ellington and James Cass. See the Directory at the back of this chapter for additional information.

THE BASIC OBJECTIVES

Regardless of your decision, there are some things that cannot be postponed or ignored. With some conditions, a diet must be followed, insulin administered, and radiation treatments given.

But, equally important, when specialized needs are dealt with, the entire life of the child must be considered and kept in perspective. Take time to find out how your child feels. Give him or her opportunities to vent frustration, anger, or disappointment. No one likes to be different. But if you take the time and effort to open yourselves up, you can help your child learn to live with difficult situations.

The kinds of services needed may vary widely, even for children with the same problem. One child with diabetes may require carefully supervised exercise, a strict diet, extra rest, and daily insulin injections. Another child may only require a special diet and insulin taken orally. The right program for one child with retarded mental development might emphasize self-help skills. The correct program for a second child might stress academic development.

Services can be long range, short range, or on a one-time basis. They may be needed for a lifetime or only for a specific period, several times a day or several times a year. Diverse resources—surgery, medication, diet, physical or occupational therapy, psychological counseling or psychiatric treatment, vocational or self-help training, specialized educational programs or settings—can be used to help children deal with particular problems and reach their greatest potentials. The availability of these services, and how they may be used, is dependent upon a number of variables, including the child, the family's finances, and the locality.

A special therapy or education program should help your child move beyond the boundaries imposed by a handicapping condition. In some cases it may even push back these boundaries. Medical treatment may gradually alleviate the symptoms of a condition or ward off the crippling effects. But sometimes the preventive treatment itself can create new problems if it involves difficult exercise, distasteful medication, or unpleasant side effects. A program must be planned in terms of the long-range emotional and intellectual effects on your child as well as the purely medical standpoint.

THE FIRST STEPS

Planning should begin as soon as you get a diagnosis. Don't be put off by well-meaning people who say, "It's too early to treat that," or, "Let's wait until the child has been more thoroughly tested." Surgery is possible immediately following birth. Glasses or hearing aids can be fitted in the first weeks of life. Retarded infants can receive extra stimulation in their early months. There are programs to help toddlers overcome the limitations of handicaps so that they will develop more normally.

You may be able to provide some of these specialized services at home. One of the symptoms of the chronic lung disease cystic fibrosis is the accumulation of excess fluids that must be removed with postural drainage, a matter of positioning the body. Lara Cole would have had to have been taken to the clinic several times a day if the clinic staff had not taught her mother how to do this. Not all her needs can be met at home, of course, and visits are still necessary for medication and other forms of therapy, but without her mother's help life at home would be a virtual impossibility for Lara.

Providing services for your child yourself is far more than a matter of saving money. It also saves wear and tear on you, your child, and your family by reducing the number of trips to get professional assistance. But how much you do must be balanced against other factors. Just as parents often make the poorest teachers, as you may have discovered when trying to help your children with homework, so the parent who tries to be therapist as well may end up being effective at neither role. It isn't simply a matter of time; there is a confusion of roles. It is difficult for a child to see loving parent as distinct from stern and persistent teacher, or disciplining parent from persuasive therapist.

Like medical programs, educational programs may be preventive as well as remedial—that is, aimed at *avoiding* problems. Whether the emphasis is on correcting deficiencies, compensating for them, or arresting their development, the common objective is to make sure your child is not closed off from normal activities or routines. The growth of a child with special educational needs can be stunted in all areas of development because of limits in one.

A child who cannot see will not reach out as readily for objects and people within his environment and thus will miss some of the essential experiences that are building blocks in learning. Extra stimulation and directed activities are needed to compensate for the incentive to explore that sight provides. Children need chances to develop to their fullest potential in all areas, and many kinds of resources can be tapped to provide these.

The professional or group that diagnosed the problem probably has considerable experience with children in need of special services and may offer such a program or be able to refer you to one. You may also be able to get assistance in long-range planning for your child's future that will show you how to make use of the available resources best suited to each stage in your child's development.

Depending on your child's needs, these programs may include

physical or occupational therapy, vocational training, tutoring, special schooling, community-based programs, foster care, residences, halfway houses, sheltered workshops, institutional care, colleges with special equipment for the handicapped, and surgical or medical services. These can be planned on the basis of your child's growth, from infancy to adulthood.

While you should survey current resources with an eye to the future, your planning should be flexible. Your child's needs may change. Developments in therapy may offer new alternatives. Changes in federal or state law, your financial status, or a relocation could make new services available. But do plan ahead. Update yourself on programs in which you are interested; at least a year in advance find out if the programs have a waiting list and how and when you can get into them.

Your local board of health may be able to provide you with information on programs that combine medical and educational services. Another prime source is your state's crippled children's program, for which you will find an address in the Resource Directory at the end of Chapter 2. Remember, such programs can provide services for a wide variety of handicapping conditions, not only crippling conditions.

In some cases your family doctor may be able to guide you to potential resources. But unless he or she is a specialist, your doctor may lack the information necessary to give you a thorough picture of the alternatives. The Knapps' doctor, for example, was an experienced physician, knowledgeable in the technical aspects of his profession, but he was not familiar with the educational and social aspects of special-needs children. He also did not share the Knapps' view of retarded children and felt it was too "idealistic." Nor did he know about the programs that existed to help such children and their families. The Knapps had to strike out on their own, counter to his advice, to get what they felt was best for their family.

If you feel dissatisfied with or uneasy about the first recommendation you receive, your state and county crippled children's program and your local department of health may be able to refer you to a professional in the field for another opinion. Parent groups, citizen groups, and professional organizations devoted to interests of special-needs children can often suggest available alternatives. They may have listings and evaluations of the local and state programs to service these children. The local chapter of the Association for Retarded Citizens (ARC), for instance, gave the Spivaks current information on several programs for their daughter, Kara.

EDUCATIONAL OPPORTUNITIES

The logical place to start your search for educational opportunities is your local board of education. Under the Education of All Handicapped Children Act, enacted in 1975, every state must provide by 1978 "free, appropriate education" for every child with specialized needs. Every child has a right to an education, and most communities today are obliged to provide it.

Still, some school officials, because of their lack of understanding or their unfounded fears about handicaps, are reluctant to accept participation of children with special needs in public schools. Peg McGrath recalls that at first the local school district in her community wanted to send her son, Kim, to classes at a children's hospital instead of at the local public school. "They were afraid of what they didn't know," she says. "They made their decision without ever having seen Kim. There was an unspoken, unrecognized prejudice toward handicapped children."

Peg finally took her son with her to a meeting with the school principal. "He met Kim and saw that he didn't have two heads and that his lack of mobility wasn't contagious," she says. "After we talked about what Kim could and couldn't do, he was convinced enough to go to bat for us with the superintendent of schools."

Kim was admitted to school on a trial basis, which soon became permanent. "The strange thing was that they would have been spending a lot more money sending Kim to the private school—over fifty dollars a day—while it costs them less than five dollars extra a day now for a school bus to transport Kim to and from school," says Peg McGrath.

Despite his leg braces and crutches, Kim participates in all of the usual school activities except gym classes. What he can't get through the school system is the physical therapy that he needs. But he attends a local clinic for such therapy twice a week after school.

Discrimination against children whose needs are special is becoming less acceptable and less widespread. But there are still marked differences in the willingness of communities and states to creatively accept the federal mandate to provide universal free education.

With the 1978 deadline looming, it is especially important to find out what your child is entitled to under the new law and how to get it. While this legislation provides you strong backing in your efforts to get local educational services, it will take time before the law's impact is fully felt and all loopholes can be closed. As with the civil rights laws of the past twenty years, translating the legislation into reality will require effort, public education, and support.

When the law was passed in late 1975, forty-eight of the fifty states already had some kind of legislation requiring public education of handicapped children. State budgets for such education had doubled in just the three previous years. So change is underway, but the effects are uneven and not yet universal.

States and localities may interpret federal laws in quite different ways. One may adhere to the letter of the law, and not go one step further. Another may follow the spirit of the law, planning and supporting innovative programs. A third may find a way to get around the mandate. Differing priorities, financial resources, and philosophies will produce widely varied programs. Even with the law on your side, in some areas you may still have to fight to get what you need. But the act does provide the base on which precedents and guidelines may be built, so it is a significant step forward.

At present, preschool programs for the handicapped are generally not as available as are those for older children. In a recent effort to bring the child with special needs into the mainstream of education, the federal government ruled that ten percent of the Head Start programs for disadvantaged preschool children must be made up of handicapped children. This is close to the estimated percentage of handicapped in the preschool population. Head Start is designed to provide a preschool enrichment experience for four-year-old environmentally deprived children.

There has been an unfortunate side effect of this requirement. Some Head Start programs attempt to fill the quota by labeling non-handicapped children unnecessarily as "behavior problems" or as "emotionally disturbed" in order to get them into the programs. One result of this sidestepping may be that children with other serious handicaps are not sought out and enrolled. And while such efforts might benefit some children now by getting them into a program, these children may be so inappropriately labeled that later school problems can result.

Some public schools provide specialized instruction within the regular school system. The school that Marc attends provides special programs for his learning disabilities. Three times a week Marc receives specialized instruction from a trained volunteer tutor, who leads Marc in forty-five-minute sessions of activities that promote coordination. Marc is excused from his regular classroom on the other two school days in order to take part in a group session run by a specialist who works in several other schools as well. This extra help is intended to make it possible for Marc to keep up with other children in his grade.

Some schools have separate classes for "disabled" students who are mildly retarded or who have learning disabilities, physical impairments, or behavior problems. Still other schools, or whole school districts, "purchase" services from private and voluntary groups who provide educational programs, either using school or outside facilities.

Following LeRoy McCall's automobile accident, his parents and physician were successful in planning a continuing program that met most of his changing needs. After his release from the hospital he returned several times a week to continue the physical therapy he had been receiving there as well as for speech therapy once a week. After several months the doctor evaluated LeRoy's progress and suggested continued therapy within a school setting. Although LeRoy's problem was the result of a childhood accident rather than a birth injury, the type of attention he required was available at a cerebral palsy center, where he could receive therapy in combination with an educational program. The McCalls have been pleased with their son's progress, and next year he will be able to attend a special class in their neighborhood school again.

Part of the funding for LeRoy's school in the cerebral palsy center comes from the local school district. The district refers students with physical and-or mental impairments to the center rather than integrating them into the public schools.

Because they are both state and federally funded, public school systems in some parts of the country may actually provide better services for the disabled than private or voluntary programs. Their funding makes it possible for them to buy costly equipment and it allows higher budgets for teachers and other staff. When a CRMD (children with retarded mental development) class can use the classrooms and other facilities—cafeteria, gym, psychologist, nurse, bus transportation—of an already existing school, this is obviously far less costly than duplicating them at a separate location.

Voluntary or private schools, on the other hand, often have more comprehensive programs to meet the needs of disabled students. Public schools rarely have resident physical or occupational specialists, psychiatrists, or medical specialists—although they may come in as consultants or on a part-time basis. Public schools are oriented to teaching rather than treating, while private programs may be able to attack the problem that limits the ability to learn or function. Furthermore, because they are in constant contact, nonpublic programs often benefit from the interdisciplinary cooperation between educators and other professionals.

What voluntary, nonprofit schools lack in capital they sometimes make up in dedication, particularly when they are the product of the efforts of parents and community volunteers. These qualities may be present in a private school that operates for a profit, but there is also the possibility of a "rip-off." Programs vary enormously, so investigate carefully before committing yourself.

APPROACHING THE EDUCATIONAL SYSTEM

In order for your child to participate in a program, the program or the school district must be aware of your child's existence and what services he or she needs. Unfortunately, in many cases, unless you initiate action yourself, nothing will get done. Although schools in some areas do take a census of school-aged children, even canvassing door to door, too often it is left to the parent to make the approach.

Before the end of the school year preceding the year your child will begin school you should contact your local board of education *in writing* to say that you have a school-aged or preschool child who requires special care. Give your child's name, age, and in simple, concise terms specify whatever recommendations and diagnoses have already been made. Secure a letter that confirms the information you have provided, and send a copy to the school board along with your letter. You may want to call in advance to find out what specifics they want. If not, you should follow the letter up with a phone call to find out if additional information is needed. Copies of all correspondence should be kept with your child's future school records.

You may need to contact a particular section within the board of education that deals with special-needs children. It might be a bureau of special education, a department of handicapped children, or simply a secretary assigned to handle this among other duties. Make it perfectly clear why you are calling and ask if you are speaking to the right person.

After one mother of a child with special needs called a school, she waited months without getting a response. Finally, after she wrote a letter of complaint, she discovered that she had talked to a secretary whose title sounded right but who was in the wrong department to act on her request. If the mother had followed up her initial telephone request more promptly, the misunderstanding could probably have been cleared up quickly. Remember, too, that once a recommendation has been made or a change requested, the paperwork may move to another desk. This increases the chances that it will be lost or misplaced.

At the same time you contact the board of education, you should talk with officials at your own neighborhood school, even though the people there may be unaware what facilities are available or how to get them. Build up a friendly working relationship. Do not wait until registration day, when everyone is swamped with paperwork and people, to introduce yourself.

The board of education or one of its components will probably ask for permission to obtain copies of all diagnostic reports and previous school records. Since these will become part of your child's permanent record, it is important that you state in writing at this time if you have any disagreements with what is contained in them or feel that further explanation is needed. You may want to add a second opinion or diagnosis to balance or rebut any questionable points.

When you send records to schools and others, never send the originals. Make photocopies and send these if you cannot get duplicates. Some officials may ask that you send the originals to be photocopied and returned, fearing that parents or other "unauthorized" persons may be tempted to alter unfavorable data. To avoid the risk of loss, you should hand-carry these to the proper office and wait while copies are made.

Even though you have a diagnosis, your school or district may require testing by its own staff or consultants prior to registration. But, even with this information in hand, school authorities may not necessarily act until prodded by a parent. Gentle reminders or insistent demands might be necessary. The problem could be an overwhelming work load, bureacratic delays, unfamiliarity with the type of request, personal prejudices or discriminatory policies, waits while others do their part in the process (doctors, school officials, state officials, etc.), or simple inefficiency. You may not have to become militant, but you will probably have to be persistent.

Some school districts hold hearings before recommendations are made to place children in special programs. Find out where and when these will be held, and how to request or file for one. In some areas these are closed to the public, in others they are open. Find out who is permitted to attend. You may want legal advice or to arrange for an "expert" to testify.

A hearing can be an informal chat over coffee or an elaborate appeals procedure with prescribed steps and rules. Your local board of education should provide information on the procedure, but if it doesn't, check with the state department of education or special education. Parent groups can be useful in steering you on the right track by providing both concrete information and behind-the-scenes tips.

Even if you are sure that your child will be entering a private program or you have verbal assurances of a position in a program from your local school, you should register your child with the school district and get a written response. Communities that compute certain taxes on the basis of a school census need this information. And you may be entitled to some additional services, such as bus transportation or the use of recreational facilities.

How to Respond to Delays

With tests in hand and records evaluated, the school board should be able to decide where your child is to be placed within the school system, or referred in the case of district-supported programs. But at that point you may encounter new snags.

● *The recommendation for placement may not be what you and others who have seen your child think best.* This may be because the type of program you prefer is not available or has a lengthy waiting list. Or it may be the result of error or because the school has a different view of your child's needs and its ability to meet them.

If you disagree with the recommendation, in whole or in part, and you believe your objections are realistic, let the school know immediately. Tell them what adjustments or alternatives you and others feel are more appropriate. The opinions of professionals can sometimes cause the initial decision to be altered. You could have your child's diagnostic team, teacher, or doctors write letters or submit additional reports to reinforce their findings and opinions, or you could have additional tests and diagnoses made.

It can be helpful if someone on the board of education or school district staff who agrees with you volunteers an opinion to those who consider such requests. Again, find out from the board of education what rights you have to a hearing. Here, especially, the help of experienced parent groups can be helpful. They can also serve as a support or pressure group if you decide to take legal action (see Chapter 7).

● *The school may make no recommendation for placement or may put your child on a waiting list.* If you have no other program you plan to use, insist on a recommendation. If your child is placed on a waiting list, make sure his or her name is not lost, misfiled, or misplaced. If you move or change your phone number, the school should be notified immediately.

When you request information from school officials, don't merely ask, "How are things going?" That wastes both their time and yours. Be specific: "This is Mary DuBois, Lisa's mother. How is Lisa's application for next year's cerebral palsy preschool moving?" Identify yourself, your child, the exact name of the program, the time and place. If anything has changed that can alter the situation favorably—such as income, age, a new diagnosis—mention it, and follow this up in writing. Better yet, have your physician, teacher, or diagnostic clinic—whoever helped you with the diagnosis—make the call. This will probably carry more weight and make you less of an annoyance.

Although laws might guarantee all children the right to an education, there are many factors that determine whether or not the schools actually meet their obligations. It does little good for a state legislature to pass a progressive law concerning special education programs if it fails to allocate funds or if guidelines are not established for carrying out the law and protecting the child's rights. If no local school, private or public, can provide appropriate services for your child, the school board obviously cannot make a referral. It is then up to you to look outside your area, to try to initiate new programs, and to join other advocates in trying to influence state officials to fund services for local schools.

Valid or not, here are some of the reasons local schools have given for not referring handicapped children or providing services: no available programs, a policy against referrals to nonpublic schools, no knowledge of existing programs, lack of funds, lack of space, waiting lists, child's age (too young, too old), child not toilet trained, child a "behavior problem," or child has limited mobility and/or intellect.

These reasons will not be valid under the 1978 law, but this does not mean that some districts or individual schools won't try to use them. Years ago, "homebound" instruction, with a tutor or special teacher coming to the child's home two or three hours a week, was the accepted means of educating a nonmobile child. Today activists have rejected even segregated schools and are pressing for the integration of these children into regular schools in which architectural barriers would be eliminated.

Checklist If You Feel Dead-Ended

If you believe you are doing the right things but are not getting the right results, review this checklist:

1. Do you have the right department, office, or official?
2. Are you sure you have sent *all* the necessary documents at the right time?
3. Do school officials have the correct and *current* address, your name and phone number, child's name and age, diagnosis?
4. Do you know local policies, official and unofficial, and have you checked to see whether they might be contrary to state and federal policies or laws?

5. Do you know at what stage to enter an appeal, how to file it, when and where a hearing is held, what the procedures are, and what and whom to send or bring?
6. Do you know of a parent or citizen group that has experienced similar problems and might help you?
7. Have you contacted influential people—board members, local officials, politicians, and so on—for their assistance?

Your next step is to try the big guns. You can approach individual staff and board members with your problems and ask them to go to bat for you. This is the tack Peg McGrath took in trying to register her son, Kim, who needs crutches and braces in order to walk. She enlisted the principal of her neighborhood school, who supported Kim's enrollment before the board of education.

Formal appeals to the board of education may also be possible. These must be in writing and may have to be submitted in a particular form at a particular time. Your board will give you this information.

If you can't get positive action with local influence and appeals, move up to the next level, county or state. Even though there may be no procedural or legal basis for intervention, your request may focus enough attention on local programs to get them expanded, changed, or given adequate funding.

As a last step, you can try the legal remedies discussed in Chapter 7.

Parent groups will be a great help to you, for they can often point out sympathetic school officials and advise you on the most efficient courses of action.

EVALUATION PROGRAMS

If a program is recommended to you, how can you judge whether or not it will be suitable for your child? How do you choose among available programs? We all want our children to have the best, to have experiences that will be positive influences on their development. To keep up in a complex world, they must develop both academic skills and physical dexterity. And they need opportunities to become self-reliant. Children especially need the chance to build self-confidence and develop positive self-images—to feel good about themselves. These are important to all children but even more so to those who have special needs.

Your view of what experiences are likely to make these things possible will probably be shaped by a combination of influences: professional diagnosis, your own observations of your child on a daily basis, and plain gut feelings. All these can be used in deciding whether or not a particular program is appropriate for your child's needs. One of the best strategies is for you to pay a personal visit and spend time just observing the program at work. Guided tours, fancy equipment, and pretty brochures full of popular theories are only part of the picture. What you are really looking for are intangibles, such as a cheerful, relaxed atmosphere in which your child will feel comfortable.

It is not enough to look at a program through an adult's critical eyes. You must also try to see it from a child's point of view. How will he or she react to it? Those vivid, multicolored posters and exciting activities that seem so appealing could be overwhelming to a hyperactive, minimally brain-damaged child with a need for structure, continuity, and discipline. Multilevel classrooms and a carpeted library loft may look modern and challenging, but for a child with limited mobility they can be sources of additional frustration.

Yet, as a parent you also know that some challenges can be a necessary enticement to a reluctant child, giving a push in the right direction. Some situations are too restricting and discourage experimentation.

"Of course we don't let sight-impaired children finger-paint," you are told at one school. "It's silly." At another, they explain, "Our children can't see, but we encourage them to explore a variety of textures with paint and other materials to use their senses of touch and taste, to learn to use what they have to the greatest extent possible."

The administrator of one program says, "We let children have chances to succeed and to fail as well. Both are important. The most important thing is to try." In contrast, another remarks, "These kids become frustrated so easily we don't want to let them try too much, so that they won't have to experience failure."

It is the teachers who make much of the difference in most programs. They can work miracles on a shoestring budget, or merely provide high-priced baby-sitting. The relationship between them and the children is the crucial factor. It is vital that they enjoy and feel comfortable with children as well as that they have the professional competence to deal with the children's needs.

Although it is important that a program have at least the supervision of trained professionals and adhere to educational standards for staff and administration, the essentials are a genuine enthusiasm for the whole learning process with children and a personal interest in each. When there is a warm concern for children, paraprofessionals and volunteers often do excellent jobs even though their training is minimal. They free the trained teacher to deal with children who have individual problems, to provide special therapies, and to help with emergencies. Even the most creative teacher has only so much time. And, since the needs of children with handicaps often require special handling, it is especially important that these children have a number of adults with whom they can interact.

Volunteers can be skilled or unskilled, senior citizens or boy scouts. A good program will have a well-organized screening-orientation process to make sure that volunteers and staff are not tripping over each other but that they work with coordination. Volunteers are asked to show up at scheduled times or find a replacement. But a program should not become so dependent upon them that it disintegrates when they fail to show up. One disadvantage in a voluntary or experimental program is the possibility that funding may vanish, leaving your child without a badly needed program.

In experimental or demonstration programs, which are usually affiliated with a university or hospital, try to judge whether children might get lost in the shuffle of statistics, tests, and professionals. The program's primary concern should be for the child, not the research grant or graduate program. These should contribute to the children's benefits, not detract from them.

Ask administrators and staff what they see as the program's goals. Answers may range from the acquisition of self-help and vocational skills to overcoming academic problems so that the children can return to regular classrooms. These goals can be compared to those you have for your own child, and they give you a basis for observing classroom activities. Is their work really aimed at accomplishing their objectives? Activities should have a purpose, not merely keep children busy or entertained until it is time to go home. It is sometimes difficult, however, for a parent to distinguish between "play" and "learning."

At the same time, don't overlook the more practical aspects of the administrator's job. Check the staff's credentials and experience, the program's licensing, salary scales, food service, and so on. If it is a private, profit-making program, look at the financial statements and try to get an evaluation of it by state or other outside authorities. Check with your department of education to see whether it provides reports.

If therapies, tutoring, or treatments are part of the program, you will need to know the names, qualifications, and experience of those providing them and how often and where they are conducted. If the emphasis is on therapy, education may be neglected. "Normal" activities, such as music and art, or recreational opportunities may be overlooked, even though they could be especially important to special-needs children. The program should be tailored to the needs of each child.

There should be periodic progress reports on students, and reviews at least yearly if not quarterly. Reevaluation should be every other year, or more often if improvement, decline, or any unusual situation indicates the need for it. Children should not be locked into an inflexible program; they should be moved as their needs and potentials change. The program should provide, be affiliated with, or cooperate with a professional who provides diagnostic or evaluative services. This could be your child's doctor or clinic.

The school may make available the names of other parents whose children are in the program, or you may have to find them on your own. Talk to them and get their reactions to the program. Talking to several, you could find some reactions that are all negative or some totally positive. But remember that each child has individual needs and each parent a different viewpoint.

These methods will give you a good feeling for the program in general, but you will probably have other questions you will want answered, questions directly related to your own child. All these elements must be weighed and measured, and you may want to draw up a list of priorities.

An expensive private school may have certain advantages, for example. But if you have four children and you can only spend a limited amount on your children's education, you may have to settle for something less. You're impressed by the teachers in one program, say, but an hour-and-a-half bus ride is too much for a five-year-old, so you choose a closer school. The school system will pay for eduction but not for therapy, so another gets preference. Many personal, often complex, factors go into the choice of a program.

INTEGRATION VERSUS SEGREGATION

In evaluating schools you should be aware of a controversy over an increasingly used concept known as mainstreaming, or integration of programs for children with special needs. This means including children with special needs in a regular classroom situation rather than isolating them in special classes or schools. Thus, children who would have been excluded only a few years ago are now part of classes in which there are ordinary, nonhandicapped students.

Proponents of this new trend assert that the old segregated system was in fact "separate but unequal" in many cases. Because children with handicaps were out of sight, they were easily discriminated against, and they often received inferior instruction in second-class facilities. The proponents claim that segregating children with special needs tends to make them feel isolated and inferior and aggravates their special problems.

But more conservative educators argue that, for example, adding children who are retarded to the so-called "normal" classroom may only frustrate the handicapped children more because of the contrast with their nonretarded peers. The retarded children will also become victims of prejudice, this view holds. In addition, such educators contend that large numbers of students with special needs would overwhelm the classroom teacher, disrupt the learning situation for the other children, and benefit no one.

The moderate viewpoint holds that while mainstreaming can be a valuable educational tool, it should not be considered as a panacea. You must remember that children are not all alike. This is as true of children with special needs as it is of others. Abilities, disabilities, and personalities vary widely. Mainstreaming should not, therefore, be a mass movement in which *all* children are taken from specialized settings and integrated into ordinary classrooms. At different stages in their educational development it could be the wrong step for many.

Nor is it less costly in every respect. Some teachers feel that for every child mainstreamed, class size should be reduced by three "regular" students. And the special services required in the segregated setting must follow the mainstreamed students to the regular classroom. Supports from consultants, aides, and visiting teachers are still needed, as well as resource rooms where mainstreamed students (and sometimes their teachers and classmates) can receive extra attention from resource personnel.

The special needs remain, and "regular" facilities and programs must be changed to accommodate them. The child with mobility limitations requires a physical setting that may include ramps, wider doorways, or elevators. A child with retarded mental development may benefit more from vocational training than from the college-oriented academic activities of some of his peers.

Which system is best for your child is something you may want to consider when you evaluate private and public programs. Sometimes, when children with handicapping conditions attend schools where there also are nonhandicapped children, the child may be subjected to pressures, subtle or otherwise. The Spivaks, for example, initially sent their retarded daughter, Kara, to a CRMD (children with retarded mental development) class at the local public school. But eventually they decided to move Kara to a private program because they were aware that other students at the public school called the CRMD class the "dummy class" and made fun of the children in the program. The Spivaks felt Kara needed opportunities to succeed at her own level, to develop self-esteem, before she would be capable of dealing with ostracism.

In other cases the situation may be just the reverse. Ellen Schwartz found that while her son Adam went to a private school for children with handicaps, he remained somewhat isolated from the public school children who lived in his neighborhood.

"There was some flack from one or two of the rougher kids on the block about Adam going to a 'school for stupids,'" she remembers. "When he was finally transferred into the new classes the public school started, he was much more relaxed and comfortable about dealing with the other kids. Now he walks home with some of the boys in our building and shares lunch with them. He also belongs to a cub scout pack after school. It's much better for him."

If classes are not "integrated," public schools may have planned activities shared with nondisabled children. One boy scout troop sponsored jointly by a public school and a school for children with limited mobility has a wheelchair basketball team. All the children, mobile or not, must use the chairs.

If there are no occasions for mixing, you may want to take the initiative and plan activities in which both disabled and nondisabled children may participate. Your PTA or parent council might be willing to take this on as a project. Other parents may have suggestions on how to go about this without you appearing to be "interfering" parents.

This brings us to an important part of the school program—the parents. Children benefit more when parents are an integral part of the educational team. The program should encourage their participation on many levels. In addition to the traditional roles of class mother, cookie baker, and fund raiser, a parent should serve on the school board or the board of trustees or directors. Real parent-teacher cooperation means parent classroom volunteers, parent members of school committees, and a more active PTA and advisory board or other liaison unit.

GETTING WHAT ISN'T THERE

Maybe there are no programs to choose from, and hopes to get one are slim. The problem could be lack of funding, lack of understanding, or other reasons more complicated.

In a later chapter we will look at how parents, educators, and other concerned citizens have fought in the courts, before the legislatures, and before the public for the rights of all children to an education. But at the moment we are concerned with your child today, how to get services *now* without lengthy court battles or extensive public education campaigns. Working together with other concerned individuals and groups, you may be able to open the right doors. And if these efforts are not successful for your child, at least others may benefit.

When you try to present your case for a program in your community, it will be useful if you have models of those that have succeeded elsewhere. If you can show how they were developed, and how they provided services such as those you need, you could light a flame under a potential supporter in a position to accomplish something. Check with your state crippled children's program, state or county department of health or education, your parent group, and professional organizations concerned with your child's problem to see if they can provide you with examples.

You should be able to point out, using accurate figures, how much such programs have actually *saved* money in other communities, by training and educating handicapped children to become self-supporting citizens rather than dependents on welfare programs. A good program is actually preventive in the social sense, conserving rather than wasting taxes. The best alternatives are often those that in the long run are the most economical.

One child development center in New York State made its case by presenting the state legislature with facts and figures showing how many retarded children were being kept out of state institutions by their program, and how many of them would later be able to contribute to society, if only in small ways. They got their state funding.

If you are really determined, you could try to start your own program from scratch, but it is usually easier to become part of an already existing structure. One group of parents managed to get a preschool for emotionally disturbed children made part of an existing church-affiliated nursery school. The church gave them the use of an extra classroom, and they were able to rely for supervisory and advisory support on the nursery school staff and board of directors. Volunteers from various church groups and organizations pitched in to help. Since the school was already established, there were no initial problems with licensing, taxes, rent, zoning, or similar technicalities.

In another case a mother convinced a private elementary school that it should apply for a grant for a learning disabilities program. Today it has a staff of four professionals, six paraprofessionals, and thirty volunteers.

To start your own school, you need classroom space, equipment, teachers, possibly a license or zoning permit, insurance, financial support, and—most important—students. Before you do anything else, make sure there are potential students whose families are interested in participating in a program. You can get started on an informal basis in someone's family room with a group as small as three or four children. Programs have a way of growing once people know their services are available.

Your state department of education or health may be able to help you locate the appropriate regulations, laws, and program aids. Also, contact your community government for local zoning regulations and other applicable ordinances.

To gauge the need and interest in such a program, you should first gather interested parents and potential volunteers at an informal meeting. You can advertise it in your local newspaper's classified section or current events column:

> *A meeting for parents and others interested in a recreation program for children with limited mobility will be held Thursday evening at 8:30 P.M., at the home of Mrs. George Ellis, 20 Cleveland St., Kirkland. For information or directions, call (602) 555-1212.*

It's a good idea to get RSVPs because you might find more attending than your living room can hold. Or you could have only a handful show up to sit in the front row of a large church hall.

If you have gotten the names of prospective students through a school or some other source, you may find that some will resent a telephone call. They may consider you strangers intruding in their personal affairs. Some parents may be disturbed that others are aware their child has a problem. A letter is usually less threatening. Be sure to indicate who suggested that you contact the individual family.

Have an agenda for your meeting, even though it's just a get-together to discuss possibilities for fund raising, types of programs, or locations. But remain open to other ideas and directions. To accommodate the needs and goals of others, compromises will probably have to be made. It may take several such gatherings before people feel comfortable enough to commit themselves to working together.

Sort out those in your group with special skills—doctors, secretaries, lawyers, educators. Find out who has experience in public speaking or fund raising and whether any are members of influential groups. Remember that it will take a tremendous effort by many dedicated people over a long period of time to turn your plans into a reality. Be patient, but persevere.

Good organization from the start is important. Keep records of all who attend meetings or offer to help. Get listings of the pertinent regulations and work out ways to deal with them systematically. If some regulations seem too stringent, there may be ways to get around them, just as the group that affiliated with the church nursery school was able to do. If a door is closed, try a window.

You may find that your efforts will help put public pressure on the local schools to recognize that a need actually does exist. A more enlightened attitude could lead to a solution so that you won't have to start your own program. But that would not mean that your organization should break up. You would have a new function: to assure that valuable programs are continued and ineffective ones are improved.

LIVING A FULLER LIFE

While parents worry about their children's educational progress, they are also concerned about their social development, in school and after. How do you balance your child's special needs, which often seem so overwhelming and time-consuming, with his or her need for "normal" childhood activities and friendships?

In your rush from doctor to therapist to school, there may seem to be no time left in which to sandwich these important aspects of your child's life. They sometimes get overlooked because, intent on compensating for a liability, you may fail to give your child's assets the attention they deserve. Your child is a complex, whole individual who simply happens to have a disability, not merely a "handicapped child." If you ignore these other needs, you may end up with a child crippled in spirit, a child with a handicapped personality.

We all have heard of people who have overcome great obstacles to reach their goals: Helen Keller was one, Franklin D. Roosevelt another. The list is long. But we also know of so-called "healthy" adults whose emotional development has been twisted or stunted, who are in fact mentally unhealthy or immature. As a person with a disability, your child faces the challenge of overcoming the prejudices directed toward him. It would hardly be fair if you, their parents, gave him the added handicap of a limited social development.

You cannot make friends for your child, but you can find situations in which this could happen naturally. Some of the best social opportunities lie in the established school and after-school programs and organized recreational activities.

Almost any child can take part in a scouting program, which makes an excellent starting point. The scouts have a long history of involving in their programs youngsters who have mild or even severe disabilities. The most recent innovation is cooperative or integrated troops. Contact the local boy or girl scout council through your telephone directory. If there isn't a program at present in your area, they will most likely be willing to help you find one for your child.

At times, particularly if your child is severely limited or very self-conscious about a disability, it might be best to start with a program especially for disabled children. But don't become over-protective. If your child seems ready, or if a teacher suggests it, consider a mixed program or one in which there is the possibility of competing on some level with nonhandicapped children. Your local church, "Y," or recreation center might have a program or might be willing to start one.

Simply because your child has special needs does not mean she must be excluded from such programs. Possibly your local programs seem negative, uncertain, or even hostile. Regrettably, the burden will then be on you to find a way to get what you need without making your child a target. Be positive. Offer concrete suggestions on how a program could easily be adapted to allow integration, or how your child could add to the experience for other participants. Get the backing of a friend with a child in the program. Integration has often started from the other side.

SUMMER ACTIVITIES

When most educational programs close for the summer, parents feel at loose ends, unsure what to do with their child until school reopens. If progress has been made, they may perhaps want some way for it to continue. Or perhaps they simply want their child to find opportunities for socializing and recreation. But for at least part of the day they would like to find a structured activity in which their child can participate during the summer.

There are existing programs and camps for children with special needs. The U.S. Department of Health, Education, and Welfare's Office for the Handicapped can provide you with information on where to look for specific kinds of summer programs. You should also contact the voluntary health group or parent group that is concerned with your child's problem, organizations such as United Cerebral Palsy or Mothers of Mongoloids. They are often aware of programs. Other sources for specialized programs or open programs into which your child might fit and be welcome include the local "Y," recreation or park departments, community centers, boys and girls clubs, Jaycees and Rotarys, and other civic and fraternal groups as well as the boy and girl scouts.

In a very few areas there are year-round sleep-over centers where severely or moderately retarded children may be left under the supervision of a professional staff while their families go on outings or trips. Sleep-away summer camps can be especially useful in giving a child with special needs and his or her family a breathing spell apart. It gives the child an opportunity to experience a certain degree of independence and the parents a break from the physical and psychological pressures.

If there is no local program open to your child, you may find yourselves again in the position of having to strike out on your own—influencing, cajoling, pressuring, or starting your own. Existing programs may expand to include your child, or new ones might be created.

In helping your child adjust to a handicapping condition, to its particular limitations and necessary treatments, and to the larger world's view of both of these, you will encounter many problems. Your child may become shy and withdrawn or aggressive and rebellious. He may be excluded from the activities of other children, or he might deliberately withdraw. Time-consuming special therapy, treatment, schooling, and concentrated special programs may result in the normal activities of childhood being overlooked. Or there may be a lack of the specialized activities she needs.

Many times these problems may seem overwhelming and more than you can handle. You may feel genuine discouragement and even despair. How do you cope with these situations, these feelings that affect your child, your family, and your own equilibrium? You will need to be able to accept help, and to seek it when you need it. It could be an informal chat over a cup of coffee with another parent with similar experiences, or you may require more formal and structured assistance. The next chapter will discuss techniques for handling many of these problems and will offer some solutions.

DIRECTORY

Whom to Contact

Questions on Education
State Director of Special Education
State Department of Public Instruction
Capitol City, Your State

or

Closer Look
Bureau of Education for the Handicapped
Box 1492
Washington, D.C. 20013

Questions on the Education for All Handicapped Children Act
Your Congressperson or Senator
U.S. House of Representatives or U.S. Senate
Washington, D.C. 20515

Your elected representatives in Washington should provide you with a copy of the act if you requested it by name and number (P.L. 94-142). Copies are also available from the U.S. Government Printing Office. Also contact
Children's Defense Fund
1520 New Hampshire Avenue
Washington, D.C. 20036

for a copy of *Your Rights Under the Educational for All Handicapped Children Act.*

Also See: Chapter 7 Directory for listing state guides on education and due process and Chapter 2 Directory for listing of Crippled Children's Services

Chapter References

Directory of Resources on Exceptional Child Education (ERIC, 1971). Report of the Day Care and Development Council of America, 1971 (1426 H Street Northwest, Suite 340, Washington, D.C. 20005).

Great Atlantic and Pacific School Conspiracy. *Doing Your Own School: A Practical Guide to Starting and Operating Your Own School.* Boston: Beacon Press, 1972.

Kirk, Samuel A. *Educating Exceptional Children.* Boston: Houghton Mifflin, 1972.

Kugel, Robert B. and Wolfensberger, Wolf, eds. *Changing Patterns in Residential Services for the Retarded.* President's Committee on Mental Retardation, 1969. Single copy free.[1]

Lurie, Ellen. *How to Change the Schools: A Parent's Action Handbook on How to Fight the System.* New York: Vintage, 1970.

National Association for Retarded Citizens (NARC). *The Right to Choose: Achieving Residential Alternatives in the Community.* 1973. (Available from: National Association for Retarded Citizens, 2709 Avenue E East, Arlington, Tex. 76011; $1.50.)

Directories of Residential Facilities for the Handicapped (primarily for the mentally handicapped)

National Association of Private Schools for Exceptional Children Directory. P.O. Box 928, Lake Wales, Fla. 33853. 1975.

U.S. Facilities and Programs for Children with Severe Mental Ill-

[1] All U.S. government publications are available from the Superintendent of Documents, U.S. Government Printing Office, Washington, D.C. 20402.

nesses—A Directory. Compiled by the National Society for Autistic Children for the National Institute of Mental Health, 5600 Fishers Lane, Rockville, Md. 20852. 1974.

Directory of Services for Handicapped Children. Compiled by the Kennedy Council of the John F. Kennedy Institute for Habilitation of the Mentally and Physically Handicapped Child, 707 North Broadway, Baltimore, Md. 21205. First edition 1973. R362.025 Z3D

Directory of Facilities Providing Special Education in the United States. U.S., Department of Health, Education, and Welfare, Office of Education, Bureau of Education to the Handicapped. June 1973. Information available from Closer Look, National Special Education Information Center, Box 1492, Washington, D.C. 20013.

Registry of Private Schools for Children with Special Educational Needs. National Educational Consultants, Inc., 711 Saint Paul Street, Baltimore, Md. 21202. 1971. Revised and augmented spring 1973. Microfiche copies available. ($30) R371.9 N2765r.

Directory for Exceptional Children. Porter, Sargent, Inc. 11 Beacon Street, Boston, Mass. 02108. Seventh edition 1972. $7.50. R371.9 D598d7.

Directory of Catholic Special Facilities in the United States for Handicapped Children and Adults. National Catholic Educational Association, One Dupont Circle Northwest, Washington, D.C. 20036. Fifth edition 1971. $5.

Directory of State and Local Resources for the Mentally Retarded. U.S., Department of Health, Education, and Welfare, Secretary's Committee on Mental Retardation, Washington, D.C. 20201. June 1970.

Directory of Residential Facilities for the Mentally Retarded. The American Association on Mental Deficiency, 5201 Connecticut Avenue Northwest, Washington, D.C. 20015. 1968.

U.S. Private Schools Classified. Robert J. Leib. Shebourne Press, Inc., 8063 Beverly Boulevard, Los Angeles, Calif. 90048. 1968.

New York Association of Private Residential Facilities for the Mentally Handicapped, Inc. c/o Mrs. Grace L. Dubendorf, Secretary, Gra-Mar Hall, 99 South Main Street, Churchville, N.Y. 14428.

State Rehabilitation Agencies

ALABAMA
Vocational Rehabilitation Agency
State Board of Education
2129 East South Boulevard
Montgomery 36111

ALASKA
Office of Vocational Rehabilitation
Department of Education
Pouch F
Alaska Office Building
Juneau 99801

ARIZONA
Rehabilitation Services Bureau
Department of Economic Security
1535 West Jefferson
Phoenix 85007

ARKANSAS
Department of Social and Rehabilitative Services
P.O. Box 3781
Little Rock 72203

CALIFORNIA
Department of Rehabilitation
California Human Relations Agency
714 P Street
Sacramento 95814

COLORADO
Division of Rehabilitation
State Department of Social Services
916 Social Services Building
Denver 80203

CONNECTICUT
Division of Vocational Rehabilitation
State Board of Education
600 Asylum Avenue
Hartford 06105

DELAWARE
Vocational Rehabilitation Service
Department of Labor
1500 Shallcross Avenue
P.O. Box 1190
Wilmington 19899

DISTRICT OF COLUMBIA
Bureau of Rehabilitation Services
Social and Rehabilitation Administration
Department of Human Resources
122 C Street Northwest
Washington 20001

FLORIDA
Division of Vocational Rehabilitation
Department of Health and Rehabilitative Services
1309 Winewood Boulevard
Tallahassee 32301

GEORGIA
Division of Vocational Rehabilitation
Department of Human Resources
17 Trinity Avenue
Atlanta 30334

GUAM
Division of Vocational Rehabilitation
Board of Control for Vocational Rehabilitation
Department of Education
P.O. Box 3009
Agana 96910

HAWAII
Vocational Rehabilitation and Services for the Blind
Department of Social Services
P.O. Box 339
Honolulu 96809

IDAHO
Vocational Rehabilitation Services
State Board for Vocational Education
1501 McKinney
Boise 83704

ILLINOIS
Division of Vocational Rehabilitation
State Board of Vocational Education and Rehabilitation
623 East Adams Street
Springfield 62706

INDIANA
Rehabilitation Services Board
17 West Market Street
Indianapolis 46204

IOWA
Division of Rehabilitation Education and Services
State Board of Public Instruction
801 Bankers Trust Building
Des Moines 50309

KANSAS
Division of Vocational Rehabilitation
Department of Social and Rehabilitation Services
State Office Building
6th Floor
Topeka 66612

KENTUCKY
Bureau of Rehabilitation Services
State Board of Education
Capital Plaza Office Tower
Frankfort 40601

LOUISANA
Division of Vocational Rehabilitation
State Board of Education
P.O. Box 44371
Baton Rouge 70804

MAINE
Bureau of Rehabilitation Services
Department of Health and Welfare
32 Winthrop Street
Augusta 04330

MARYLAND
Division of Vocational Rehabilitation
State Board of Vocational Education
P.O. Box 8717
Friendship International Airport
Baltimore 21240

MASSACHUSETTS
Rehabilitation Commission
296 Boylston Street
Boston 02116

MICHIGAN
Vocational Rehabilitation Services
State Department of Education
P.O. Box 1016
Lansing 48904

MINNESOTA
Division of Vocational Rehabilitation
State Department of Education
1745 University Avenue
Saint Paul 55104

MISSISSIPPI
Division of Vocational Rehabilitation
Department of Education
1304 Walter Sillers State Office Building
P.O. Box 1698
Jackson 39205

MISSOURI
Section of Vocational Rehabilitation
State Board of Education
Farm Bureau Building
1616 Missouri Boulevard
Jefferson City 65101

MONTANA
Rehabilitation Services Division
Department of Social and Rehabilitation Services
506 Power Block
Helena 59601

NEBRASKA
Division of Rehabilitation Services
State Department of Education
233 South Tenth Street
Lincoln 68508

NEVADA
Rehabilitation Division
State Department of Human Resources
Union Federal Building
308 North Curry Street
Carson City 89701

NEW HAMPSHIRE
Vocational Rehabilitation Division
105 Loudon Road
Building 3
Concord 03301

NEW JERSEY
Rehabilitation Commission
Department of Labor and Industry
John Fitch Plaza
Trenton 08625

NEW MEXICO
Vocational Rehabilitation Agency
Department of Education
P.O. Box 1830
Santa Fe 87501

NEW YORK
Office of Vocational Rehabilitation
State Education Department
99 Washington Avenue
Albany 12210

NORTH CAROLINA
Division of Vocational Rehabilitation Services
Department of Human Resources
620 North West Street
P.O. Box 26053
Raleigh 27611

NORTH DAKOTA
Department of Vocational Rehabilitation
State Board for Social Services
1025 North Third Street
P.O. Box 1037
Bismarck 58501

OHIO
Rehabilitation Services Commission
4656 Heaton Road
Columbus 43229

OKLAHOMA
Division of Rehabilitative and Visual Services
Department of Institutions
Social and Rehabilitative Services
P.O. Box 25352
Oklahoma City 73125

OREGON

State Vocational Rehabilitation Division
Department of Human Resources
2866 Center Street Northwest
Salem 97301

PENNSYLVANIA

Bureau of Vocational Rehabilitation
Labor and Industry Building
Seventh and Forster streets
Harrisburg 17120

PUERTO RICO

Vocational Rehabilitation Division
Department of Social Services
P.O. Box 1118
Hato Rey 00919

RHODE ISLAND

Division of Vocational Rehabilitation
Vocational Rehabilitation Services
40 Fountain Street
Providence 02903

SOUTH CAROLINA

Vocational Rehabilitation Department
State Agency of Vocational Rehabilitation
400 Wade Hampton State Office Building
Columbia 29201

SOUTH DAKOTA

Division of Vocational Rehabilitation
State Board of Education
200 West Pleasant Drive
Pierre 57501

TENNESSEE

Division of Vocational Rehabilitation
State Board of Vocational Education
1808 West End Building
Suite 1400
Nashville 37203

TEXAS

Texas Rehabilitation Commission
1600 West 38th Street
Austin 78705

UTAH

Division of Rehabilitation Services
State Board of Vocational Education
1200 University Club Building
136 East South Temple
Salt Lake City 84111

VERMONT

Vocational Rehabilitation Division
Department of Rehabilitation
Agency of Human Services
56 State Street
Montpelier 05602

VIRGINIA

State Department of Vocational Rehabilitation
Board of Vocational Rehabilitation
4615 West Broad Street
P.O. Box 11045
Richmond 23230

VIRGIN ISLANDS

Division of Vocational Rehabilitation
Department of Social Welfare
Saint Thomas 00801

WASHINGTON

Vocational Rehabilitation Services Division
Department of Social and Health Services
P.O. Box 1788
Olympia 98504

WEST VIRGINIA

Division of Vocational Rehabilitation
State Board of Vocational Education
P & G Building
2019 Washington East
Charleston 25305

WISCONSIN

> Division of Vocational Rehabilitation
> Department of Health and Social Services
> One West Wilson Street
> Madison 53702

WYOMING

> Division of Vocational Rehabilitation
> State Department of Health and Social Services
> State Office Building
> Room 305
> Cheyenne 82001

5

Where to Find Support

When you discover that your child has special needs, you may feel very alone, set apart, and somehow singled out. Feelings of guilt, anger, and frustration over the difficulties involved with meeting those needs or the lack of services can increase your sense of isolation. You may even contribute to your own isolation by retreating from familiar routines and by pushing others away.

You do not have to be alone unless you want it that way; you are not the only ones in the world who have problems. Indulging in self-imposed isolation and self-pity, a form of "martyrdom," ultimately hurts your child, yourselves, and your family.

LEARNING TO ASK FOR HELP

It is essential that parents of children with special needs learn to recognize their own very valid and real needs for emotional support and practical assistance in day-to-day living. Some people are shocked to realize that they have to be dependent upon others, that they must turn to others in order to meet basic needs. Those of you who have always prided yourselves on your self-sufficient, independent way of life may find it difficult to admit that you need outside support to cope with the special needs of your child. People who consider themselves "private" or introverted have additional barriers to overcome before they can accept or reach out for help.

As part of your overall adjustment to a new situation you will begin to seek resources. At first, you may search to confirm or deny your suspicions about your child's development; you may then search for a cure. Gradually, you try to find ways to alleviate the problems—

including personal support. You may not recognize this at first, so you must begin with a good look at yourselves; you must make an assessment of your needs. There are the technical needs related to the handicap, the practical aspects of money, transportation, housing, and daily life disruptions, and your emotional needs that are tangled up with all of this.

Even if you accept the fact that you can't do it all by yourselves, you may still not be able to ask for help. You may be ashamed or embarrassed; you may feel humiliated by your child's handicap or by your need to ask others for help with your own lives. Our society often makes us unaccustomed to being dependent and you may not know how to reach out. You have to learn to ask.

Support Starts at Home

You can start with your own family. Since so often a husband and a wife go through stages of adjustment at different times, in different sequences, with different intensities, it may at first be hard for you to respond in positive, constructive ways to each other. The needs of one of you at any one moment could be out of mesh or in direct conflict with those of the other.

The Burnses had a good start in their mutual support when they attended prepared childbirth classes together before the birth of their second child. The loving cooperation established then helped to carry them through the shock of giving birth to a child who had a missing forearm and sustained them through the difficult months that followed. Because they had learned to depend upon as well as to help each other, each could more easily respond to the changing needs and emotions of the other.

The special needs of a child with a handicapping condition can create challenges that seem insurmountable, particularly in dealing with such major considerations as diagnosis, treatment, and finances. But nagging small details in your daily life also can build into a crescendo of frustration unless you find ways to cope with them. Often it takes a little more ingenuity and an ability to see your life together from a slightly different perspective in order to deal with the demands that are made upon you.

The Burnses, for example, while teaching their son Kevin the basic self-help skills of feeding and dressing had to make allowances for Kevin's special needs; they wanted him to be able to accomplish these tasks independently, using his one arm and stump. They found ways to make these tasks simpler for Kevin without doing them for him, ways that encouraged his independence and prepared him for more complicated demands to come as he grew older.

After a number of bumps and bruises Michael Fine learned to tell where all the furniture was situated in his house, even though he could not see, but learning to tell his jeans and T-shirts apart from his brother's was too difficult. The name tapes Michael's mother put on their clothes obviously didn't help because he couldn't see them. Michael's parents could have given the boys separate bureaus or laid out Michael's clothes each day. These would have been simple solutions, but they wanted to find a way to deal with the situation that would not deny him opportunities for normal responsibility appropriate to his age. Michael's father came up with the idea of punching a little hole in the size label or name tape of Michael's things. Michael could easily feel the hole and thus identify his clothes. Later his parents used a more elaborate system to help Michael tell the difference between his play clothes and his school clothes, and between colors.

Both of these families found ways on their own to deal with situations complicated by special needs. But you, alone, will not always be able to come up with solutions to problems, you will need help from others. You will eventually feel comfortable enough with yourselves, your child, and the handicap to be willing to accept help from friends, neighbors, and relatives.

Others Reach Out to Help

The help others can offer can be invaluable even if you may not be always able to define it in concrete terms. The emotional support they can offer just by being there, regardless of what other services they may be able to provide for you, can be a blessing. The grandmother who will take the other children for a weekend visit, the friend who will sit with you in the hospital, the neighbor who drops off a casserole so you won't have to cook—all are offering small things, but these small gestures of caring can mean so much at the time.

When the immediate crisis period has passed and you begin to settle into a routine pattern that perhaps differs in subtle, or signifi-

cant, ways from former routines, your friends and relatives can continue their support in other ways. A friend who will listen may
provide an outlet for you to share your feelings or vent your
emotions. A neighbor may help out by baby-sitting or by providing
transportation. A relative might come up with a seemingly simple
solution to worrisome problems. Frequently, others can help you
simply by lending a hand with the practical aspects of your daily
living and special needs and by enabling you to take advantage of
needed social and leisure activities.

You will find, however, that some advice and help so generously
offered, sometimes without our asking for it, can be less than helpful.
The lady next door who keeps bringing over strange home remedies
and spouting old wives' tales can be annoying, if not depressing. The
grandparent who tries to move in with you and take over the care of
your children can be difficult to deal with. The good friend who
cries every time she comes over for coffee can be draining on your
patience and strength.

All of these "helpful" people mean well, but they can cause extra
problems that you don't need during a time of stress. You end up
trying to comfort, educate, and work through their emotional needs
just when you are least able to do so. You may have to learn how to
tell do-gooders, well-wishers, and others gently but firmly that the
help they insist upon giving is appreciated, but "Not now, thank
you."

Some people may not be able to take a hint, or even a strong
suggestion, and you will have to be more direct with them: "Thank
you, Mom [or neighbor, or old chum], but right now we feel that we
have to do things *our* way. It may be right, it may be wrong, but it's
something that we have to do on our own."

You may also find yourselves trapped in the opposite situation,
where you have become so dependent upon the kind services of
others that you cannot stand on your own feet. The whole situation
has become so paralyzing to you that you are immobilized, and others
around you are carrying on for you.

There has to be a balance between asking and giving. This is often
hard to achieve when there are so many and often conflicting, needs
to be met. If you find your needs becoming overwhelming, you may
have to spread out your requests for help beyond your circle of
friends, relatives, and neighbors.

EXPERIENCED ADVICE FROM PARENT GROUPS

As you seek out needed resources, you will not always have to blaze a trail on your own. There may be in your area an organized group of parents of children with special needs who have already experienced and who are still dealing with the questions you are asking now. People in such parent groups can share their experiences with you. Even if your particular need seems unique, other parents may be able to help you find a solution that is just as unique by relating their responses to their own challenges.

You may find that smaller, special-interest groups within large parent organizations can provide the most direct and practical advice. Friendships established among individuals belonging to such groups often develop into an informal support system. What started as a conversation over coffee during the refreshment period of a meeting is continued through telephone calls, social events, and shared interests.

You may be surprised how other parents of children with handicaps respond to your feelings with great understanding, whereas longtime friends may have little or no comprehension about your situation or how you feel. Another parent of a child with special needs, even if those needs are very different from your child's has probably experienced many of the conflicts and satisfactions that you have. Sometimes you really have to experience something to understand it.

Starting a Group

If there is no parent group in your area, or if there's no group that deals with your particular interest, you might consider starting one. You could aim for either a small discussion group or a more organized educational or action-oriented association. Either way, take your time. You can't expect instant success. It may take several months just to contact interested parents, professionals, and others and then to establish mutual concerns and goals. Then, it may take a couple more months after the first meeting to build up momentum. Most groups don't consider themselves really established until after the first year. You can recheck Chapter 2 of this book for some specific suggestions about starting groups.

SUPPORT FROM COMMUNITY MEMBERS

In addition to parent groups, there may be certain individuals in your community with special skills and talents whom you can tap for help in dealing with your needs. Perhaps, someone who knows carpentry could build special equipment that your child needs at a far cheaper price than a ready-made model that you may not be able to afford. Or an architect might be willing to draw up plans for modifying your house or apartment to fit your child's needs. Often, teachers can suggest special activities for your child, or they may provide tutoring.

The Walters, for example, found ways to meet some of their son's special needs with the help of his nursery school teacher. Troy Walters was born with a heart defect that specialists hoped could be corrected surgically. However, the doctors delayed his surgery because they felt that as long as there was no immediate risk to his life, there would be a better chance for successful surgery when he was older. In the meantime, his parents tried to avoid overprotecting him while at the same time they attempted to make sure that he did not overexert himself. They found that as Troy grew older, they didn't need to monitor or nag him constantly because he tended to find his own level of activity, and he would voluntarily rest if he felt tired.

But as Troy reached nursery school age, Karol, his mother, became concerned about his development. He couldn't keep up with the rough and tumble games of the other children, he would lag behind and play quietly by himself rather than join them.

Karol realized that Troy's handicap could limit his social and even his educational development if some way were not found to include him in the activities appropriate to his age within the limits of his physical capabilities. So she and her husband, Dan, sat down with Troy's teacher and planned a strategy for him.

The teacher agreed to try to include enough "sit-down" play on the two mornings Troy attended school so that he could have a sense of being part of the group. She also would provide alternatives during those times when more rigorous play proved too much for him, or when he was particularly fatigued.

At home Dan set up a workbench in the playroom for his son,

with real tools scaled to child size. Karol cleaned out a low shelf in one of her kitchen cabinets, which she stocked with a variety of simple arts and crafts materials. Both of these innovations provided creative outlets for Troy's energies within acceptable limits. They also attracted other neighborhood kids in to play.

In your community you may be able to find people who are interested in providing services or help during their free time on a volunteer basis or at a low cost. Senior citizens are a good source of potential volunteers. Retired professionals from many fields may welcome the opportunity to work on a limited basis. Often, you can find volunteers by putting up a notice on bulletin boards at churches, shopping centers, community centers, libraries, and schools.

One family even advertised in their local paper for a grandpa. Their help-wanted ad read:

> *Wanted, a grandfather—someone experienced in life and raising boys—to provide occasional attention and love to a boy with special needs whose grandpas are far away.*

The family received several responses, and they found a nearby gentleman who was delighted for the chance to become the designated grandfather to a young boy.

COMMUNITY RESOURCES

Other sources of help in your community include civil and social groups. You may be involved with some of these groups already, while others may be unfamiliar to you. But even if many of the individuals in such groups are strangers to you, or if most haven't experienced a child with special needs, they often stand ready to pitch in and provide help.

When Bobby Rosa was hospitalized with a possibly terminal disease, members of the church his parents attended organized a car pool so his mother could get to and from the hospital during the day. Members of a women's group at the church volunteered to sit with the other Rosa children. And when Bobby needed blood donors, several civic groups and churches sent volunteers.

Such groups often stand ready to provide other services when the crisis period is past. If you aren't a member of such an organization, you may be able to seek their aid through a member whom you know. Even if you don't know anyone in a civic or service group you think may be able to help, don't be shy about contacting the organization by letter or telephone in order to present your problem. Ask if they can suggest ways to help you deal with your problem. Even if they can't provide the service you need, perhaps they will suggest another group that can.

Public and private agencies also can provide various kinds of supportive services. The McCalls were able to get baby-sitting services for their son LeRoy through the cooperative service established at his school by a parent group. The Lees got suggestions for adapting their family's food habits to accommodate their son's dietary needs from the visiting nurse program of their county's department of health. The DuBois family found counseling services available at their diagnostic center.

You may be able to find services easily, or you may have to search for them. You may discover some services at such traditional resources as the school, the local recreation department, or the youth center. Others may turn up in unexpected places, such as the homemaker services at the department of health. The agencies and organizations listed in the Resource Directory at the end of this and other chapters of this book will give you some ideas on where to look for help.

PARENTING TECHNIQUES

In addition to services, there may be special courses or educational programs available in your community that will help you learn to cope with your situation. Some libraries and schools, for example, offer courses on effective parenting, including structured approaches to child management that may be especially useful to parents of children with special needs.

You sometimes can find out about such programs through libraries, churches, schools, your diagnostic center, community mental health centers, family therapy centers, or your own parent group. Your parent group may even be able to sponsor its own parenting program that is especially tailored to meet the situations faced by parents of children with special needs.

These courses go by different names, ranging from effective parenting or child management to "behavior modification in the family." Some courses are based on established theories and have published texts approved by national organizations. Other courses are more informal and may draw upon several philosophical viewpoints as well as the experiences of the people running the course. Such programs can consist of one-time lectures or a series of workshops an discussions. The fees range from nothing to one hundred dollars or more per couple for some elaborate programs.

These courses tend to teach philosophies about dealing with children, and they usually involve specific, practical techniques for parenting children. The proposed techniques can be adapted to your own family situation as you choose. If your usual patterns of responses to your children have become confused or difficult now that you are parenting a child with special needs, you may find that such a course may bring things back into perspective. This can be true even if you decide that the specific recommended techniques are not appropriate for your family.

SEEKING PROFESSIONAL SUPPORT

Even with support from friends and relatives and from other resources in your community, you may still have difficulties in dealing with certain aspects of your life as parents of a child with special needs. It is then that you may decide to seek professional assistance.

Sometimes, finding professional help can be more difficult than finding medical services. One reason is that the term *professional help* covers a wide area of specialities, and it isn't always easy to decide what kind of professional to turn to. The search is further confused by the fact that just about anyone can use such titles as "counselor" and "therapist" with little formal training or experience. This doesn't necessarily mean that people with a minimum of formal training can't be helpful, or that they are unscrupulous, but you should be aware that just because someone sticks an impressive-sounding title on their door doesn't automatically qualify him or her as a professional in the field of counseling.

There are several basic types of specialists in the helping professions who provide counseling. Some are super-specialists dealing only with a particular type of problem; others deal with a variety of concerns. Which type of specialist you pick depends upon your needs, your view of life, and perhaps upon your finances. In many communities, professionals can be found in private practices and lower-cost group practices or clinics. Some of these programs may be affiliated with schools, hospitals, diagnostic services, or public agencies.

Many Professionals to Use

Since titles can be confusing, here is a list of the types of professionals you may want to consider and the types of problems they deal with:

A psychiatrist is a medical doctor. He or she has an M.D. degree as well as training in psychiatry. Psychiatrists deal with severe emotional disturbances as well as less serious problems from a medical frame of reference, and treatment is usually long-range. Because they are physicians, psychiatrists can readily prescribe drugs or other medications.

A psychologist has studied human behavior and can apply this knowledge in many ways in addition to counseling. There are many specialties within psychology. A psychologist may teach, do research, do testing (usually with a M.A. degree), or provide consultations to business and government. Not all psychologists are trained or experienced in counseling. Those who are usually have a Ph.D. degree.

A social worker deals more with individuals within his or her own environment, building upon people's strengths in order to establish coping mechanisms for problems they face. Social workers are concerned with practical approaches to concrete problems as well as more complex long-range situations. A social worker has a masters degree (a M.S.W.) or a doctorate (a D.S.W.). A social worker who is affiliated with the Academy of Certified Social Workers may use the initials C.S.W., which indicates he or she has met the academy's qualifications of experience and knowledge. Not all people who call themselves social workers are actually qualified to do so.

A guidance counselor is a professional, usually with a M.A. degree, who works with students in school settings. Primarily through testing and other techniques, he or she seeks to assist a student with academic planning. A vocational counselor deals strictly with vocational planning.

A pastoral counselor is a member of the clergy with a degree in divinity and with training from a specialized counseling program. A clergyperson might have more advanced training and degrees in psychology or social work, but then he or she would tend to use those titles rather than pastoral counselor.

A family counselor may be any of the professionals we have mentioned except guidance counselor. Family counselors specialize in working with family problems. Most are social workers.

How to Use Support

Whichever type of professional you approach, don't be afraid to ask questions. Ask for degrees, accreditations, affiliations, and licenses. Find out what experience they have had with your type of situation and how they feel about it. After all, it's your money and your life.

Many professionals have probably received training in work with emotional problems. They may see anything out of the ordinary as being a sign of pathology, or they may have had very little if any experience with the myraid special needs of children with handicaps and their families. You may have to educate them about the child's medical condition and special needs as they help you with your reactions to these.

Unlike well-meaning friends and relatives, professionals are specifically trained to help people deal with their problems. They may have decided to enter their field because they felt they had an aptitude or talent in that area, and in their professional training they have learned to build upon these skills and have increased their knowledge about people and their problems.

With a professional you run very little risk of having your confidence come back to you at a party or in a moment of anger. In establishing a relationship with a counselor you are often more free to speak honestly than you are with a friend. The professional counselor is not there to judge but to help you work out a problem. He or she will not solve it for you but rather will help you to find the solution on your own.

You may already have access to a counselor at your child's school, diagnostic center, or hospital. You may already have an established relationship and feel quite comfortable working with that person. If you don't or if this counselor is not able to help you, perhaps he or she can refer you to someone who can. Members of your parent group may suggest someone useful as well as advise you who to avoid. Also try your local mental health council, community chest, and so on.

In this age of increasing specialization, you may find it will take several people to help you with your needs. For example, a good family counselor may know very little about vocational assistance yet may be able to help you work out other problems. You could end up with a vocational counselor for that type of planning, a doctor to prescribe drug therapies, and a family counselor to help you deal with the added stress of special needs or a long-standing family problem. It is not uncommon for families in counseling for one problem to bring up and deal with other older problems that have perhaps become more burdensome when added to the tensions of adjustments to a child with special needs.

In order to work successfully with a counselor, you have to be willing to work on the problem. At times it can be uncomfortable to dredge up feelings and frustration, but you will have to decide that the effort will bring you a better future.

But it is impossible to solve a problem if you have not established trust in the professional. Some professionals may not have dealt much with problems and emotions of parents with handicapped children and may not fully understand them. If you feel that you cannot establish this trust or that your counselor does not understand your problem, you will need to find a new counselor. But first, make sure that *you* are not avoiding the problem.

SPECIAL NEEDS LEADING TO SPECIAL CONSIDERATIONS

Eventually you will probably be able to find most of the special services you need to help you cope with the physical and emotional demands of a child with special needs. Indeed, sometimes it is finding routine services that can most challenge your ingenuity and perseverence. For example, almost any competent dentist can care for most children. But it may take an especially understanding and patient dentist to treat a child whose involuntary muscular movements pose special problems during dental treatments.

Similarly, such routine activities as vacations and recreation and such normal services as baby-sitting or day care often require special adjustments when they involve children with handicapping conditions.

Family vacations that include your child with special needs may require extra planning. At first some parents assume that former activities and pursuits have to be abandoned, but most eventually find that these actions only need to be adapted, not eliminated. With a little creativity and extra planning, vacations can be arranged that take limitations into account. The Febros discovered, for example, that most state and federal parks and many museums have wheelchairs and that most public roadside rest stops now have special restroom facilities for the handicapped as well as reserved parking for car carrying handicapped persons. The U.S. Department of Health, Education, and Welfare's Office for the Handicapped and the National Park Service can both provide information about tourist facilities adapted for people with handicaps. These agencies also have information about tours and other programs for handicapped visitors and their families. Even the White House has special visiting hours set aside for visitors with handicaps.

A local travel agency may not be familiar with the many different organized programs for travelers who have disabilities, but most agencies are usually willing to find out about them. Your travel agent or their contacts may be able to make advance arrangements for special cars or baby-sitting services.

Recreational opportunities in your own locality may be more difficult to find because many communities don't have programs that include activities for children with handicapping conditions. If this is the case in your community, you have several options: You can try to get established recreational programs to include your child; you can push to have specialized programs initiated; or you can try to start one of these programs on your own, with or without the support of established resources.

"INTEGRATION" VERSUS "SEGREGATION" IN UTILIZING COMMUNITY SERVICES

An "integrated" activity may be the best opportunity for one child with a handicap, but it may be disastrous for another child with the same type of handicap. Each may react differently to the same disability or have a different degree of severity. One handicapping condition may fit into certain activities, another may not. It is not only the handicap and its limits, but also the effects the activities have upon the personality of your child that will determine your best approach. If possible, try existing programs first. You may heighten the program staff's awareness of the special needs that many children have, and you may open up an untried resource for your child and others. Even if it doesn't work out this time, you are laying the groundwork for the future.

Preschool programs sometimes are considered by parents more in terms of their social value than for their educational benefits, and for that reason they are occasionally lumped together with recreational opportunities. In Chapter 4 we discussed getting into or starting preschool programs, but basically the same advice on recreation applies to nursery school or to play groups. Try existing resources, attempt to educate them to your needs, but be ready to initiate a group yourself.

STARTING A PLAY GROUP

One possible alternative to established programs is for you to seek out other parents in your area who also have children with special needs and together arrange a play group for your children. Such groups can be a tremendous help if no such recreation program exists or if existing programs are prohibitively expensive. It is best to keep such groups small; about six children or so should be the maximum. You may be able to get extra adult supervision from a civic group, church league, or ladies club whose members would like to become involved in daytime service projects with children.

A play group shouldn't be designed just to provide a baby-sitting service but to initiate children into new experiences essential for normal development. Activities can be planned to develop hand-to-eye coordination and motor abilities as well as to promote social interaction.

RECREATION

Some people think that sports and other recreational activities are beyond the capabilities of children with disabling conditions. Anyone who has ever seen amputees wheel up and down a basketball court playing wheelchair basketball knows nothing could be further from the truth. Children with special needs, just like all kids, enjoy shooting a basketball, throwing a football, racing, and taking part in all kinds of games and play. True, some children may be limited in their abilities to engage in many of these activities, but that doesn't stop them from trying and, often, doing surprisingly well, as is demonstrated every year in the Joseph P. Kennedy Foundation "Special Olympics" for children with handicapping conditions. At these Olympics members of the Kennedy family and famous athletes lead children with special needs in a day of competitive events. The emphasis is on fun, which shows that the spirit of competition is not limited by whatever physical disabilities a child might have.

Like most of us, children with handicapping conditions aren't likely to grow up to be star athletes. But more than a few children with handicaps have made great strides in the area of professional sports. For example, the longest field goal in the history of professional football was booted by Tom Dempsey, a man who is without both forearms and who kicks with a stump for a foot. His record, by the way, was a last-second, sixty-three-yard kick that won a game for the New Orleans Saints against the Detroit Lions on November 8, 1970.

BABY-SITTING AND DAY CARE

Baby-sitting and day care services can also be areas of concern. Parents sometimes feel guilty about leaving their handicapped children with others. They shouldn't. All parents need time for adult pursuits. When both parents work, sitters or day care are a necessity, not a luxury. Parents who are chained to the home by the real or imagined needs of a child with a disability will find themselves physically and emotionally drained, making it difficult to respond in positive ways either to their children or to their own lives.

Day care for the child with special needs may be difficult to find outside of part-day school programs. Often, however, day care centers are already caring, on an individual basis, for children who have disabilities. At these centers, the first consideration is a child's need for day care; special needs are basically considered only in terms of how this child could fit into the program. Unfortunately, there are few day care programs operated specifically for disabled children and few that offer integrated programs for both disabled and nondisabled children on other than an individual basis.

If you work, you may need to find someone to take care of your child during the day. In any case you will need someone to provide part-time baby-sitting services.

Again, baby-sitting is one of those seemingly routine services that may require extra effort. A child with special needs sometimes requires a sitter with special qualifications, either because of the child's needs themselves or because of the parents' worries about the sitter being able to handle everything. Often, however, the best sitter is a person who is used to your child and who understands any special treatment or behavior.

Your doctor, therapist, or people at your diagnostic center might be able to suggest someone who has experience caring for children with special needs and who is available to take care of your child on a daily basis. You can probably find reliable sitters by contacting local schools or a university, youth groups, and church groups.

Starting a Co-op

Your best option may be to establish a baby-sitting cooperative with parents of other children with special needs. In this way, you can insure that your child will be cared for by an adult who understands a child's special needs and who won't be frightened or overwhelmed by such needs. A co-op can also save you money.

Setting up a baby-sitting co-operative requires organization in the beginning as well as someone to take responsibility for it as it grows. It is best to limit the group to less than a dozen children, preferably about six. If the group grows too large, particularly in the early stages, it can become unwieldy. You may later have to divide the group into two or more smaller ones, perhaps on the basis of geography or the age of the children. You should make one person in charge of setting up a rotating baby-sitting schedule for parents involved in the co-op.

One schedule for a baby-sitting co-op might have each couple sitting one week night every two weeks and one weekend night every three weeks. (Weekends are difficult to schedule because of their popularity and because most couples like to spend that time together, even if at home.) In return, one member of each couple is responsible for reciprocating for this sitting. (It's good to gently prod husbands to take their turn at this reciprocal sitting.) You may want to develop a different type of scheduling, but remember that it will take a while and require some adaptations in your original plan before you find a system that will please everyone. The same type of co-op system can be used for daytime sitting.

Occasionally there are unexpected results from such a co-op. When the McCall's became involved with a baby-sitting co-op that the parent group at their son's school had established, they discovered that they benefited more than just socially. Edna McCall found that when she had to deal intimately with another child who had a handicap similar to her son's, she gained some additional insight into her son's needs and her own.

She noticed ways in which she could help her son by watching what other parents did, and she also learned what to avoid. By observing another child with limits and his family, she felt less isolated: Others, she discovered, had the same challenges, worries, and experiences. When situations are shared, they can sometimes become more bearable.

Developing Community Resources for Skilled Child Care

If you belong to an active parent group, you could suggest that it offer a minicourse jointly with a school or youth group in baby-sitting, which would feature the basics of child care and emergency care as well as a little about special-needs children. It could be part of a service project or a college or high school course in home economics, education, sociology, civics, or some other area. The young people would learn and benefit, and so would your group.

Some courses like this may already exist in your community, sponsored by schools, churches, or youth groups. In some areas of the country a government-sponsored project called Education for Parenthood (EFP) has initiated high school courses in child development and management. There is a package of curriculum materials available called "Exploring Childhood," which could be used as a basis for a program you develop. The address for further information is at the end of this chapter. If you are planning a minicourse, try to get someone who is experienced in education or training to help you or your group plan it out carefully. The course should probably be short in order to keep interest high. Also, at least for the first time, you shouldn't try anything too ambitious. Several consecutive weekends, or coursework over a month's period, would probably be enough to handle. One evening or afternoon session might even suffice. You can always plan a sequel program if the response is high enough to warrant it.

Preparing a Sitter

Even if you are able to find a sitter who has had some experience with, or has taken some courses in, caring for children with special needs, you'll still want to make some special preparations the first time she or he cares for your child. When a child who has special needs meets a sitter for the first time, it is a good idea to have the sitter come early so the two can become acquainted with each other. Perhaps even a separate visit prior to the first sitting would be helpful. The sitter should be told what medicine, if any, your child needs. And she or he should be shown how to handle eyeglasses, hearing aides, artificial limbs, braces, or other items that need to be put on, taken off, or otherwise manipulated. Even if the sitting is scheduled for a time when such services will not be required, the sitter should be informed of their existence and how they operate in case of an emergency.

Make sure your sitter is prepared, but don't frighten her or him to death. Sometimes parents bombard sitters with so much negative information that they can be overwhelmed by the task. Don't overprotect your child to the extent that a sitter is frightened to deal with the child.

As with a baby-sitter for any child, you should naturally prepare your sitter to deal with the routine and possible emergency situations in your household. Give the sitter a phone number where you can be reached, as well as a list of emergency numbers for fire, police, and doctor. Make another list of routine instructions for taking care of your child. Because of your child's special needs, you should also leave a telephone number of someone who is experienced in handling your child in case you cannot be reached.

Getting Ready for Day Care

Most of the same preparations just described also apply when you enter your child in a day care center. In this case, you will probably want to arrange at least one advance visit between your child and the new caretaker at the day care center itself. Not only will this benefit the caretaker, but it will also help your child adjust more easily to the strange new surroundings. If possible, go to the center for several short visits with your child and try leaving the room for gradually lengthening periods of time. Let the child see the entire facility and its activities.

Just as you may need to overcome certain feelings of guilt and anxiety when you leave your child alone with others, even for a short time, your child may also have uneasy feelings about being left without you. You may have to prepare your child slowly for this new experience, but do not overprepare her and thus create anxieties. Some parents paint such a rosy picture of the wonderful time the child will have that it becomes a disappointment. Others repeat "You musn't be afraid" so many times that the child decides that there must be something to be afraid of.

Negative Reactions of Others

When you prepare your child for a new sitter or day care center, there are other influences upon both of you besides your own intertwined emotions. Friends, neighbors, and even members of your own family may be shocked that you are even thinking of leaving your child with strangers. If you are actually returning to work or enjoying yourselves, they may be completely horrified. They see the child as something to wrap in cotton protected from the cruel world and hidden in shame from others. They do not realize the need of the child to experience many different situations and to be exposed to different people.

Outsiders may still be working through their own feelings and guilts about handicapped children, and often they cannot conceive how you can deal with it successfully. They can only see heartless, selfish, uncaring parents instead of responsible, loving, and caring ones. Where you see steps toward independence, they see callousness. They see the child somehow chained to you forever by a strange umbilical cord of guilt and responsibility.

While all this may rekindle your own guilts and concerns to a degree, you have to live your own lives. Unfortunately, you will most likely have to deal with this on an on-going basis, since few people who have not shared a similar experience will condone your actions. This may include your employer and even the very professionals involved with the services you use.

There are many resources for the support you need when you parent a child with special needs. Some of these come from strengths and talents within yourselves and your family. Others come from friends, neighbors, extended family, and the neighbors you have yet to meet within your community.

You may have to search, demand, improvise, and innovate. But if you persevere and are willing to share the burdens of the challenges that special needs can bring, you just might find solutions to many of these challenges. At the very least, you will discover that you are seldom really alone when you allow others to reach out and allow yourselves to be open to them.

DIRECTORY

Professional Resources

Check local telephone listings under these headings:

Community Chest	County Mental Health
Community Council	Associations
Community Planning Council	Family Counseling Service
Community Services	Family Service
Council for Community Services	Family Service Association
Counseling Clinic	Health and Welfare Council
Counseling Service	Information and Referral Service
County Department of Health	Mental Health Clinic
	United Way, United Fund

Chapter References

Books for Parents

Ayrault, Evelyn West. *You Can Raise Your Handicapped Child.* New York: G. P. Putnam's Sons, 1964.

Gordon, Thomas. *P.E.T.—Parent Effectiveness Training.* New York. Peter H. Wyden, 1970.

Gutman, Ernest M. *Travel Guide for the Disabled.* New York: Charles C. Thomas, 1967.

McDonald, Eugene T. *Understanding Those Feelings.* Englewood Cliffs, N.J.: Prentice-Hall, 1964.

National Park Guide for the Handicapped. U.S. Department of Interior, 1971, publication no. 1.29.9 2/H19. $.40.[1]

Paige, Marianna. *Respite Care for the Retarded: An Interval of Relief for Families.* 1971. $.25.

"A Practical Guide to Coalition Building." Institute on Pluralism and Group Identity, 1976 (165 East 56th Street, New York, N.Y. 10022). $.25.

President's Committee on Mental Retardation. *People-Live-In Houses: Profiles of Community Residences for Retarded Children and Adults.* 1975. $1.50.

Rowlands, Peter. *Children Apart: How Parents Can Help Young Children Cope with Being Away from the Family.* New York: Pantheon Books, 1973.

Styon, Gail. *Heartaches and Handicaps: An Irreverant Survival Manual for Parents.* Science and Behavior Books, 1976 (P.O. Box 11457, Palo Alto, Calif. 94306).

Wentworth, Elsie H. *Listen to Your Heart: A Message to Parents of Handicapped Children.* Boston: Houghton Mifflin, 1974.

Books for Children

Berger, Terry. *I Have Feelings.* New York: Behavioral Press, 1971.

Brightman, Alan J., Ph.D. *Like Me.* Boston: Little, Brown & Co., 1976.

Fassler, Joan, Ph.D. *Howie Helps Himself.* Chicago: Albert Whitman, 1975.

---

[1] All U.S. government publications are available from the Superintendent of Documents, U.S. Government Printing Office, Washington, D.C. 20402.

Fassler, Joan, Ph.D. *One Little Girl.* New York: Behavioral Publications, 1968.

Lasker, Joe. *He's My Brother.* New York: Albert Whitman, 1974.

Mack, Nancy. *Tracy.* Chicago: Raintree Publications, 1976 (P.O. Box 11799, Chicago, Ill. 60611).

Stein, Sara Bonnet. *About Handicaps.* New York: Walker & Co., 1974.

Wolf, Bernard. *Connie's New Eyes.* Philadelphia: Lippincott, 1976.

Wolf, Bernard. *Don't Feel Sorry for Paul.* Philadelphia: Lippincott, 1974.

Travel and Recreation Resources

Directory of Camps for the Handicapped
American Camping Association
Bradford Wood
Marysville, Ind. 47141

Boy Scouts of America
New Brunswick, N.J. 08902

Girl Scouts of the U.S.A.
840 Third Avenue
New York, N.Y. 10022

Camp Fire Girls
16 East 48th Street
New York, N.Y. 10017

Education for Parenthood Information

Public Affairs Pamphlets
381 Park Avenue South
New York, N.Y. 10016
("Preparing Tomorrow's Parents" by Elizabeth Ogg, Public Affairs Pamphlet No. 520, $.35)

Education for Parenthood Curriculum Planning

EFP Project
Office of Education
Room 2089-G
400 Maryland Avenue Southwest
Washington, D.C. 20202

EFP Project
Division of Public Education
Office of Child Development
P.O. Box 1182
Washington, D.C. 20013

Organizations

Committee on Parenthood Education (COPE)
P.O. Box 9533
San Diego, Calif. 92109

Day Care and Development Council of America
1426 H Street Northwest Suite 340
Washington, D.C. 20005

Effectiveness Associates (P.E.T. Information)
110 South Euclid
Pasadena, Calif 91101

Parent/Advocate Groups

This listing is meant to be a starting point, not a comprehensive listing. Some addresses will have changed and some groups disbanded; other groups will have started up after publication of this book. Also check for parent/advocate groups in the *Directory of Organizations for the Handicapped in the U.S.* (Massachusetts Council of Organizations of the Handicapped, Inc., Harold H. Reemes, 41 Woodgren Road, Hyde Park, Mass. 02136) .

Association for Children with Learning Disabilities
2200 Brownsville Road
Pittsburgh, Pa. 15210

Association for Education of the Visually Handicapped
1604 Spruce Street
Philadelphia, Pa. 19103

Association for the Aid of Crippled Children
345 East 46th Street
New York, N.Y. 10017
(spina bifida booklet)

Association for the Visually Handicapped
1839 Frankfort Avenue
Louisville, Ky. 40206

Candlelighters
123 C Street Southeast
Washington, D.C. 20003
(For parents of children with potentially fatal conditions)

Children in Hospitals
c/o Barbara Popper
31 Wilshire Park
Needham, Mass. 20970

League for Emotionally Disturbed Children
171 Madison Avenue
New York, N.Y. 10017

Little People of America, Inc.
P.O. Box 126
Owatonna, Minn. 55060

National Aid to the Visually Handicapped
3201 Balboa Street
San Francisco, Calif. 94121

National Association for Retarded Children
2709 Avenue E, East
Arlington, Tex. 76011
(State offices)

National Association for the Deaf
814 Thayer Avenue
Silver Springs, Md. 20970

National Information and Referral Service for Autistic and
    Autistic-Like Persons
101 Richmond Street
Huntington, W. Va. 25702

National Multiple Sclerosis Society
257 Park Avenue South
New York, N.Y. 10010

National Society for Autistic Children, Inc.
621 Central Avenue
Albany, N.Y. 12206

Natonal Tay-Sachs and Allied Diseases Association, Inc.
200 Park Avenue South
New York, N.Y. 10003

Osteogenesis Imperfecta, Inc.
1231 May Court
Burlington, N.C. 27215

Parents Anonymous
2930 Imperial Highway
Inglewood, Calif. 90303
(Child abuse)

Parents Concerned with Hospitalized Children
176 North Villa Avenue
Villa Park, Ill. 80181

Groups Concerned with Down's Syndrome

Association for Children with Down's Syndrome
589 Patterson Street
East Meadow, N.Y. 11554

Monday's Mothers
349 Fitch Street
Monterey, Calif. 93940

Mongoloid Children's Association
14867 Stadler Road
Sterling Heights, Mich. 48078

Mongoloid Development Council
11 North 73rd Terrace
Kansas City, Kan. 66111

Mongoloid Development Council
307 Bender Avenue
Roselle Park, N.J. 07204

Mothers of Children with Down's Syndrome
P.O. Box 217
Allap Station, Miami, Fla. 33142

Mothers of Mongoloids
6817 Circleview Drive
Saint Louis, Mo. 63123

Mothers of Young Mongoloids
713 Ramsey Street
Alexandria, Va. 22301

National Association for Down's Syndrome
628 Ashland Avenue
River Forest, Ill. 60305

National Association for Down's Syndrome
Southern Maryland Chapter
1800 Rhodesia Avenue
Friendly, Md. 20022

National Mongoloid Council
P.O. Box 140
Park Ridge, Ill. 60068

National Association for Retarded Citizens (NARC)

NARC is a national group concerned with the welfare of retarded persons. It started as a parent support group and has become an activist group, fighting for the rights of all retarded citizens and their families. Local and state associations may be involved in supportive counseling, information and referral, social and recreational activities, and fund-raising for these. Some groups may provide concrete services such as educational or training programs, diagnostic services, and financial assistance. The state associations are listed below:

Alabama ARC
4301 Norman Bridge Road
Montgomery, Ala. 36105
Phone: (205) 288-9434

Alaska ARC
Drawer 8-1
Anchorage, Alaska 99508
Phone: (907) 277-1522

Arizona ARC
2929 East Thomas Road
Room 216
Phoenix, Arizona 85016
Phone: (602) 955-8940

Arkansas ARC
University Shopping Center
Little Rock, Arkansas 72204
Phone: (501) 562-0558

California ARC
1225 Eighth Street
Suite 312
Sacramento, Calif. 95314
Phone: (916) 441-3322

Colorado ARC
8000 East Gerard
Suite 702
Denver, Colo. 80231
Phone: (303) 751-4641

Connecticut ARC
21-R High Street
Hartford, Conn. 06103
Phone: (203) 522-3379

Delaware ARC
P.O. Box 1896
Wilmington, Del. 19899
Phone: (302) 764-3662

D.C. ARC
405 Riggs Road Northeast
Washington, D.C. 20001
Phone: (202) 529-0070

Florida ARC
P.O. Box 1542
Tallahassee, Fla. 32302
Phone: (904) 222-0470

Georgia ARC
1575 Phoenix Boulevard
Suite 8
Atlanta, Ga. 30349
Phone: (404) 761-5209

Hawaii ARC
245 North Kukui Street
Honolulu, Hawaii 96817
Phone: (808) 536-2274

Idaho ARC
P.O. Box 816
Boise, Idaho 47893
Phone: (598) 345-8190

Illinois ARC
6 Michigan Avenue
Chicago, Ill. 60602
Phone: (312) 263-7135

Indiana ARC
752 East Market Street
Indianapolis, Ind. 46202
Phone: (317) 632-4387

Iowa ARC
1707 High Street
Des Moines, Iowa 50309
Phone: (515) 283-2359

Kansas ARC
6100 Martway
Suite 1
Mission, Kan. 66202
Phone: (913) 236-6810

Kentucky ARC
P.O. Box 275
Frankfort, Ky. 40601
Phone: (502) 564-7050

Louisiana ARC
7465 Exchange Place
Baton Rouge, La. 70806

Maine ARC
269½ Water Street
Augusta, Maine 04330
Phone: (207) 622-7502

Maryland ARC
55 Gwynns Mill Court
Owings Mills, Md. 21117
Phone: (301) 356-3410

Massachusetts ARC
381 Elliot Street
Newton Upper Falls,
Mass. 02164
Phone: (617) 965-5320

Michigan ARC
416 Michigan National Tower
Lansing, Mich. 48933
Phone: (517) 487-5426

Minnesota ARC
3225 Lyndale Avenue
Minneapolis, Minn. 55408
Phone: (612) 827-5641

Mississippi ARC
P.O. Box 1363
Jackson, Miss. 39205
Phone: (601) 353-4326

Missouri ARC
320 West Dunklin
Jefferson City, Mo. 65101
Phone: (314) 634-2220

Montana ARC
P.O. Box 625
Helena, Mont. 59601
Phone: (406) 442-2421

Nebraska ARC
620 North 48th S-318
Lincoln, Neb. 68504
Phone: (402) 467-4408

Nevada ARC
1800 Sahara
Suite 102
Las Vegas, Nev. 89104
Phone: (702) 732-1354

New Hampshire ARC
52 Pleasant Street
Concord, N.H. 03301
Phone: (603) 224-7322

New Jersey ARC
92 Bayard Street
New Brunswick, N.J. 08901
Phone: (201) 246-2525

New Mexico ARC
8200½ Menaul Boulevard
NE Suite 3
Albuquerque, N.M. 87110
Phone: (505) 298-4009

New York ARC
200 Park Avenue South
New York, N.Y. 10003
Phone: (212) 254-8203

North Carolina ARC
P.O. Box 18551
Raleigh, N.C. 27609
Phone: (919) 782-5114

North Dakota ARC
514½ First Avenue North
P.O. Box 1494
Fargo, N.D. 58102
Phone: (701) 235-4479

Ohio ARC
61 East Gay Street
Columbus, Ohio 43215
Phone: (614) 228-6689

Oklahoma ARC
P.O. Box 14250
Oklahoma City, Okla. 73114
Phone: (405) 842-8834

Oregon ARC
3085 River Road North
Salem, Ore. 97303
Phone: (503) 588-0095

Pennsylvania ARC
1500 North Second
Harrisburg, Pa. 17102
Phone: (717) 235-4479

Rhode Island ARC
Now Building
2845 Post Road
Warwick, R.I. 02886
Phone (401) 738-5550

South Carolina ARC
P.O. Box 1564
Columbia, S.C. 29202
Phone: (803) 765-2431

South Dakota ARC
P.O. Box 502
111 West Capitol
Pierre, S.Dak. 57501
Phone: (605) 224-8211

Tennessee ARC
2121 Belcourt Avenue
Nashville, Tenn. 37212
Phone: (615) 298-4487

Texas ARC
833 West Houston
Austin, Tex. 78756
Phone: (512) 454-6694

Utah ARC
2952 South Seventh East
Salt Lake City, Utah 84106
Phone: (801) 486-0073

Vermont ARC
323 Pearl Street
Burlington, Vt. 05401
Phone: (802) 864-0761

Virginia ARC
909 Mutual Building
909 East Main
Richmond, Va. 23219
Phone: (804) 649-8481

Washington ARC
213½ East Fourth
Suite 10
Olympia, Wash. 98501
Phone: (206) 357-5596

West Virginia ARC
Union Building
Room 614
Parkersburg, W.Va. 26101
Phone: (304) 485-5283

Wisconsin ARC
351 West Washington Avenue
Madison, Wisconsin 53703
Phone: (608) 256-7774

Wyoming ARC
P.O. Box C
Buffalo, Wyo. 82834
Phone: (307) 684-2373

National Voluntary Health Agencies

Arthritis
Arthritis Foundation
1212 Avenue of the Americas
New York, N.Y. 10036

Birth Defects
National Foundation—
March of Dimes
1275 Mamaroneck Avenue
White Plains, N.Y. 10605

Cancer
American Cancer Society
219 East 42nd Street
New York, N.Y. 10017

Cerebral Palsy
United Cerebral Palsy
Associations, Inc.
66 East 34th Street
New York, N.Y. 10016

Cystic Fibrosis
National Cystic Fibrosis
Foundation
3379 Peachtree Road
Northeast
Atlanta, Ga. 30326

Diabetes
American Diabetes
Association[1]
18 East 48th Street
New York, N.Y. 10017

Epilepsy
Epilepsy Foundation
of America
Suite 406
1828 L Street Northwest
Washington, D.C. 20036

Hearing and Speech Disorders
Alexander Graham Bell
Association for the Deaf
1537 35th Street Northwest
Washington, D.C. 20007

Deafness Research Foundation
366 Madison Avenue
New York, N.Y. 10017

John Tracy Clinic
807 West Adams Boulevard
Los Angeles, Calif. 90007
(Education of deaf children)

National Association of
Hearing and Speech Agencies
814 Thayer Avenue
Silver Springs, Md. 20910

National Association of the Deaf
814 Thayer Avenue
Silver Springs, Md. 20910

Heart Disease
American Heart Association
44 East 23rd Street
New York, N.Y. 10010.

---

[1] This is actually a professional association, but since it performs many of the functions of a voluntary health agency, it is listed here.

Hemophilia
National Hemophilia
Foundation
25 West 39th Street
New York, N.Y. 10018

Huntington's Chorea
Committee to Combat
Huntington's Disease
200 West 57th Street
New York, N.Y. 10019

Kidney Disease
National Kidney Foundation
116 East 27th Street
New York, N.Y. 10010

Mental Health
Joseph P. Kennedy Jr.
Foundation
Suite 205
1701 K Street Northwest
Washington, D.C. 20006
(Mental retardation)

National Association for
Mental Health
1800 North Kent Street
Rosslyn, Va. 22209

Multiple Sclerosis
National Multiple Sclerosis
Society
257 Park Avenue South
New York, N.Y. 10010

Muscular Dystrophy
Muscular Dystrophy
Associations of America, Inc.
810 Seventh Avenue
New York, N.Y. 10019

Orthopedic Disorders (General)
Foundation for Child
Development
345 East 46th Street
New York, N.Y. 10017

National Easter Seal Society
for Crippled Children
and Adults, Inc.
2023 West Ogden Avenue
Chicago, Ill. 60612

Paraplegia
National Paraplegia Foundation
333 North Michigan Avenue
Chicago, Ill. 60601

Pituitary Disorders
National Pituitary Agency
Suite 503-7
210 West Fayette Street
Baltimore, Md. 21201

Poliomyelitis
National Foundation—
March of Dimes
1275 Mamaroneck Avenue
White Plains, N.Y. 10605

Respiratory Disorders
American Lung Association
1740 Broadway
New York, N.Y. 10019

Sickle Cell Anemia
Center for Sickle Cell Anemia
College of Medicine
Howard University
520 W Street Northwest
Washington, D.C. 20001

Foundation for Research and
Education in Sickle Cell
Disease
421-431 West 120th Street
New York, N.Y. 10027

Visual Disorders
American Foundation
for the Blind
15 West 16th Street
New York, N.Y. 10011

National Council to
Combat Blindness
41 West 57th Street
New York, N.Y. 10019

National Society for the
Prevention of Blindness
79 Madison Avenue
New York, N.Y. 10016

Professional Associations

American Academy of Pediatrics
1801 Hinman Avenue
Evanston, Ill. 60204

American Association for Health, Physical Education and Recreation
1201 16th Street Northwest
Washington, D.C. 20036

American Association for Maternal and Child Health
116 South Michigan Avenue
Chicago, Ill. 60603

American Association on Mental Deficiency
5201 Connecticut Avenue Northwest
Washington, D.C. 20015

American College of Obstetricians and Gynecologists
79 West Monroe Street
Chicago, Ill. 60603

American Diabetes Association
18 East 48th Street
New York, N.Y. 10017

American Medical Association
535 North Dearborn Street
Chicago, Ill. 60610

American Occupational Therapy Association
251 Park Avenue South
New York, N.Y. 10010

American Personnel and Guidance Association
1607 New Hampshire Avenue Northwest
Washington, D.C. 20009

American Physical Therapy Association
1156 15th Street Northwest
Washington, D.C. 20036

American Psychological Association
1200 17th Street Northwest
Washington, D.C. 20036

American Public Health Association
1015 18th Street Northwest
Washington, D.C. 20036

American Rehabilitation Counseling Association
1607 New Hampshire Avenue Northwest
Washington, D.C. 20009
(A division of the American Personnel and Guidance Association)

American Speech and Hearing Association
9030 Old Georgetown Road
Washington, D.C. 20014

American Vocational Association
1510 H Street Northwest
Washington, D.C. 20005

Council for Exceptional Children
1201 16th Street Northwest
Washington, D.C. 20036
(A department of the National Education Association)

National Catholic Educational Association
One Dupont Circle
Washington, D.C. 20036

National Council for Homemaker–Home Health Aide Services, Inc.
1740 Broadway
New York, N.Y. 10019

National Education Association
1201 16th Street Northwest
Washington, D.C. 20036

National Rehabilitation Association
1522 K Street Northwest
Washington, D.C. 20005

National Vocational Guidance Association
1607 New Hampshire Avenue Northwest
Washington, D.C. 20009
(A division of the American Personnel and Guidance Association)

Government Agencies

Closer Look
P.O. Box 19428
Washington, D.C. 20036
(A national Special Education Information Center to help parents
and others find services for children with mental, physical, emotional, and learning handicaps, sponsored by the U.S. Department
of Health, Education, and Welfare)

Health Services and Mental Health Administration
Rockville, Md. 20852

Library of Congress
Division for the Blind and Physically Handicapped
Washington, D.C. 20542
(Free library services for the visually and physically handicapped)

U.S. Civil Service Commission
Washington, D.C. 20415

U.S. Department of Health, Education, and Welfare
Children's Bureau
Washington, D.C. 20201

U.S. Department of Health, Education, and Welfare
Office of Child Development
P.O. Box 1182
Washington, D.C. 20013

U.S. Department of Health, Education, and Welfare
Office of Education
Washington, D.C. 20202

U.S. Department of Health, Education, and Welfare
Office of Education
Bureau of Education for the Handicapped
Seventh and D Streets Southwest
Washington, D.C. 20036

U.S. Department of Health, Education, and Welfare
Rehabilitation Service Administration
Washington, D.C. 20201

U.S. Department of Labor
President's Committee on Employment of the Handicapped
Washington, D.C. 20542

U.S. Public Health Service
National Institutes of Health
Public Information Officer
Bethesda, Maryland 20014
 (Information about specific birth defects)

U.S. Social Security Administration
Division of Disability Operations
6401 Security Boulevard
Baltimore, Md. 21235

Other Organizations

American Legion
National Child Welfare Division
P.O. Box 1055
Indianapolis, Ind. 46206

American Printing House for the Blind
P.O. Box 6085
Louisville, Ky. 40206

B'nai B'rith Career and Counseling Service
1640 Rhode Island Avenue Northwest
Washington, D.C. 20036.

Child Study Association of America
50 Madison Avenue
New York, N.Y. 10010

Federation for the Handicapped, Inc.
211 West 14th Street
New York, N.Y. 10011

Foundation for Child Development
345 East 46th Street
New York, N.Y. 10017

Goodwill Industries of America, Inc.
1218 New Hampshire Avenue Northwest
Washington, D.C. 20009

National Association for Education of Young Children
1834 Connecticut Avenue
Washington, D.C. 20009

National Association of State Programs for the Mentally Retarded
c/o Mr. Robert Gettings, Executive Director
20010 Jefferson Davis Highway
Arlington, Va. 22202

National Committee on Employment of Youth
145 East 32nd Street
New York, N.Y. 10016
(A division of the National Child Labor Committee)

National Health Council
1740 Broadway
New York, N.Y. 10019

National Parents and Teachers Association (PTA)
700 North Rush Street
Chicago, Ill. 60611

National Urban League
55 East 52nd Street
New York, N.Y. 10022

Spastic Children's Foundation
1307 West 105th Street
Los Angeles, Calif 90044

Vocational Guidance and Rehabilitation Services
2239 East 55th Street
Cleveland, Ohio 44103

6

Financial Problems—
Financial Solutions

Finances are one of the first problems that hit families of a child with special needs. We envision—sometimes all too accurately—a staggering, unending financial burden that drains a family completely. But for many families this is not the case. Often the combination of government and private services, proper medical insurance, and frugal budgeting can help ease the financial pressures.

Specific situations vary. But often "with all the resources available, handicapped kids aren't any more expensive to raise than other children. And they have so much to give," says Jack Becker, who, with his wife, Steffi, adopted a six-year-old daughter, Melanie, who is partially paralyzed as the result of spina bifida.

A national health insurance plan might be able to alleviate many of the financial worries of a family with special medical needs, but, as yet, we do not have this kind of plan in operation in the United States. Until then one of the major supports for a family with a child having special needs is adequate health insurance.

MEDICAL INSURANCE

You may be participating in a company-sponsored insurance plan, or you may have chosen your insurance on your own. Either way, you need to determine in detail, right down to the fine print, specifically what your policy can cover for your family. If the policy does not meet all of your needs adequately, you will have to consider switching to another insurance company, or adding other coverage.

You can get some of this information on your coverage, and its limits, by reading the policy and whatever booklets or brochures accompany it. But since much of the policy may be subject to interpretation, and since policies tend to be written in a very technical language, it is imperative that you get an insurance agent, or the person in your company or union in charge of insurance, to explain the coverage in detail to you. Any questions that that person cannot answer should be referred directly to the company. And it's a good idea to get policy explanations in writing.

If you decide to switch policies, remember that having an independent insurance agent write your new policy doesn't automatically mean that your policy will cost more than if you write a policy directly with an insurance company. What's more, an independent insurance agent, who handles policies from different companies, may be helpful because he can review the advantages and disadvantages of a variety of choices regarding your special needs. Also, that agent may be able to act as your advocate in case there is a claim problem.

There are also several government-sponsored insurance plans that are available only to specific groups of people. Medicare is limited by the age of the person to be insured; medicaid by the income of the family. Military insurance covers only those serving in the armed forces and their dependents. In addition, there are a number of medical benefits available to veterans of the armed forces and their dependents. You may be eligible for some of these programs. Check with your local health or welfare department and with the Veterans Administration.

You should know that you could be eligible for assistance for your medical bills from the government even though you are not eligible for welfare benefits. If your uninsured medical bills are more than one fourth of your income, you may be able to receive medical or other assistance. There is also a growing trend to include coverage for potentially financially debilitating conditions even when income limits are exceeded. For example, medicaid will now pick up the costs related to kidney disease for a patient or his family. The philosophy behind such coverage is that a family should not be drained of all resources before they can obtain aid. SSI, (Supplemental Security Income), based on the family's income, is another federal program that provides direct assistance to families with a child who has special needs.

Checking Your Medical Coverage

When you review your health insurance and how it covers your child with special needs, there are important questions to ask yourselves and your insurance representative. They include:

● Which members of our family are covered and for how long?

Some policies exclude children over or under a certain age, or children who are married, or those who hold jobs. If your child needs psychological counseling, braces, medication, or other services through adolescence and is still living with you after his eighteenth or nineteenth birthday, your policy may exclude the coverage that you may have taken for granted all these years.

Children from a previous marriage of the spouse who is not the policy holder, adopted children who had medical problems before being placed with you for adoption, and other relatives you might be legal guardians for may be excluded from coverage.

Some policies do not cover a child during the first days after birth. If your newborn infant needs emergency surgery at two days of age and your policy does not begin coverage until the twenty-eighth day or until the mother of the child leaves the hospital, you could be stuck with thousands of dollars of uncovered bills. A few states now require insurance carriers to provide coverage for the first twenty-eight days of life of a child.

● What types of services are covered? Are there limits on the length of time, amount of allowable coverage, deductions, place of treatment, waiting periods, or any other special exclusions?

Your policy could cover expenses for surgery, but if you're not careful, you could find yourselves in financial trouble when you try to claim these expenses because of qualifiers in the policy that you were unaware of. One of the most common qualifiers is the "deductible," a certain amount of money that you must pay each year, or on each bill, before the insurer will start the coverage you need. Some policies will cover only a certain amount of expenses each year, or they have a waiting period after you start your policy before you are allowed to use the benefits. This can be a problem if, for instance, you conceive a child right after you start a policy that requires you to wait ten months before you'll be covered by maternity benefits. You may be required to use only certain clinics, hospitals, dentists, doctors, or other approved personnel. Again, if your policy does not meet your needs, you will have to adjust, amend, or add to it if you do not want to carry the cost on your own.

● Are there any renewal or cancellation provisions, particularly if you must switch jobs or locations?

Because of such provisions, you might find yourself in the frightening situation of suddenly being without medical insurance and with many bills coming in. Always renew your policy well in advance of the date of expiration, checking to make sure you still meet the company's current eligibility requirements. If you must switch policies, allow for time to compare policies carefully. It's also a good idea to check your policy periodically for any changes that may have been instituted in the coverage. An item the policy covered last year may not be covered this year, or it may not be covered at the same rate or with the same standards. With the rising costs of medical services and insurance, it is common for companies not only to raise premiums but to reduce services as well.

● Is my coverage adequate? Am I getting what I am paying for?

You may have too little coverage for your family. Or, you may have too much. You may have coverage that overlaps; for example, car insurance may pay for your medical bills in case of accident, and medical insurance may cover the same costs. Check your insurance costs against the benefits available to you under the policy. A premium that is a terrific bargain may not be so terrific if it excludes your largest medical expenditure when you need it. A policy that initially seems expensive may not really be that costly when you consider how much of the total expenditure it actually covers. You must weigh everything in light of your projected expenses, not just the initial premium costs or deductibles.

Health Insurance Plans

Basically, there are two types of health insurance plans offered by insurance companies—profit-making and nonprofit plans. About one thousand commercial insurance companies, such as Prudential and Allstate, offer plans that primarily cover hospital expenses, either through individual or group coverage. In order to realize a profit, such companies prefer to concentrate their coverages on a "low-risk" population—that is, people least likely to use the coverage. Their rates are higher if you or your family fall outside this select group.

Blue Cross and Blue Shield are two of the most widely used of all group-insurance plans. They each originated as nonprofit plans willing to accept a higher-risk population at lower rates than commercial plans. They are willing to cover high-risk individuals as part of large groups primarily because such groups include many low-risk individuals too. Generally speaking, the larger the insurance plan, or group, that you belong to, the easier it will be to obtain coverage at a reasonable rate if your child has special needs.

There are also both profit and nonprofit independent health insurance plans—often administered on a prepaid basis—for hospital, surgical, dental, or medical care. Some plans include costs of drugs and appliances, such as braces, hearing aids, and glasses. One type of coverage is the nonprofit community plan, usually affiliated with a clinic or group practice, that services a specific area or group. There may or may not be a choice of doctors or dentists. Private group clinics can be organized by physicians or dentists as private business ventures. Either kind of prepaid group systems for health care coverage and delivery may sometimes be organized into what is referred to as a health maintenance organization.

Unions, company employee groups, or companies can operate group or individual insurance and health plan systems. These plans serve a select specific group of employees or union members and are usually operated and administered out of the welfare funds of the company or union.

Types of Health Insurance Coverage

Within the various kinds of insurance plans there are several general types of coverage, each for slightly different needs. These include straight medical insurance, insurance for hospital costs, surgical costs, maternity care; major medical or extended benefits; dental insurance; and comprehensive prepaid medical care.

Most people need or use a combination of these. Here is an outline of some of these types of health insurance coverage plans:

Medical: Medical insurance covers the costs of a doctor's fees at home, in the hospital, or in the doctor's office that are not surgical in nature. It can include lab fees for tests and X rays.

Surgical: Surgical insurance covers necessary surgical costs. This means that "cosmetic" surgery is usually not covered unless the purpose is to correct a medically related problem, such as repair of a cleft lip or burn scars. You should attempt to check about the cost in advance of the surgery, if possible, since you are usually required to pay the difference between what the insurance policy will allow you and what the surgeon will ask. Sometimes you can negotiate with the surgeon for lower costs or for time payments. Blue Shield is an example of surgical insurance. It covers over seventy-one million people for medical and surgical care, making it by far one of the most often used types of policies.

Hospital: Hospital insurance covers inpatient hospital expenses, such as room, board, and standard nursing care. Occasionally intensive care and outpatient services, such as emergency room fees, X rays, and lab tests, are also covered.

How much of your bill and how long you can continue to be covered, as well as any ceiling imposed upon your total yearly medical expenses, vary greatly from policy to policy. Policies often have a deductible clause, which means that you will have to pay a percentage of the total bill or an initial amount, such as fifty or one hundred dollars, before the insurance coverage will pick up the remainder. Blue Cross is the largest insurance carrier for hospital care; its policies cover more than seventy-nine million people.

Maternity: Expenses of maternity care are usually not covered in your standard medical, surgical, or hospital insurance plan. It must be specifically included in order to have your doctor and hospital expenses for maternity-related services covered. If it is unlikely that you will be conceiving a child, this may be unnecessary coverage for you, and you may want to eliminate it from your policy if it was included during a previous time when pregnancy was a consideration. This is especially important coverage, however, if you have already had a child born to you with special needs, since you could have another. Your policy may or may not cover your newborn child as part of its maternity or other insurance. As mentioned before, some policies exclude the very young infant from coverage under your family plan. Only a handful of states now require that such coverage be included without extra high costs, and few policies include it voluntarily. Since the early 1970s, the American Academy of Pediatrics has encouraged legislation to guarantee insurance coverage of a child's first month of life.

If your newborn child with special needs is not covered by insurance, there are available a limited number of intensive infant care projects funded by the U.S. Department of Health, Education, and Welfare. These are listed at the end of this chapter. Also included are the regional HEW offices, which may have information on additional projects being developed. If you do not have adequate insurance coverage, the professional staff at HEW or at one of the projects may be able to make some suggestions to you.

The eligibility clause for maternity benefits often trips up some prospective parents. Sometimes a policy includes a clause that states that you must be insured for the better part of a year before maternity benefits in your policy can be used. So if you are expecting a child at the time of initiating the policy or shortly thereafter, you could be out of luck with this type of policy. Also, certain complications of pregnancy and certain services may or may not be covered.

Major medical–extended benefits: Major medical covers many items not included by other health plans, so it is used in addition to a basic insurance policy. Comprehensive major medical includes both types, basic and extended. This is the area where costs mount up for the family with special needs—counseling, testing, appliances, therapy, and special care of various types. This is important coverage, so check it carefully to make sure you are adequately covered.

Dental: Dental benefits may be included within your regular health plan or a similar affiliated plan. If your children are approaching orthodonture age (over nine), your policy should include orthodontic coverage, since this type of work can be very costly. You might have coverage in a prepaid group insurance plan, which may or may not give you a choice of dentists and dental specialists.

Comprehensive prepaid medical: We previously discussed insurance administered by profit or nonprofit groups that ask you to pay for health services before you receive them. They attempt to provide total health care, not just emergency services, with the emphasis on keeping people healthy rather than treating people after they are no longer healthy. For this reason they are referred to as "health maintenance" plans.

At the end of this chapter you will find contacts where you can obtain additional information on insurance policies, both general information and information on specific types of policies.

GOVERNMENTAL MEDICAL COVERAGE

Adequate medical insurance is a fundamental prop for families with children having special needs. But insurance usually won't cover all the extra costs of medical care as well as the expenses of therapy or special equipment. These costs can be a strain if you cannot find financial help. And the availability of that help is not always obvious.

At first the McGraths were struggling along with the bills and insurance coverage for their son Kim's physical therapy at a private hospital where their doctor had referred them. Then a therapist at the hospital mentioned to them that there were other programs, public and private, in the area that might be able to provide the therapy at a lower or subsidized cost. The McGraths subsequently discovered that their county had a "medical rehabilitation program," part of their state's crippled children's services, and that it would pay for whatever services their child received that their insurance did not cover.

State and county services for handicapped children, usually funded by the federal government, vary widely from state to state and from locality to locality. But they are usually administered by a community's department of health, although other agencies, such as the department of welfare or education, may also be involved. The major aid program in most states are the crippled children's programs. These are administered by the states but are jointly funded by federal and state governments. Remember that they cover a multitude of special needs, not just crippling handicaps.

To qualify for the services of a crippled children's program, a child must be under twenty-one years of age and have a heart disease, cerebral palsy, orthopedic problems, accidental injuries, burns, birth defects, a handicapping condition caused by heart disease, epilepsy, vision or hearing problems, or one of many other handicapping conditions. Most states also include such conditions as cystic fibrosis and other chronic diseases.

Services under such programs—usually coordinated through local departments of health, education, or public welfare—may include free diagnostic services as well as medical and surgical services. The array of services vary. So do the costs, which usually are based on an income formula. In one county you might receive total financial coverage of costs for therapy, surgery, and special education; the next county may require the family to make a partial or total payment for such services.

As a result the burden of costs falls unevenly on families of children with special need depending on where they happen to live. For example, the crippled children's program in the county where the McGraths live covered all of their expenses directly related to Kim's handicap that were not covered by their medical insurance. The McGraths were required to fill out a yearly financial statement to determine if they still met the program's income criteria. At first they paid nothing for the care their son needed beyond insurance coverage. But a few years later, when they moved into a higher income bracket, they were obligated to pay a percentage of the total bill. But the amount was only about twenty-five dollars, a fraction of the total cost.

In contrast, the DuBois family, who lived in the same state but in a different county from the McGraths, found that their local department of health administered the crippled children's program with more stringent financial regulations. As a result they received little financial help and had to rely heavily on their medical insurance.

Still another family, the McCalls, found that their state's guidelines for the crippled children's program excluded them. So three families with similar needs for services for their children found that existing programs responded in varying degrees.

To find out about the services, programs, and eligibility requirements of your state's crippled children's programs, contact the agency in your state that administers the program. These are listed at the end of Chapter 2.

COMMUNITY RESOURCES FOR SERVICES

There are also other potential sources for the medical or other services your child needs. Among them are programs available at many universities and colleges and at many dental schools and medical schools. Some universities and colleges have counseling, therapy, hospital services, recreational or day care programs, and other specialized programs for the handicapped through centers that are affiliated with them. Some medical and dental schools have clinics staffed by students under the supervision of trained and qualified professors.

The fees for programs affiliated with universities and schools vary, depending on how much the program is subsidized by either government or private funding. Few diagnostic programs are entirely supported by such funding because of the high cost involved. So there probably would be some cost to you. But the charges probably wouldn't be as high as at a private facility.

The quality of services can also vary. Since clinics are used, for example, to help train students as future doctors, the question sometimes arises of which comes first: the training or the patient? But most programs are able to achieve a balance allowing excellence in patient care along with excellence in preparing future practionioners. Programs involved chiefly with direct services—rather than teaching or research—also can have excellent staff and facilities. You will have to check in your area for such programs, but those in some cities are listed at the end of Chapter 2.

Other sources of financial help for medical and other costs include private foundations, civic groups, hospitals, clincs, and medical centers. Such organizations may provide loans, grants, financial aid, or special treatment. Some fund programs that enable others to provide benefits to children with special needs and their families. For example, the DuPont Foundation funds the A. I. DuPont Institute in Wilmington, Delaware. The institute operates a children's orthopedic hospital that provides, at little or no cost, outpatient and inpatient services to residents of the state and, sometimes, to out-of-state people as well. To find such services, you will have to search diligently because there is no central listing of these private programs. Your local parent group, department of health or education, or social service agency may be aware of some of these programs.

Religious Groups

You may also be able to find religious groups in your community that can help provide some of the services you need for your child. Often a religious-affiliated group will provide services for special-needs children of any religious background. Roman Catholic Saint Agnes Hospital in suburban White Plains, New York, for example, has an early infant stimulation program for retarded children and a preschool nursery and therapy program for orthopedically handicapped children, including retarded children who also have orthopedic disabilities. Both programs are open to any child who has such needs in the county where the hospital is located, regardless of his or her religious affiliation. Some of the families involved with the programs use a combination of their insurance and the county's crippled children's services funding to pay for the costs.

There are many religious agencies and programs that aid children with special needs, and they are sponsored by almost every religious group. You can contact your local church to find out what is available for families of your religion in your area. But you also can contact groups affiliated with other religions. Three you might look for are the Catholic Charities, Federation of Protestant Welfare Agencies, and Federation of Jewish Philanthropies. While you are asking about programs, also check into low-interest or noninterest loans, grants, or other financial services such groups might be able to provide.

How to Get Help from Community Groups

Civic and fraternal groups are another potential source of financial aid in your community. Many such groups have long been known for their involvement with community programs for special-needs children. The Shriners, for example, have several specialized hospitals. The Lions Clubs and Rotary Clubs for many years have sponsored programs for handicapped persons. These and other groups can provide such help as obtaining kidney machines, wheelchairs, tutors, swimming lessons, psychiatric counseling, and other needed equipment or services.

Even if your local groups haven't become involved with such services, don't despair. You may only have to make the need known to them. Contact them and let them know about your child and the help you need. You can start with an informal personal or telephone contact, but follow that up with a letter explaining who you are, what your problem is, and what kind of help is needed for your child and for other handicapped children. If you are part of a parent group, get them working on prodding local clubs into action, especially through personal contacts with club members.

Sometimes it helps to interest such clubs if you have specific plans for projects that would aid children with handicapping conditions in your community. For example, if your parent group needs funds, supplies, and manpower to construct a playground for handicapped children, break the problem down into several steps—fund raising, purchase or donation of supplies, initial groundbreaking, construction, and maintenance. Then ask if they could help with any or all of these steps over a period of time.

The same strategy applies to a personal need in your family. If you need a specially constructed chair for your child but it is beyond your means, ask the civic group if they could help you raise the money, donate the money themselves, or help build a chair from purchased or donated materials. Even if they could simply help you publicize your need, you might be able to reach others who can assist you.

If there is a need for support and services for the special needs of children like yours, contact the city editor of your local newspaper or the news director of the nearest television station. They may assign a reporter to tell your story. With such coverage, you will discover that there are scores of people out there who are anxious to help but who were unaware that the need existed.

Don't be afraid to ask. Don't be afraid to try. It's true, you may only spin your wheels and get nowhere. But you could also meet some sympathetic new supporters who will steer you to the help you need.

There are other community service groups that you may be able to tap for certain services for your child with special needs. These groups are often funded by umbrella, community charitable organizations that go under such names as United Way or United Fund. Many of these community services groups—such as YWCA and the YMCA, the Visiting Nurse Association, and the Homemaker–Home Health Aid Services—offer various youth, counseling, recreational, and medical programs. Such organizations may also be able to refer you to an agency that can provide counseling about financial problems or about planning a budget suited to your family's financial situation.

You can find these groups by contacting your local United Way or United Fund. Or look in your telephone directory for organizations with such titles as the following:

Community Chest
Community Hotline Service
Community Planning Council
Council for Community Services
Family Service Association
Health and Welfare Council
Information and Referral Service
Mental Health Clinic
Also see the Directory at the end of Chapter 5.

For more general aid, you can also lobby your local government to make them aware of the needs of handicapped individuals when planning public projects. Many communities are providing ramped curbs, signal bells at traffic signals, and other simple modifications that open up ordinary life to the handicapped. Attend public hearings on planned expenditures for federal revenue sharing and community development funds to make sure the needs of the handicapped are considered.

SPECIAL CONSIDERATIONS OF SPECIAL NEEDS

Architectural barriers may require some adjustments in the way your family copes with life, and they may also mean extra costs. Some home improvements and other costs, such as transportation, may be tax deductible. Others will not be. And there is also the annoyance factor. A planned trip to a museum may have to be changed at the last minute because the old building doesn't have elevators wide enough to accommodate wheelchairs. You may have to make special arrangements to enter a building by the back door if steep flights of steps are too much for a child with respiratory problems. A compact car may be eliminated in favor of a station wagon that can accommodate a Seeing Eye dog.

When you are looking for an apartment or a house, keep architectural barriers in mind. Older two-story houses may be more in your price range, but a contemporary one-level home may be necessary. On the other hand, some barriers may be difficult but not impossible, and they may provide opportunities for the child to experience and cope with the larger world. The McGraths were living in an older two-story home when their son Kim was born, and they could not afford to move. They found, however, that although the stairs were a difficulty, Kim learned how to climb them, and they provided a daily source of exercise as well as training in dealing with barriers in the outside world. Their large old-fashioned bathroom proved to be an advantage over smaller modern types because it could accommodate a wheelchair.

Other adaptations to your apartment or home might include removal of sharp-edged furniture, dust-prone materials, or pets; installation of fencing, window bars, handrails, or air conditioning; or perhaps just a special organization of a child's room to facilitate use and cleanup of toys and clothing.

THE COST OF AN EDUCATION

In addition to medical costs and services, you may also be faced with the expense of special schooling for your child with a handicapping condition. Although the right to a free education will soon be mandatory nationwide, it is not yet an accomplished fact. And the availability varies widely from locality to locality.

The state where Michael Fine lives pays for the education of blind children, starting at age two. Michael is now attending a private school for the blind, which is funded entirely by the state. Later, when Michael reaches five years of age, he will attend a regular school in his community that has special facilities for blind students. But if Michael's family lived just a few miles away, across the state border, they would not be so fortunate. In the neighboring state the Fines would only be reimbursed for part of Michael's schooling cost at a fixed rate well below the cost of private school tuition. And he would have had to wait until he was six years old to begin this schooling.

The new law should resolve such problems by establishing uniform, national guidelines for minimal services for the handicapped children and by requiring free and appropriate public education for such children.

Meanwhile, some parents of children with special needs may wish to continue their children's education in private schools, feeling that there they will get better care and attention. But many families with children having handicapped conditions can't afford the extra expense of private schooling. While it is true that private schools can sometimes offer superior programs, we sometimes get caught in the trap of thinking that money talks. In fact, a co-op nursery program may make up in enthusiasm and dedication what it lacks in furnishings. And the education of children in the private school might not be significantly better, or even better at all, than in a public school, even though the cost is higher.

When one private school for handicapped children closed its doors because of financial problems, many of the parents decided—as a last resort—to try integrating their offspring into the local public schools. The schools were open, albeit hesitant, to accepting students in wheelchairs and on crutches at the single-floor elementary, junior high, and senior high schools. To their surprise, the parents found that their children did well in the new public school, both academically and socially. Despite some rough spots the school officials, the students, and the parents were satisfied that integration of handicapped and nonhandicapped children can work. In fact, the reading scores of the handicapped children improved dramatically after the move.

CREATIVE BUDGETING

The type of schooling you decide on for your child may depend on how it can fit into your budget. A family with a child who has special needs has to be especially careful to budget wisely for family expenses—including the expected and the unexpected. There are a number of extra costs involved in raising a child with special needs that may not be obvious at first but that can add up. Both these and more obvious costs can often be held down and sometimes avoided.

For example, as we discussed in Chapter 5, sharing baby-sitting assignments with other parents of children with special needs—or with parents of nonhandicapped children—can be one way to cut costs. Baby-sitting expenses are not one of the first services that you might think of as an extra cost involved with a special-needs child, but it is a necessary expense that can add up.

To budget money well, you have to be creative about your resources. This extends to children's clothes and entertainment as well as the grocery list and menu. When you have special needs that pinch your finances, your imagination really has to work overtime. You have to be able to provide experiences to compensate, stretch, and enrich, but you also have to work within tighter limits than usual. If you have difficulty with your family finances, there may be a local service agency that can provide counseling on balancing your budget. Check with the agencies you are presently dealing with or the service organizations mentioned on page 182. If none are available through a service agency or group, you might be able to obtain this help through a certified public accountant, perhaps a member of your parent group. The cost may seem unnecessary to you, but it is a one-time cost that can possibly save you money in the long run. A budget is like a diet, however; it does you no good unless you intend to stick to it.

Parents sharing in other formal and informal ways will also reap financial as well as emotional benefits. Hints on clothing, toys, special equipment, and other items that can be purchased more economically, built, borrowed, shared, or "passed on" are always welcome. One parent group compiled a list of discount stores in their area that stocked educational toys, inexpensive children's clothing, and other items that the entire family could use. They included on their list "thrift" stores and secondhand stores that had quality merchandise, as well as exchange programs sponsored by a local school for sports equipment. Other parents may pass on this information in less formal ways.

Beware When Buying

There is one aspect of family buying where parents tend to go overboard; they buy too many toys. When there is a child with special needs in the family, toys and other purchases are sometimes made more often, and are more costly, than might have otherwise been the case. Sometimes "educational" toys and materials are bought in larger quantities than they could ever be realistically used by a child. Sometimes special gifts or toys are bought for the child or for other children in the family as almost a compensatory gesture. True, children with special needs may require extra stimulation and extra experiences to compensate for what has been denied them. And they may need to look extra neat and well dressed to overcome prejudicial attitudes. But you should make sure other children in the family don't feel left out because of the extra attention given to the child with special needs.

Lots of toys, "educational" or otherwise, can be "passed down" from friends or relatives or can be bought at garage sales. Some excellent toys can be made at home without the benefit of a fancy workshop or a handy husband; some of the longest-wearing toys can be made from everyday scraps, such as cardboard boxes, plastic containers, and juice cans. Games can be developed from simple household items: clothespins and a bottle can become a toss game that develops hand-eye coordination; flour, salt, water, and food coloring can be mixed into a modeling substance (not too tasty, but nontoxic); and cutouts from magazines can be made into lotto games. You may have a friend or relative who is handy and who could build more elaborate things, perhaps a needed piece of equipment.

As part of his Christmas present to his niece, Mari, Tom Febro gave two hours of cementing work to eliminate a curb in the sidewalk leading to her house. Now Mari can go go in and out of the house in her wheelchair unaided. It is one more step toward Mari's achieving independence, and her Uncle Tom is proud to have contributed.

The end of this chapter has a listing of books that can help you put together inexpensive toys and games for your children. Some of the books listed in the bibliography that deal with specific handicaps also have suggestions and hints about toys and other equipment for children with special needs.

Purchasing Medicines

Another area where careful planning can help family finances is in buying prescription medicines. If your major medical or other coverage does not pay for out-of-hospital medicines, you need to shop with extra attentiveness. If you need medicine for any member of your family, request that the doctor or dentist consider prescribing the drug by its generic name, rather than by a brand name. In most cases this can save you money, depending upon the drug. Also, shop around at drugstores in your area and compare prices. In some areas of the country drugstores are required to post their prices. Where they don't, you can ask. Make sure that you check the prices periodically for changes. Rarely should you receive a bottle of pills with the wrong count, but if you do, bring it to the druggist's attention. If it happens more than once, change pharmacies.

If you are regularly using a drug that has a long shelf life, buy it in bulk. Check with your doctor for approval and with the druggist to find out which size is the most economical. The size that the drug comes from the manufacturer, whether it is in units of one hundred, five hundred, one thousand, is usually the best buy. Your druggist can tell you whether the medicine you want can be stored safely, and for how long. It is extremely important to remember, however, that when you have medicines on hand in large doses, you are increasing the chances of accidental poisoning in your home. Always store medicines in a place inaccessible to children, which is usually *not* the bathroom medicine cabinet. Too many children quickly learn how to climb onto the sink or drag over a chair to reach the "pretty pills." Choose a place that would be difficult for an adult to reach, such as the top of a closet shelf. For convenience you can keep a smaller amount in a "childproof" bottle in a more accessible place. Something as seemingly harmless as fluoride tablets to strengthen children's teeth, or vitamin pills, can be lethal in large enough doses.

Make sure that you ask for and keep all of the receipts of pre-scription medicines for income tax purposes. Perhaps you could put them in a large envelope, box, or jar, so that you won't forget where they are come tax time.

INCOME TAX DEDUCTIONS

Income tax deductions can be especially important to a family with the extra costs of a child with special needs. State and federal income tax regulations change from year to year, so it is wise to check with your local Internal Revenue Service and state tax offices for the most current information. Here are some of the deductions you should be considering long before it's time to file your yearly income tax. Notice that almost all are related to expenses that occur because of a prescribed medical reason. If you decided to do something on your own, it is usually not considered valid to claim the expense on your income tax.

Medical insurance: You can claim the cost of premiums for medical care. You may not claim the cost of premiums for life insurance or disability income.

Medical care: You can deduct the cost of medical or dental expenses that were not paid for or reimbursed by insurance or other means. Usually you cannot claim the total amount but must compute a percentage based on adjusted gross income. Your local tax office can give you the details for the current year.

Prescription medicines: You can deduct the cost of prescription medicines, that is, drugs you purchased and were not reimbursed for and were prescribed by a doctor. Anything you bought because you felt you needed it or because a nonmedical person advised you to, cosmetics, and other items that can be purchased in a drugstore are not deductible. This deduction, too, is usually computed in relation to adjusted gross income.

Home care: Care at home that is prescribed by a doctor, including the cost of nursing care and special appliances, is deductible.

Institutional care: Institutional care or outpatient hospital care prescribed by a doctor is deductible.

Transportation: Transportation to and from prescribed medical care and to and from special schooling prescribed by a doctor is deductible. Also included would be the costs of tolls, parking, and other related transportation costs. Transportation can be by any means, but if you travel by car, there is usually a standard formula for computing the cost, based on the number of miles involved in driving. Parking tickets or other fines are not deductible.

Education: Tuition for special schooling or for remedial help for a child in regular school, if diagnosed and recommended by a doctor, is deductible. Private school tuition or private lessons such as dancing, recreation, or hobbies, which are not specifically recommended by a doctor as necessary for the child's development are not usually deductible.

Home Costs: Costs that you incur at home for improvements, such as ramps or special heating or air filtration systems, or that you incur to operate special equipment, such as air conditioners or mist tents, which are recommended or prescribed by a doctor for medical reasons, are deductible. This can be a sticky area. Some recommendations by doctors, primarily those for psychological reasons, are not considered by the IRS or state tax officials to be deductible. Before you claim these, or perhaps even before you buy or install some of these appliances or make major adjustments to your home, check with the tax officials.

There may be other deductions allowable from your state tax, or some we have listed that your state will not accept. New reforms occur yearly with federal taxes as well. As we mentioned before, check directly with the state and federal tax offices for the most current standards.

When you prepare your income tax, here are some general tips:

● Prepare and file early; avoid the April rush. Don't forget that the earlier you file, the earlier you get your results back. It is important to begin early if you have questions to ask about recent changes or current standards. The IRS will be much happier to answer your questions and help solve your problems if you contact them at the beginning of the calendar year.

● If you are unsure about something, ask. And don't ask your neighbor or your Uncle Harry, but go directly to the officials. It is unpleasant to have your return sent back or audited.

● If you need help on your return, consult a professional who is experienced and reputable. Don't depend on a well-intentioned friend or relative who may not have that much experience with your special types of deductions—or with any deductions at all, for that matter. Remember that your deductions for special needs should be for expenses incurred in relation to prescribed care recommended or performed by a doctor.

● Keep accurate records, and *all* bills and receipts. If you can't prove it, it probably won't be deductible if you are audited. If you are keeping meticulous records, or even informal records, you might check with tax officials as to what kind of record keeping they would accept in the case of an audit. A small notebook, where you can jot down such things as mileage and tolls, for which it's often difficult to get accurate receipts, may be sufficient. Whenever you can, get receipts. Try to keep all the bills in one place, even if it's the old penny jar. If you collect all your bills and then leave them in various coats and drawers and wallets, you may have a hard time trying to make a tally at tax time and an even harder time if you are audited.

PLANNING FOR THE FUTURE

While you are considering financial factors related to your special-needs child for today, you might also want to consider his needs for the future by taking the time to draw up a will that will deal with financial considerations for his future needs.

All parents are concerned about their children's futures. The possibility lurks in the back of each parent's mind that something could happen to them—death or catastrophic illness, which would leave their children destitute. Parents who have children with special needs often have an even greater concern, especially if their children need specialized attention to reach their maximum potential.

In order to safeguard your children's future, it is essential that you plan carefully now. Obtain the services of a lawyer you know and trust. Again, your parent group may be able to refer you to a lawyer, or a member may be one. Your lawyer should help you draw up a will that specifically includes every member of your family. As with insurance, children who are not born to you within your marriage—adopted children or foster children or stepchildren or children you are guardians for—could be excluded from the legal definition of children in your will unless they are specifically mentioned. An important part of your will should be the appointment of a guardian for your children should both parents pass on. You should give very careful thought to this guardian, for this person or persons will be taking your place. You must ask their permission and agreement to this before you include them, or they could decline to take on this role later. You should also talk to them about the finances, schooling, and other details that you wish to have them carry out. Many children are eligible for social security payments after the death of their parents, and this money can be very helpful for everyday expenses as well as for future plans. Your life insurance should also name benefactors clearly and possibly designate how this money is to be distributed or saved. Plan your life insurance carefully because that enormous amount you are insured for has a way of dwindling into nothing with inflation and with the climbing costs of needed services.

You may wish to have a separate person act as executor of your estate. That is, you may wish to have one person control the money and another care for the children. This can be both good and bad. If the two don't get along, or if they disagree about the way the money should be allocated, your children could be caught in the middle. On the other hand, if one person is a financial dud who is terrific with kids and another is the reverse, you may have a viable team working on behalf of your children.

Your lawyer and possibly your financial advisor or accountant can also help you set up a trust fund for your children. Trust funds and wills can become terribly complex, so have them explained to you in detail. Trust funds should also name a specific person you have checked with in advance to help be your child's advocate when you are no longer able to do so.

All of these financial considerations we have just discussed are intertwined with legal considerations, which are discussed in the next chapter.

DIRECTORY

Insurance Information: General

American Dental Association
   211 East Chicago Avenue
   Chicago, Ill. 60611

American Hospital Association
   840 North Lake Shore Drive
   Chicago, Ill. 60611

American Medical Association
   535 North Dearborn Street
   Chicago, Ill. 60610

American Public Welfare Association
   Medical Care Committee
   1313 East 60th Street
   Chicago, Ill. 60637

Health Insurance Institute
277 Park Avenue
New York, N.Y. 10017

Insurance Information: Specific

Blue Cross
Blue Cross Association
840 North Lake Shore Drive
Chicago, Ill. 60611

Blue Shield
National Association of Blue Shield Plans
211 East Chicago Avenue
Chicago, Ill. 60611

Private
Health Insurance Association of America
750 Third Avenue
New York, N.Y. 10017

Group
Group Health Association of America, Inc.
1321 14th Street Northwest
Washington, D.C. 20005

Voluntary (Canada)
Canadian Health Insurance Association
36 Toronto Street
Suite 709
Toronto 1, Ontario, Canada

Consumer-oriented Health Organizations

American Public Health Association
1740 Broadway
New York, N.Y. 10019

Health-PAC
17 Murray Street
New York, N.Y. 10007

Medical Committee for Human Rights
Physicians Forum
510 Madison Avenue
New York, N.Y. 10022

Source
P.O. Box 21066
Washington, D.C. 20007

Intensive Infant Care Projects

Newborn Services
Temple University Health Sciences Center
3400 North Broad Street
Philadelphia, Pa. 19140

Department of Pediatrics
University of Utah Medical Center
50 North Medical Drive
Room 2B-425
Salt Lake City, Utah 84112

Children's Mercy Hospital
24th and Gillham Road
Kansas City, Mo. 64108

Robert B. Green Memorial Hospital
527 North Leona
San Antonio, Tex. 78207

Neonatal Intensive Care Unit
University of Mississippi Medical Center
2500 North State Street
Jackson, Miss. 39216

Newborn Services
City of Memphis Hospital
42 North Dunlop
Fifth Floor
Memphis, Tenn. 38163

Neonatal Care
Sacramento Medical Center
Sacramento, Calif. 95817

Section of Family Health
  Pouch H
  Juneau, Alaska 99801
  (Project site:
  Providence Hospital
  Anchorage, Alaska 99504)

Regional Offices of the Department of Health, Education, and Welfare, Office for Maternal and Child Health

REGION I: CONNECTICUT, MAINE, VERMONT, NEW HAMPSHIRE, MASSACHUSETTS, RHODE ISLAND
  Room 1409
  John F. Kennedy Federal Building
  Boston, Mass. 02203
  Phone: (617) 223-6865

REGION II: NEW JERSEY, NEW YORK, PUERTO RICO, VIRGIN ISLANDS
  Federal Building
  26 Federal Plaza
  New York, N.Y. 10007
  Phone: (212) 264-4622

REGION III: DELAWARE, DISTRICT OF COLUMBIA, MARYLAND, PENNSYLVANIA, VIRGINIA, WEST VIRGINIA
  Gateway Building No. 1
  3531-35 Market Street
  (P.O. Box 13716)
  Philadelphia, Pa. 19101
  Phone: (215) 597-6686

REGION IV: ALABAMA, FLORIDA, KENTUCKY, GEORGIA, NORTH CAROLINA, SOUTH CAROLINA, TENNESSEE, MISSISSIPPI
  Room 423
  50 Seventh Street Northeast
  Atlanta, Georgia 30323
  Phone: (404) 526-3877

REGION V: ILLINOIS, INDIANA, MICHIGAN, MINNESOTA, OHIO, WISCONSIN
300 South Wicker Drive
34th Floor
Chicago, Ill. 60606
Phone: (312) 353-1660

REGION VI: ARKANSAS, LOUISIANA, NEW MEXICO, OKLAHOMA, TEXAS
1114 Commerce Street
Dallas, Tex. 75202
Phone: (214) 749-2891

REGION VII: IOWA, KANSAS, MISSOURI, NEBRASKA
New Federal Office Building
601 East 12th Street
Kansas City, Mo. 64106
Phone: (816) 374-5777

REGION VIII: COLORADO, MONTANA, NORTH DAKOTA, SOUTH DAKOTA, UTAH, WYOMING
9017 Federal Building
1961 Stout Street
Denver, Colo. 80202
Phone: (303) 837-3356

REGION IX: ARIZONA, CALIFORNIA, HAWAII, NEVADA, GUAM, AMERICAN SAMOA TRUST TERRITORY
Federal Office Building
50 Fulton Street
San Francisco, Calif. 94102
Phone: (415) 556-0653

REGION X: ALASKA, IDAHO, OREGON, WASHINGTON
Arcade Plaza Building
1321 Second Avenue
Seattle, Wash. 98101
Phone: (206) 442-0500

Books for Parents

Burack, Richard. *The New Handbook of Prescription Drugs*. New York: Ballantine Books, 1975.

Placere, Morris N., and Marwick, Charles S. *How You Can Get Better Medical Care for Less Money*. New York: Walker & Co., 1973.

Sagov, Stanley E. *The Active Patient's Guide to Better Medical Care (Strategies for Working Together with Your Doctor)*. New York: David McKay Co., 1976. (An excellent guide, also useful in terms of diagnosis.)

Books with Inexpensive Ideas for Toys and Games

FOR INFANTS AND TODDLERS

Gordon, Ira C. *Baby Learning Through Baby Play*. New York: St. Martin's Press, 1970. $6.95.

Upchurch, Beverly. *Easy-to-Do Toys and Activities for Infants and Toddlers*. Infant Care Project (Institute for Child and Family Development, University of North Carolina at Greensboro, Greensboro, N. C. 27412). $1.50.

U.S., Department of Health, Education, and Welfare, Children's Bureau. *Fun in the Making*. 1976. $.55.[1]

FOR PRESCHOOL CHILDREN

Baretta-Lorton, Mary. *Work Jobs for Parents*. New York: Addison-Wesley, 1972. $3.95

Gordon, Ira C. *Child Learning Through Child Play*. New York: St. Martin's Press, 1972. $6.95.

Marzollo, Jean, and Lenya, Janie. *Learning Through Play*. New York: Harper & Row, 1972. $10.95. (Paperback edition, 1974. $2.95).

FOR OLDER CHILDREN

Caney, Steven. *Playbook*. New York: Workman Publishing Co., 1975. $3.95.

———. *Toybook*. New York: Workman Publishing Co., 1972. $4.95.

---

[1] All U.S. government publications are available from the Superintendent of Documents, U.S. Government Printing Office, Washington, D.C. 20402.

Palmer, Bruce. *Making Children's Furniture and Play Structures.* New York: Workman Publishing Co., 1974. $8.95. (Paperback edition, $3.95).

Companies and Catalogues of "Educational" Toys

Camphill Village Gift Shop
Chrysler Pond Road
Copake, N.Y. 12516
(Soft dolls and other toys made by a working community of retarded
  adults)

Child Craft Educational Corporation
964 Third Avenue
New York, N.Y. 10022

Community Playthings
Rifton, N.Y. 12471
(Catalogue no. 202 and exceptional equipment leaflet)

Constructive Playthings
Early Childhood and Special Educational Materials
1040 East 85th Street
Kansas City, Mo. 64131

Creative Playthings
P.O. Box 1100
Princeton, N.J. 08540

Dick Blick
P.O. Box 1267
Galesburg, Ill. 61401
(Enrichment aids catalogue)

National Easter Seal Society for Crippled Children and Adults
2023 West Ogden Avenue
Chicago, Ill. 60612
("Your Child's Play" [parent series] by Grace Langdon, $.35)

Also, try some toys by the following companies:

Fisher-Price Toys
606 Girard Avenue
East Aurora, N.Y. 14052

Playskool, Inc.
4501 West Augusta Boulevard
Chicago, Ill. 60651

Books on Baby-sitters and Play Groups

Kraft, Ivor. *When Teenagers Take Care of Children.* U.S. Department of Health, Education, and Welfare, Children's Bureau, 1974. $.70.[1]

Winn, Marie, and Porscher, Mary Ann. *The Playgroup Book.* New York: Macmillan Co., 1967.

---

[1] All U.S. government publications are available from the Superintendent of Documents, U.S. Government Printing Office, Washington, D.C. 20402.

7

Legal Rights of Those with Special Needs

Securing the legal rights of people with special needs and obtaining services to meet those needs has been a long and hard struggle. Much of the progress has come through legal actions in the courts or as the result of laws passed by Congress or state legislatures. Social acceptance sometimes preceded court decisions and laws and sometimes came after these actions. But almost every success was marked by the common denominator of unrelenting efforts by the handicapped and their advocates, including parents of children with special needs. By organizing, publicizing, pressuring, and demanding the rights of people with handicapping conditions, they were able to force progress by going to the public, the courts, and lawmaking bodies. For children with handicaps, it has been the dedication, skill, and plain hard work of their parents that has meant the most.

You may run into problems in meeting the needs of your special-needs child that will require both understanding and the exercise of your child's rights. Before you consider specific legal solutions and obligations, it is helpful if you have a clear picture of how these rights developed.

DEVELOPMENT OF LEGAL RIGHTS OF THOSE WITH SPECIAL NEEDS

It was not until the mid-1800s that the federal government began assuming any responsibility for the needs of individuals with disabilities. In 1857 Congress created and funded the Kendall School as the first school for the deaf, "dumb," and blind. In 1864 Gallaudet, a national college for the deaf, was established. Both schools remain in operation today.

In 1867 the first federal Office of Education was begun. But it was not until the 1930s that the U.S. Office of Education created a Section for Exceptional Children and Youth. Its successor division was abolished in 1963 and then reestablished in 1967 as the Bureau of Education for the Handicapped, with separate divisions for research, educational services, and training programs.

Around the turn of the twentieth century individual states began to accept some legal responsibilities for individuals with special needs. In 1911 New Jersey became the first state to legislate special education for mildly retarded children, and it later extended the law to moderately retarded children.

Veterans Lead the Way

The next real surge at the federal level came after World War I, when American veterans began returning home with war-related disabilities. The public felt an obligation to help these men, who had become handicapped as the result of fighting for their country. The public awareness about the special needs of veterans later spread to the needs of workers with disabilities and eventually to others with handicapping conditions. In 1918 Congress passed the Smith-Sears Vocational Rehabilitation Act, which provided medical, surgical, and psychiatric treatment as well as vocational rehabilitation for disabled servicemen. In 1920 the law was expanded to include disabled workers. Annual appropriations to all disabled people were increased in 1939 by an amendment to the Social Security Act.

During World War II the federal government again took action to aid returning disabled veterans. The Vocational Rehabilitation Act of 1943 provided full federal reimbursement to the states for necessary costs of vocational rehabilitation for disabled war veterans. In addition, one half of the necessary expenses for other disabled persons was made reimbursable by the federal government. Each state had to administer its own program according to approved specifications, but administrative expenses were not included in the federal reimbursement.

The returning World War II veterans brought handicaps into the open. Praised as heroes, they pushed aggressively for their rights.

Even if they still encountered the same old prejudices and road-blocks, they did not return to the ways of the past, when families hid their members with handicaps and meekly accepted whatever meager allowances were offered.

Increased Social Acceptance

The 1950s marked a continuation of this increased awareness and acceptance of handicaps. Congress passed additional legislation dealing with mental retardation and other handicaps. And this climate of change spawned increased parental involvement in seeking public acceptance of the needs and rights of handicapped persons, especially children with special needs. Groups such as the National Association of Retarded Children (NARC), which today is sometimes called the National Association for Retarded Citizens, and the United Cerebral Palsy (UCP) began organizing on the local and state level. They soon became national in scope, and they were followed by other groups concerned with children who were emotionally disturbed, who had learning disabilities, and who may have been afflicted with any number of disabling conditions. Such groups pressed not only for increased public awareness about handicaps but also for better service programs and public education programs. Their impact over the years was documented in a 1968 study that reported that parental pressure was the single major reason for beginning programs for children with learning disabilities in over half of the states queried about such programs.

The early 1960s was a period of presidential leadership in the area of handicaps. President Kennedy established the President's Panel on Mental Retardation, which in 1963 declared that "all rights normally held by anyone are also held by the retarded." Efforts to extend that declaration to all disadvantaged persons were mounted by those who demanded that society share the responsibility for such essentials as education and the preparation of children for useful, independent, and fulfilling lives.

A New Militance—A New Civil Rights Movement

The 1960s was also the era of the civil rights movement and of growing militance by many groups, including handicapped persons, who were beginning to reject the failure to extend full rights to many minorities. The War on Poverty during the Johnson administration followed. The militance and the government activism demonstrated during this period led to social action, court decisions, and legislation during the late 1960s and the 1970s that has greatly advanced the rights of people with handicapping conditions.

LEGISLATION FOR SPECIAL NEEDS

The major impact on special needs has probably been in the areas of education and employment. Two of the more important laws passed by Congress were the 1968 Partnership for Learning and Earning law and the 1973 Vocational Rehabilitation Act .

The Partnership for Learning and Earning law provides federal funds to states for job training, vocational guidance and counseling, construction of vocational educational facilities, teacher training, and other vocational education programs for persons with handicaps. The 1973 Vocational Rehabilitation Act outlaws discrimination against individuals with handicaps in employment and education, and it also requires the elimination of certain architectural and transportation barriers. The Rehabilitation Act of 1973 has been called the first civil rights law to protect the rights of the twenty-five million individuals in the United States with handicaps. It specifically applies to every public or private agency that receives over twenty-five thousand dollars a year in federal funds, but it can be invoked to prevent discrimination in every area of community life.

THE COURTS AND SPECIAL NEEDS

Other advances in education have come through the courts. In a landmark decision in 1971 a Pennsylvania court established that all children, regardless of handicap, deserve an education. This "Right to Education" ruling resulted from a suit brought by parents of mentally retarded children and the Pennsylvania State Association for Retarded Children (ARC) against the state of Pennsylvania. The court's ruling was based on the historic 1954 Supreme Court decision, *Brown* v. *Board of Education,* that outlawed "separate but equal" racial segregation in public schools. That Supreme Court ruling said, in part: "In these days, it is doubtful that any child may reasonably be expected to succeed in life if he is denied the opportunity to an education. Such an opportunity . . . is a right which must be made available on equal terms to all."

Significant Court Decisions for Children with Special Needs

The Pennsylvania court ruling seventeen years later affirming the right of all handicapped children to an equal opportunity for an education was as momentous for such children as the 1954 ruling was for blacks and other minorities. Other court decisions also have significantly affected the rights of children with special needs in the area of education. Here are some of them:

Diana v. *California Board of Education* (1970): Nine Mexican American children charged that their placement in classes for the educable mentally retarded (EMR classes) was based on prejudical testing. The case was resolved by the following requirements: Children must be tested in their primary language; children not so tested must be retested; efforts must be made to aid children misplaced in readjustment; and California must develop and standardize appropriate tests.

Wyatt v. *Stickney* (1971): The federal government appeared as amicus in this case. The court ruling had several provisions for persons with handicaps, and it ordered: (1) the provision of habilitation, education, and treatment; (2) the principle of normalization be employed in education and treatment—that is, these should be administered in as normal a fashion as possible; (3) the imposition of the least restrictive conditions necessary; (4) education must be provided regardless of age, degree of retardation, disabilities, or handicaps; (5) that individuals with disabilities or handicaps be guaranteed prompt and adequate medical treatment, dignity, privacy, humane care, no unnecessary or excessive medication, and protection against indiscriminate use of physical restraint.

LeBanks v. *Spears* (1973): This case attacked Louisiana's failure to provide education for many children in need of special education. The suit did not come to trial because the defendents agreed to provide free, publicly supported education for all children. Other provisions of the agreement were that education must have as its goal to make every child self-sufficient or employable and that educational opportunities must be provided for retarded adults who were not given opportunities for education as children.

Maryland ARC v. *Maryland* (1974): This was a class action brought on behalf of mentally and physically handicapped children denied access to free public education. The court found that the state has an obligation to provide appropriate educational facilities and services to all children between the ages of five and twenty.

In re H.G. (1974): The North Dakota Supreme Court concluded that the state constitution and the equal protection clause of the Fourteenth Amendment of the U.S. Constitution required educational opportunities for all children.

Mills v. *Board of Education of the District of Columbia* (1975): This case alleged that seven children had been denied public education without formal determination of the basis of their exclusion and without periodic review of their status. The court ordered that education be provided for the children, that other children excluded from public education be identified, that the school board propose an educational program including compensatory education, and that parents who object to the proposed program be granted a hearing. Furthermore, since suspension is one common way to exclude children with special needs, safeguards against suspension must include a hearing within ten days of suspension, and during those ten days there must be educational assistance or a diagnostic test. (In 1972 the District of Columbia Board of Education adopted a resolution that was quite influential. It said that every child must have a free, publicly supported education suited to his or her needs "regardless of the degree of his mental, physical, or emotional disability or impairment.")

THE EDUCATION OF ALL HANDICAPPED CHILDREN ACT

The mounting legal and public pressure from such cases as those just described culminated in the passage by Congress of the Education of All Handicapped Children Act in 1975. Under this law radical changes should take place in many states. Here are some of the basic requirements of the law, which is due to go into effect September 1, 1978, in all states:

● The highest priority in the act is given to handicapped children not now receiving education, and secondarily to the most severely handicapped children whose education is inadequate. Prior to the passage of the act not all states had mandated, or funded, education for *all* students regardless of handicap.

● Strong safeguards are required for due process in the rights of parents and children. For example, a school must provide notice in writing before taking any action to change a child's school program. There must also be parental access to all records related to identification, evaluation, and placement of the child, and parental right to voice complaints about educational services. There must be an impartial due process hearing when the parent and the school don't agree on the type of program for the child, and there must be adequate appeals procedures to the state department of special education and the courts.

● Children with special needs have the right to the "least restrictive environment" commensurate with their needs. This can mean that children with handicaps are to be educated with nonhandicapped children to the maximum extent possible; or it can mean that they could be provided special education and services. This requirement will be interpreted in different ways by different groups, and perhaps it will be clarified as time goes on. Basically the intent is to open options to all children.

Those who favor integrated education, also called mainstreaming, feel this approach is better not only because handicapped children will benefit from association with nonhandicapped children and from access to services available at local schools but also because nonhandicapped children need this association as well. They further assert that even if a child must attend a residential school, local community resources, such as the regular public schools, should be used for as much of the necessary services as possible. A child participating in an integrated educational program should be moved only for serious reasons related to his particular needs, not the needs of the setting, and labeling should apply to the settings and programs themselves, rather than to the children. This last point means that categorization for financial aid and other reasons should be related to the educational functions, not to individual children.

Those who take a more moderate approach to special education point out that integration means additional training and supervision as well as specialized programming. Many, if not most, schools will need additional support, direction, training, and funding to be able to cope adequately with the additional burdens that special-needs children will place on the system.

● Educational planning must be individualized, with active parental participation, and it must focus on both long- and short-range goals. The plans must be reviewed at least once a year. Some feel that the school should coordinate services in fields outside of education, such as health, recreation, and guidance, and should develop new methods to achieve this coordination. Others feel that while children and families certainly need these services, this is not the proper role of the school. The act does not directly comment upon such comprehensive planning via educational systems.

● Private school assignment of pupils by the state or local educational system must be provided at no cost to the parent. This will be a radical change for some states. In Kentucky and Arkansas, for example, only deaf-blind children were eligible for reimbursement of tuition for private schooling. According to the mandates of the act private programs must also guarantee safeguards to the rights of children and parents.

● Preschool programs for handicapped children should be made mandatory. Before the passage of the act only a little over half of the states had provisions for mandated preschool programs. The act encourages development of such programs through special incentive grants of up to three hundred dollars per child to states providing services to handicapped children aged three to five years old. Some states—such as Kansas, Kentucky, Mississippi, Montana, North Carolina, Oregon, South Dakota, Vermont, and Wisconsin—had already made educational provisions for at least part of their handicapped child population from birth on.

● Each state is required to have an advisory board, which is to include handicapped persons, parents, teachers, and others, to advise the state on unmet needs, rules and regulations, and evaluation of programs. In part this board will fill the need seen by many for advocacy separate from the deliverer of services in order to break through bureaucracy so that needs can be met and rights protected. Both Nebraska and North Carolina have citizen advocate programs already, allowing concerned individuals to put their commitments to children into action.

● The act also includes directives on the use of racially and culturally nondiscriminatory methods for testing and evaluation. It has been demonstrated in many studies and court cases that some testing techniques are prejudicial to certain groups and tend to give a biased view of abilities and disabilities.

● One of the most essential components of the act is its enforcement power. The U.S. Department of Health, Education, and Welfare can withdraw federal funds for programs under the law if a state, after notice and opportunity for hearing, is found not to have complied with provisions of the law; in turn, payments by the state to local systems may be suspended for noncompliance by the localities. Without this monetary safeguard much of the programming outlined in the law might have a low priority in the educational planning of individual states.

The Education of All Handicapped Children Act obviously has many far-reaching consequences in the lives of millions of children with special needs, probably for your child as well. However, it is not the only avenue for action or the total answer to all needs. The courts will no doubt continue to play a major role in making sure that states live up to their responsibilities to educate children with special needs. In early 1977, as one example, a three-judge federal panel ruled unconstitutional a Virginia law requiring parents to give up custody of their handicapped children to the state if they cannot afford to pay for private special education. The panel ruled that the law "is violative of the right to family integrity," and it ordered the state to provide adequate and free private or public schooling for all handicapped children in Virginia.

Under the Virginia law struck down, the state gave partial grants for private schools to parents with children who require special education outside of regular public schools. The grants were as high as $1,250 a year for nonresidential schooling and up to $5,000 a year for programs in the home. But the Fairfax County (Virginia) Legal Aid estimates that the cost of nonresidential private programs in Virginia averages $3,515 annually, and the cost of residential private education averages $10,345 a year. That means, on an average, that parents had to make up the difference of between $2,265 to $5,345 a year. Parents who were unable to pay the full difference had to relinquish custody of their children in order to receive full funding for private education, and the children were then sent to state facilities.

The federal panel's ruling requires the state of Virginia either to improve the public education system to include more and better special education programs for students with handicapping conditions or to pay their full tuition to private schools. The state may appeal the ruling. But advocates for persons with handicaps are hopeful that the decision will result in improved educational opportunities for the twenty-five to thirty-five thousand handicapped children in Virginia as well as eliminate the uprooting of children with disabilities from lower-income families.

Some legal rights of children in educational settings have been won through action on the part of those concerned primarily with nonhandicapped students. These basic rights are applicable to children with special needs as well, so you should be familiar with them. Some may be familiar to you because handicapped children have had to fight for these rights even after they were established as basic for other children.

THE LEGAL RIGHTS OF STUDENTS

One of the most basic rights under our Constitution is freedom of speech, as well as its companion right, freedom of the press. In a 1969 landmark case, *Tinker* v. *Des Moines Independent Community School District,* part of the final court ruling stated that "students in schools as well as out of school are persons under our Constitution." This means that they are entitled to basic freedoms as well as the accompanying obligations. In actuality, however, these rights are more clearly defined for college students than for students in lower grades.

Due process for a student means that school rules must be clearly and definitively written, with punishment fitting the crime. A student must have a hearing, with advance notice to prepare for it, if a charge against him or her is serious enough to have an effect upon future educational or job opportunities. In 1975 the Supreme Court ruled that when a school suspends a student for ten days or more, he or she must be given oral or written notice of the charges and an opportunity to present his or her side of the story along with the school's evidence. The student has a right to a lawyer at disciplinary hearings for serious charges that would result in expulsion, suspension, or transfer. Suspension has been used sometimes as a "catch-all" device to exclude children with special needs from school entirely. For example, a child was expelled from school as "disruptive" because he had a seizure.

Under the Buckley Education Amendment, also known as the Family Educational Rights and Privacy Act of 1974 (Public Law 93-380), only parents have access to their children's school records. Such records are not open to the students themselves if they are under eighteen years of age, or to the police, FBI, or prospective employers without the written permission of the parents. After a student is eighteen years old, only he or she has right to access, and written permission must come from the student to allow access by others. Students or parents may petition to remove damaging material, and the school must establish hearing procedures for these petitions and must grant hearings. Whether or not a petition is successful, the challenge goes on the student's school record. To file a complaint or get assistance from the federal office in charge of this act, write:

> Deputy Assistant Secretary for Management
> FERPA (Family Educational Rights and Privacy Act)
> Room 514E
> Department of Health, Education, and Welfare
> 200 Independence Avenue Southwest
> Washington, D.C. 20200

However, students do not automatically have the right to attend a school other than the one to which they were assigned. For example, if you want to go to another school across town because you feel that their curriculum is better, it is not your right to demand a transfer. An exception to this would be the case of a student whose education requires resources not available in the assigned school.

BASIC HUMAN RIGHTS

Beyond the educational rights of the student, there are also personal and civil rights to which each person is entitled. These include: the right to contract for goods and property; the right to work, to sue, to vote and hold office; and the right to use community services. All of these civil rights are affected by whether or not the person is judged as "competent." People under eighteen years of age are not generally considered competent to exercise these rights, and the retarded may also be excluded.

Adults who have special needs, particularly the mentally retarded, do have certain basic rights under the law, or through court interpretation of the legislative intent of laws. But these rights are sometimes abused or ignored without due process.

These rights include:

The right to marry
The right to bear children
The right to raise children
The right to family life—that is, the right not to be confined against one's will in an institution
The right to due process in institutionalization
The right to the "least restrictive" alternative, which means that as much as possible, individuals have the right to live as they please
The right to "normalization," to lead a life as normal as possible
The right to review of treatment or placement
The right to "habilitation," to be protected equally under the law through due process against cruel and unusual punishment

Within an institutional setting an individual has a right to: training, medical treatment, psychiatric treatment, insurance, freedom from experimentation, freedom from sterilization, protection against involuntary servitude, and adequate compensation for labor performed.

All of these rights are in turn affected by certain responsibilities. If any person cannot extend the same guaranteed protections to others—for example, if he is proven to be incapable of living in society without harming himself or others—laws may provide for adaptations or limitations of these rights.

FOSTER CARE

Foster care is intended in most cases to be a temporary, short-range alternative to stress situations. In some states foster family care or group home care is arranged so that the child returns home on weekends or holidays, and financial support is provided by the biological parents according to income. Parents are often expected to work out problems during the time their child is in foster care, so that the child can return to the home within a specific period of time and continue life in a strengthened family. In actuality, unless the agency that arranges the care is willing to intervene in positive ways to provide needed family services, foster care becomes a dumping ground for children with parents who will not be able to cope with them in the forseeable future. Although foster parents may be providing care, protection, and supportive services to the child—and this is not always the case—the child's biological parents may never be any closer to being able to resume responsible care unless concrete services are given. And even when these services are available, they are not always utilized or utilized successfully by the parents.

Because of such situations many states have begun work on legislation regarding services to families prior to and during foster care placement of children. One goal is to impose a time limit on foster care with the assumption that long-term care and separation are not in the best interests of either the child or the family. New York, for example, has an eighteen-month review bill. This bill mandates that every eighteen months a child in foster care must have a court review of his or her case. If constructive progress is being made to solve the problems and return the child to his or her home, a reasonable extension in the time of foster care may be allowed in order to complete the plan. If a plan is completed, the child may be returned to the biological family. But if no reasonable plan has been made, or if such a plan is unsuccessful, prior parental rights should be terminated and the child should be given a chance for a permanent family life through adoption.

ADOPTION

There is also the possibility of federal action to improve the prospects of adoption of foster children who now languish in legal limbo or who may be considered "hard to place." An Opportunity for Adoption Act has been introduced in both houses of

Congress that would establish uniform adoption regulations across the United States and that would provide federal aid to states to facilitate the adoption of foster children.

It is estimated that there are at least 320,000 children living in foster homes or in institutions in the United States either because their legal status is uncertain or because they are considered difficult to place. "Many of these are 'special needs' children, generally defined as those who have not been adopted due to their age—usually over 6 years—race, ethnic group, mental, physical or emotional disability, or because they are members of a sibling group," says Rep. Yvonne Brathwaite Burke of California, the prime sponsor of the bill in the House.

By establishing nationwide regulations, the bill's backers hope to eliminate jurisdictional and legal barriers to adoption of foster children. The bill would also provide funds to state and local adoption agencies in order to subsidize adoptive parents who might lack the financial means to adopt a child, especially one with special needs, and to finance efforts by the agencies to locate and free for adoption those children who have been in foster care for long periods.

The bill includes two provisions specifically aimed at encouraging adoption of children with handicapping conditions. One provision would enable a child to continue to receive any financial or other aid to which he or she was entitled while in foster care. A second provision would allow such children to continue to receive a subsidy past their eighteenth birthday if they remain dependent upon their parents because of special needs. Many children have remained unadoptable because of medical, psychological, or other problems that will keep them indefinitely dependent upon their adoptive parents.

"These two provisions will make the adoption process available to all families and will encourage the adoption of special needs children," Congresswoman Burke says.

The bill is based on two programs that have successfully increased adoptions of foster children, including children with special needs, in California. One is the Reach Out program to identify and free for adoption children who were in foster homes for extended periods of time and who stood little chance of returning to their own homes. Another is the "aid for the adoption of children" law, which provides state subsidies for the adoption of special-needs children in foster care.

Congresswoman Burke notes that even with government aid under subsidized adoption programs, the overall cost of the state is less than if the child were to remain under state care.

Parents in all states may voluntarily give up any child for adoption, including severely handicapped children. They have the option in most, but not all, states of placing their child with an agency or private party, such as a lawyer or friend. In many states, however, parents may well be discouraged from placing a handicapped child for adoption, either because the agency feels that the parents have not explored all of the resources for other alternatives or because the state must support the child if adoptive parents cannot be readily found. In over half of the states adoptive parents are offered some type of subsidy if they are able to parent a handicapped child but do not have the necessary financial resources.

Adoption today is changing . . . and that's good. Families are opening up to children who were forgotten before, some of whom have special needs because of mental, physical, or emotional handicaps. If you are considering adoptiong a child with special needs, you can prepare in many ways.

If the following statements apply to you, you have a good start in getting ready for adoption. These are positive beginnings when you are considering adoption of a child with special needs:

● You like children and enjoy the challenge of raising a family. If you are not a parent already, you may have had other kinds of exposure to children through volunteer work, teaching, or your own extended family that have given you an insight into the daily realities of parenting.

● You are a flexible person. You usually deal with frustration with patience and are open to changes in your expectations and life-style.

● You are able to view people for what they *can* accomplish, not what they cannot, and you value them according to their own potentials.

● You have had contact with people who have handicapping conditions.

On the other hand, if the following statements apply to you, you may need more time before you are ready to approach adoption of a child with special needs:

● You see adoption of a child with special needs as a charitable gesture because you feel sorry for or pity a child or because you feel a duty toward such children.

● You think such an adoption is exciting, romantic, or a good way to make a public or personal statement.

● You feel you couldn't parent an "ordinary" or "normal" child.

● A child with special needs is second choice for you; the waiting time for children you would prefer is too long or there aren't any of the kind you really want.

● You place a high value on achievement and success, and you have set goals for your children's futures.

● You view yourself as a person who does not react to change and stress well.

● Your chosen life-style is set, and the adoption of a child with special needs would disrupt the activities that are important to you.

If you see yourself in these statements, it doesn't mean that you can't adopt, but it does mean that perhaps you should carefully examine your motivations and feelings, your attitudes and life-style, to find out what you really feel a child can give to you and your family and what in turn you can give to a child.

Along the way there are many people to talk to. The North American Council on Adoptable Children (NACAC), a continent-wide coalition of Candian and U.S. adoption groups, has a committee called "Handicapped Children Are Adoptable," which can provide information and support to families, children, and agencies. It coordinates its activities with many different local, national, and international groups, including the North American Center on Adoption, Aid to Adoption of Special Kids (AASK), National Foster Parents Association, local parent groups, and others. The committee can give you information about these groups and their services as well as provide supportive services related specifically to the adoption of special-needs children.

After you have explored the possibilities and have made your decision to adopt a child with special needs, you need to contact a licensed adoption agency. If you have already adopted a child before, you can go back to your agency or have their adoption study forwarded to a new agency. If this is your first adoption, you'll have to start at the beginning. Your local adoptive families group probably has a list of agencies near you, or contact your state department of public welfare or social services to ask for a list of licensed agencies in your state. Contact a few near you by letter or phone and tell them you are interested in adopting a child with special needs and would like to have information about adoption through their agency. Give an example of the type of child that might interest you, if you can at this point, and ask what kinds of children in their care are available for adoption. This varies, and some agencies specialize in certain kinds of children or families. For example, if you want a blind child and they have none, they may be unwilling to study you even though you are asking for a "hard-to-place" child. You may have to repeat your contact. If you have difficulty in obtaining an adoption study (also called a home study) or even an appointment to speak with them, go back to your local adoption group or NACAC. They may be able to suggest alternatives.

Once your study is started, you will discuss your feelings with the adoption caseworker assigned to you: what kind of child you feel might meet the needs of your family and how you feel you can meet the needs of a child. Before you decide on a child with a particular handicap, you might want to explore with your worker, an experienced family within an adoption group, or on your own, what such a child needs—education, medicine, treatment, and so on—and what exists within the community to meet these needs. How accessible these services are, geographically and financially, should also be considered. In terms of finances, there may be special programs, such as a state adoption subsidy or crippled children's services, that can absorb all or most of the costs.

The adoption process can sometimes seem confusing to someone who has not been through it. Adopting a child with special needs can add an extra complication, perhaps because the caseworker wants to make sure the family fully understands the difficulties involved or, in a few cases, because the worker may not understand or accept the positive choice of adopting a child with special needs. If you need more detailed information on adoption—how to go about it and what to expect—you can find it in *The Adoption Adviser*.

You have probably read about the long delays in adoption proceedings because of a shortage of children who have traditionally been considered "most adoptable"—healthy white infants. One positive result of this shortage has been an upturn in adoptions of minority children, older children, and children with special needs. For them the wait is usually not as long. However, sometimes when you are very specific about a handicap or disability, even though the child you want is considered "hard to place," you may have to wait just because there may not be that many children waiting for adoption with that specific kind of problem.

Eventually that long-awaited call comes, the day when you hear "We just may have a child for you." When your new daughter or son finally does arrive, you may sail into placement in high gear, or you may discover nagging doubts. If you have second thoughts, it could be case of new-parent jitters, or it could be something more serious. Talking to other adoptive parents can really be helpful at times like this.[1]

If you require extra help in dealing with problems that may arise in coping with the needs of your adopted child, whether they are related to the child's special needs or your own personal concerns, your agency or parent group may be able to provide or refer you to the necessary services. Other resources may be available through your state's crippled children's program; departments of health, education, or mental health, and many other organizations. NACAC's committee "Handicapped Children Are Adoptable" has listings of some of these services.

In raising a child, a parent has highs and lows, exhiliration and discouragement. Sometimes a child with special needs seems to intensify both of these. People will point to the difficulties but are unaware of the tremendous rewards. Most parents who have adopted children with special needs agree that the positive growth of their whole family through adoption has been a cherished opportunity and one they would gladly repeat. Adopting children with

[1] Joan McNamara, "Thinking About Adopting a Child with Special Needs?" *Adopting Children with Special Needs,* ed. Patricia J. Kravik, North American Council on Adoptable Children (Ossining, New York: NACAC, 1976) p. 9–10.

special needs means opening yourself to a loving challenge and to the gifts they bring.

LEGAL RESPONSIBILITIES OF PARENTS

Parental obligations to the community for their children are designed to prevent the children from becoming an economic burden to the state. This can be interpreted in many ways, but basically parents are responsible for financial support to provide food, clothing, and housing for their children; their physical and emotional health; and their education. Local school ordinances and state regulations governing school attendance will determine how much schooling parents are responsible for having their children receive.

If parents do not provide for these obligations, including opportunities for school attendance, they can be charged with neglect. In cases where the neglect is found to be extreme, such as due to starvation or other physical abuse, the charge may be one of child abuse. In one suburban community a couple refused to send their two young sons to school during bad winter weather, claiming that it was too dangerous to travel. They were charged with child neglect because, in keeping the children home for a month, they had violated local ordinances on mandatory school attendance and therefore, they had "neglected" their children's well-being. An irony is that for years children with special needs have been denied this same attendance merely because of their needs, and it was the local or state authorities who were responsible for this "neglect."

Alternatives for Parental Responsibility

When parents cannot or will not provide these necessities, there are several alternatives available. In the case of divorce or separation one parent usually is awarded custody of the child with its accompanying responsibilities, although it is fairly common for a mother to be awarded physical custody and a father to be directed to continue financial responsibility. In the case of death of one parent, the surveying parent takes on all the responsibilities. When neither parent is able to assume responsibility, another relative may take over on a formal or informal basis, either temporarily or permanently.

Parent, child, or family counseling is sometimes available to help parents or guardians cope with the responsibilities of caring for a child with special needs. Groups such as the National Association of Retarded Citizens (NARC) have good counseling referral programs. They may also be able to suggest reliable respite care, which is trained care for a disabled child for a short period of time when a parent needs assistance. Respite care may be in your home or in another's, or it may be in a specialized setting; it may also be administered in combination with homemaker or home care services for the handicapped. Respite care is also used as a type of baby-sitting when parents go shopping or on vacation. Residential care is becoming less of an option as emphasis shifts from institutional to community-based services for the handicapped.

LEGAL REMEDIES

What do you do if you have a problem that you feel requires legal help? The answer depends upon your problem, your state regulations and laws, and, to a degree, your finances. First, let's take a look at the general area of disputes about education. According to the National Center for Law and the Handicapped, the first steps will be outside of the courtroom.

Educational Appeals

You would first request a hearing with the local school superintendent, then with the state board of education should the hearing not yield satisfactory results. With a child with special needs you would probably see the state's special education division. Then you would approach the state courts. State laws differ, but all are governed by the Vocational Rehabilitation Amendment of 1973, which outlaws discrimination against the handicapped in any area, and by the new Education of All Handicapped Children Act.

Most cases are related to mistesting, misplacement, or lack of services. It is common for schools to say: "There's an ideal program for your child, but we don't have the money, so we'll give you this other program instead or no program at all. Take it or leave it." This is not acceptable, especially in the light of the new act.

Even though lawyers may not be as skilled in evaluating tests or placement as other professionals, they should enter the case as early as possible, perhaps consulting with these others. Regulations may put the burden on parents to find outside experts, but there are attempts to change this so that the state bears the cost. Your local parent or advocate group may be able to provide a lot of help here. A lawyer should have time to look at all the evidence before the case goes to court. We'll talk about finding and financing legal assistance a little further on.

Employment Discrimination

Another prime area for legal problems is employment. A person with a handicap might first bring his case to the state civil rights board or department of human relations or human resources; then an appeal can be made on a federal level. Discrimination against the handicapped in employment falls under the jurisdiction of the Federal Office of Contract Compliance of the U.S. Department of Labor.

Work done within an institution for handicapped people is a different matter. Two cases, *Wyatt* v. *Stickney* and *Soder* v. *Brennan*, produced the following rulings that apply to employment within an institutional setting:

First, all labor must be voluntary in residential facilities. Second, labor must be part of a recognized treatment plan. Third, workers must be paid according to the minimum wage standards. However, the Supreme Court subsequently ruled that states do not have to comply with federal minimum wage standards, so cases concerning the payment of wages may return to court. But, this is still not a return to the concept of work without compensation or to involuntary servitude.

These are just two broad areas of concern to individuals with special needs and their families, and we have merely skimmed the surface. You will need specific assistance in attempting to deal with legal matters and the needs of your special child. Local advocacy or parent groups are often better equipped to help here than lawyers may be, even though you still may need legal services. These groups may know special lawyers or organizations that are experienced or sympathetic to your concern.

Finding Legal Services

You may have access to free or lower-cost legal services through your job. The Directory at the end of this chapter lists several organizations that may be able to help in referrals or concrete services. The National Center for Law and the Handicapped in particular can refer you to lawyers specializing in cases involving the handicapped. It can also advise you about free, or sliding-scale, legal services. Although the Center primarily offers only assistance and consultation to local attorneys and advocates, it will on occasion offer direct service.

Try your local telephone directory for legal referral services, legal defense funds, children's defense funds, the legal aid societies, and civil liberties union.

The Legal Aid Society has a one-dollar registration fee. If you qualify, that may be all you pay. The scale for fees varies according to your income. There is no additional charge for up to an eighty-five dollar-a-week salary for one person, one hundred dollars per week for two people, and so on. In order to qualify you cannot own a home or have more than three hundred dollars in the bank.

The Civil Liberties Union takes only cases they are interested in because of "new" or possibly landmark decisions. If they do take a case, all legal services are free.

Again, your local parent or advocate group may be able to provide the most useful information to you prior to your contacting a lawyer. If there is no parent group in your area that deals specifically with your interest, try another local group that is concerned with children who have other kinds of special needs. Even though you may have different focuses and be concerned about different handicaps, there may be legal experience you can share.

It may take money, and it will certainly take time and effort, but to get what you want, you have to be willing to work for it in many different arenas, including the courts and lawmaking bodies. But the fight will be worth it when your child gets the services and rights he or she deserves and needs in order to grow and develop as a full human being.

DIRECTORY

Organizations Concerned with Legal Rights

American Civil Liberties Union (ACLU)
  85 Fifth Avenue
  New York, N.Y. 10011

Association of Voluntary Bureaus of America
  P.O. Box 7253
  Kansas City, Mo. 64113

Center for Law and the Deaf
  Seventh and Florida Avenues Northeast
  Washington, D.C. 20002
  Phone: (202) 447-0445

Children's Defense Fund
  1763 R Street Northwest
  Washington, D.C. 20009

Committee for the Handicapped
  People to People Program
  Suite 610
  LaSalle Building
  Connecticut Avenue and L Street
  Washington, D.C. 20036
  (Directory of organizations)

Coordinating Council for Handicapped Children
  407 South Dearborn Street
  Chicago, Ill. 60605

Governmental Relations
  Council for Exceptional Children (NEA)
  1920 Association Drive
  Reston, Va. 22091

Human Policy Press
  Center on Human Policy
  Syracuse University
  Syracuse, N.Y. 13210

National Center for Child Advocacy
  U.S. Department of Health, Education, and Welfare
  Office of the Secretary
  P.O. Box 1182
  Washington, D.C. 20013
  (List of local advocacy centers)

National Center for Law and the Handicapped
  1235 North Eddy Street
  South Bend, Ind. 46617
  Phone: (219) 288-4751

National Center for Voluntary Action
  1735 I Street Northwest
  Washington, D.C. 20006

National Committee for Children and Youth
  1145 19th Street Northwest
  Washington, D.C. 20036

National Legal Aide and Defender Association
  National Law Office
  1601 Connecticut Avenue Northwest
  Washington, D.C. 20009

Office of Civil Rights
  U.S. Dept. of Health, Education, and Welfare
  North Building
  330 Independence Avenue Southwest
  Washington, D.C. 20201

President's Committee on Employment of the Handicapped
  Washington, D.C. 20210

President's Committee on Mental Retardation
  Seventh and D Streets Southwest
  Washington, D.C. 20201

Youth Organization United
912 Sixth Street Northwest
Washington, D.C. 20001

Copies of Federal Laws

For copies of laws concerning education, the handicapped, or other interests, write to your congressperson or senator. It is helpful to know the number of the bill. If you know it, you can also contact the U.S. Government Printing Office. The Education of All Handicapped Children Act is P.L. 94-142.

Information on State Laws

The following are brochures on rights at the state level written by various groups. Most are free for the asking.

CALIFORNIA
   *Opportunities and Rights in the California Master Plan for
      Special Education*
   (English and Spanish)
   California State Department of Education
   Publications Sales
   P.O. Box 271
   Sacramento 95802

CONNECTICUT
   Educating the Special Child
   Mental Health Association of Connecticut
   c/o Capitol Region Mental Health Association
   123 Tremont
   Hartford 06105

FLORIDA
   Your Handicapped Child's Right to Education
   Florida Association for Retarded Citizens
   Florida Coalition for Education of Exceptional Children
   Florida Association for Retarded Citizens
   220 East College Avenue
   P.O. Box 1542
   Tallahassee 32303

IDAHO

Idaho's Exceptional Children . . . Education for All
Mental Health Association of Idaho
3105½ State Street
Boise, Idaho 83703
> or

Idaho Department of Education
Len B. Jordan Office Building
Boise 83720

ILLINOIS

Is Your Handicapped Child in School?
Coordinating Council for Handicapped Children
407 South Dearborn
Chicago 60605

INDIANA

Public School and the Special Child
Mental Health Association of Indiana
1433 North Meridian Street
Indianapolis 46202

IOWA

A Parent Guide to Special Education
Iowa Association for Retarded Citizens
1701 High Street
Des Moines 50309

MARYLAND

Facts for Parents: Special Education Programs in Maryland
Maryland State Department of Education
P.O. Box 8717
Baltimore-Washington International Airport
Baltimore 21240

MASSACHUSETTS

*Parents & 766: A Parent's Guide for Children Needing
  Special Educational Services*
Massachusetts Department of Education

Division of Special Education
182 Tremont Street
Boston 02111

MICHIGAN
Your Handicapped Child's Right to Education
Michigan Association for Emotionally Disturbed
668 Pallister
Detroit 48202

MINNESOTA
Information for Parents of Students Who Are Handicapped
Minnesota Department of Education
550 Cedar Street
Saint Paul 55101

NEW HAMPSHIRE
*Procedure for Enrolling Your Handicapped Child in a
    Special Program*
New Hampshire State Department of Education
Vocational Rehabilitation Division
Special Education Section
105 Louden Road
Building 3
Concord 03301

NEW YORK
*For Parents: A Guide to Education Services for Handicapped
    Children in New York State*
State Education Department
New York Office for Education of Children with Handicapping
    Conditions
Albany 12234

OHIO
*A Step-by-Step Guide for Parents of Handicapped Children:
    How to Correctly Place Your Child in School*
Southwestern Ohio Coalition for Handicapped Children
P.O. Box 43217
Cincinnati 45243

PENNSYLVANIA
Due Process and the Exceptional Child
Education Law Center
2100 Lewis Tower Building
225 South 15th Street
Philadelphia 19102

Your Child's Right to Education Depends on You
Pennsylvania Association for Retarded Citizens
127 Locust Street
Harrisburg 17101

TENNESSEE
Equal Educational Opportunities for All: Parent Information
Tennessee Department of Education
Room 103
Cordell Hull Building
Nashville 37219

VIRGINIA
You Can Get Your Child into School
Virginia Association for Retarded Citizens
909 Mutual Building
909 East Main Street
Richmond 23219

WASHINGTON
Parents Guide to Special Education in Washington State
c/o Superintendent of Public Instruction
Old Capitol Building
Olympia 98504

WISCONSIN
Chapter 89: A Primer for Parents
Wisconsin Mental Health Association
P.O. Box 1486
Madison 53701

8

The Future
of Your Child
with Special Needs

Parents look forward to the future of their children with hopes and aspirations, and with some reluctance. They have dreams for their children yet regret the passage of each stage of their childhood. When your child has a disability, it may be difficult at times for you to contemplate the future. Your greatest fear may be: Will our child be able to make it in the larger world outside our protection?

When parents do think about the future, they often think in terms of what solutions will come to allow them to return to their old sense of normality, or of what new medical procedures will drastically rearrange their lives in ways they would prefer. There is no reason you should not dream of cures or medical breakthroughs, but it would be foolish to pin your hopes on such dreams. If you just sit and wait for possible miracles, you will be totally unprepared to deal with the real needs of your child should those hoped-for cures and breakthroughs fail to materialize.

There is another kind of "miracle" that you can create yourselves, and that is to help your children develop their abilities and talents to their fullest potential within whatever limitations they may have. This requires the hard work of preparing for expected realities, and, admittedly, there will be roadblocks. It is difficult to prepare any child for the future in these times of great uncertainties about where the world is heading. Preparing for the future of a child with special needs can add to those uncertainties.

How can you help your child prepare for those uncertainties? First, be sure your expectations for your child are realistic. Different people have different skills. Take into consideration the abilities as well as the disabilities of your child. Don't overestimate your child's abilities because of your own aspirations for him, but be careful not to underestimate your child because of misplaced concern that he might fail.

It is never easy to be honest when you deal with your hopes and fears for your child, but you must try not to let your dreams and disappointments cloud your judgment. For example, don't insist that your child be placed in a college preparation school program if what she really needs is intensive remedial reading help. On the other hand, don't let the fact that your child will never be the champion athlete you dreamed he might have been, blind you to the many things he can achieve.

Keep in mind that your child needs to obtain the skills necessary to live as independently as possible in the adult world. Ask your child's teacher, school psychologist, counselor, and doctor for their opinions on where your child's abilities lie. They may be able to suggest tests that will help you determine those abilities. But developing skills will largely depend on getting a good education for your child.

EDUCATION—A BASIC RIGHT

Parents of children with handicapping conditions have also learned that they no longer must tolerate discrimination. As your children grow, you can hope and expect that many of the barriers will fall, especially if you help to topple them. Your children are entitled, for example, to an education backed by the power of the federal government through the Universal Education Act. You may still have to contend with a local school board that resists spending money on children with handicaps, but at least you now have a law on your side. You will have to work hard to convince people that a child with a handicap deserves an even break, even though an even break may require more resources than those used for the average child.

Boards of education are made up of local citizens; you elect them, and you therefore have a voice in their decisions. You yourselves could be members of such a board. It is true that children with special needs are a minority, but they are a significant minority. You may find many supporters of fair treatment in your community.

How many of you have ever been to your local school board meetings or even voted in a school election? You can always point out, truthfully, that you are overburdened by doctors, therapies, and so on, but you can still find some time to attend an occasional meeting that could effect your child. If you do go to a meeting, do you bother to speak up and be heard? Do you speak only from a parochial viewpoint of your child's particular needs, or are you interested in supporting quality education for all children? Parents of children who have special needs can spend all their energies squabbling with one another over limited resources—or they can work together with others to see that *all* children receive a quality education.

Separate-but-equal education has proven to be very unequal for minority students. Many who are concerned about education for children with special needs feel strongly that segregated education is the only way to achieve equality, while others feel just as strongly that integration, or mainstreaming, is the one solution. Federal law now requires that education for a child with a handicap be in the least restrictive environment possible.

There are many arguments on both sides, but in reality no one approach will solve problems for all children. Many children need specialized services that cannot be obtained in every school, and many children need the specialized services that only a regular school can provide. A child with a hearing loss may have to learn several languages: finger spelling, sign language, lip reading, oral speech, and written language. This requires hard work and concentration by the student and by a teacher with specialized skills. It would be difficult to integrate this special program into every schoolroom. But segregation does have its price: Both the nonhandicapped child and the child with the hearing loss are strangers to one another, which presents problems to both in adult life.

Such a unique program could be housed within a local school, and this is being done in some areas. But when a program is separated from the mainstream of school activities, and is not really a part of the school population, segregation still exists within the same building.

MUTUAL COMMUNICATION

There have to be ways to involve students and faculty with each other, to break down barriers in order to be able to say that a program is integrated into the mainstream of school life. For example, if a program for hearing-impaired children is housed in a local school, courses in sign language could be made available to all students and staff. Not only is this a way for others to share the problems and demands upon the hearing-impaired students, but it opens up a new channel of communication. People need opportunities to interact, to learn about one another, and how they are alike. If they never get opportunities, they will never get to know one another and will always feel uncomfortable, separated by real or imagined differences.

Alan Brightman, author of the children's book *Like Me*, brings this out in the personal note to his book:

> When I think back to grammar school, I remember *the special class* as a worse place to be threatened with than the principal's office. But I don't remember why. Perhaps I never really knew. Perhaps the mysteries of unexplained difference (I remember that "they" weren't like the rest of "us") have a message all their own. Surely the fact that those mysteries were never to be acknowledged by six years of teachers had to make us all wonder.
>
> Looking back, I guess the only thing my teachers could have done would be to have noticed those kids in that room. They really didn't have to look away.
>
> I saw those kids now and again: walking hand-in-hand along the hallways, sometimes sitting on the far edge of the playground, never riding on the bus. I knew it was them because there was always an adult or two close by, sort of a human fence.

I realize now that my teachers must have seen those kids, too, more often than I. They probably knew all about all of them. I wonder if they ever shook hands or stopped to chat.

Couldn't my teachers have let me know, somehow, that those kids in that room were more like me than unlike me? that all of us were in school for the same reasons? and that just as I was having some trouble with arithmetic, so might one of those kids have found reading, writing, or shoe tieing a little difficult as well?

Now that I think of it, I would have loved to know that those kids also laughed just like I did, and cried, and even got into trouble once in a while, too. I didn't know any of that then. And I didn't know any of them.

I guess I was being protected.

How often is this true, that no one speaks of shared feelings, shared expectations? As a result a whole area beneficial to society through education is lost. Students with special needs might be tolerated, but they are not welcome into school life. We must strive to change these old attitudes so that our children, all children, can be recognized first as people and only second as people with special needs.

PLANNING A FUTURE THROUGH EDUCATION

In times of fiscal constraint parents and other concerned individuals need to be especially wary because each level of government tends to shift responsibility for costly programs to another level. The state says the county must pay, the county defers to the local school boards, but the local boards may be without funds. At this point they all turn toward Washington and wait.

The cost of educating a child with special needs may be as much as two or three times the cost for the average child. In difficult financial situations many government agencies and school boards may consider such a program too expensive and perhaps unnecessary as well. They tend to forget that all education is an investment in the future. Even from a purely monetary point of view the extra money may be well spent, since in the long run much less will be spent on the special needs of adults with disabilities if we can help children reach their full potential now.

Since children do not vote, they often receive fewer services than other segments of the population. So you must be their voice. The responsibility rests with you to change things for your child and for all children. While you will never be able to do all that is needed, you can help in many ways, including the mundane chore of attending local meetings on education, zoning, and so on. You do not have to be, and should not be, limited to the role of parent of a child with a handicap, since a concern for education of all children will be the most positive force for your child with special needs. At the same time, the responsibility for the rights and needs of children with handicaps is not yours alone. It is everyone's, even though you may be the most knowledgeable at the local level.

As your children grow older, your focus becomes directed more on specific school preparation for the adult world. Some schools may have met the mandates of federal and local laws on education, but, in actuality, their programs may lack substance. They may emphasize outdated skills for jobs now automated out of existence and courses that don't adequately prepare students for the demands of college-level work or meet college requirements for admission. The days when students with handicaps were taught only basket weaving are not that far behind us.

A student who has special needs will require an education that will adequately prepare him or her to lead as full a life as possible. At the elementary level this means acquiring the basic skills necessary for academic or vocational training at the secondary school level. Education need not be academically oriented only. It should be geared toward accomplishing many of the tasks a person will face in daily living as an adult. These include self-help skills and the ability to cope with others and to earn a living.

Some parents demand more than is possible from the schools and from children, especially when they are worried about deficiencies they perceive in certain areas. Just as it is not appropriate to try to teach reading to a child who still needs work on prereading skills, a child who is ready for academic work would be inappropriately placed in a program that would best be described as advanced baby-sitting. At times it is hard for parents to distinguish between the two, however, because what seems to us to be a waste of time may actually be part of a valuable learning experience. An example of this is an innovation such as the open classroom concept by which the old system of assigned seats and group teaching gives way to individualized instruction in more informal settings. It can look like pure chaos, but with a skilled teacher it can be a well-organized educational experience. With yet another teacher it may actually be chaos.

If, after having met with teachers, specialists, and other school personnel, you still feel that your child is not receiving the education she needs, it sometimes helps to get an outside opinion. You may be able to return to the diagnostic source that originally worked with your child, if this is other than the school itself. They may not agree with you, or with the school either, and then it is up to you to find out why. You may also be able to get referrals to other resources through the school or diagnostic source, from special educational programs or consultants, and from national organizations and groups. You may be able to find qualified individuals who are experienced with just the kinds of questions you want answered, or you may find yourselves on your own again with only your own judgment to depend upon. It could be that you are unrealistic, and perhaps you need to reexamine your goals and motivations.

However, should you decide that the school is unrealistic in its approach to your child, don't be reluctant to press for changes. If, for example, you feel the school's program is not ambitious enough, or too ambitious, discuss your concern with the school staff and with other parents. By getting the problems out in the open, you may be able to work together with others to improve the program. If the problems stem from poor communication between the staff and parents, you can encourage better rapport by arranging informal parent-staff meetings, luncheons, workshops, or rap sessions. If your concern is outdated attitudes and programs, meetings with outside speakers from other schools or groups with different perspectives might be useful. If the cause of a weak program is lack of funds, you and other parents could mount a fund-raising project.

If it is difficult to get your school's cooperation, you may need to go outside for help. Often it helps to return to the school officials armed with respected professional opinions. In some cases, however, nothing short of a presidential decree will make a difference. When the school is resistant, there is a whole process of appeals usually available to you, if necessary, through the courts. Meanwhile, you may be able to fill your child's needs by hiring a tutor or by getting the child involved with community social or recreational programs.

At times like this the support of an active parent group can be beneficial. Many other parents could be facing similar problems, and there is strength in numbers as well as comfort in shared experiences. It is through parent groups, too, that you can often learn about changing trends in services for your children as well as changing outlooks for their future.

Disappearing Barriers in Colleges and Universities

Within the last few years changes have taken place within colleges and other institutions of higher learning that will yield positive results for many students with special needs. Faced with declining enrollments, many schools have expanded their programs and facilities to include nontraditional applicants beyond the successful high school graduate. Middle-aged students are being attracted by opportunities either to begin college-level studies or to resume interrupted studies with programs for continuing education. People on split or rotating shifts, such as nurses and policemen, are being offered courses on schedules that parallel their unusual work demands, with subjects offered both day and evening. Business courses are being taught on commuter trains.

The colleges have also discovered students with special needs, including those with physical disabilities and cultural disadvantages. They have moved to erase barriers that previously blocked these students' progress, often with welcome funds from federal and private grants. When one school discovered that the two small steps at the front door were the same as a ten foot wall to the student in a wheelchair, ramps were added. Other schools have lowered telephones so that students in wheelchairs could make calls. Students previously excluded because of architectural barriers are now made welcome at many schools through adaptation of existing buildings and consideration of their needs when new ones are built. Students who need special assistance with academic skills or with the English language now receive this preparation.

Many social barriers are also breaking down. Often students volunteer to read to fellow students who are blind or to take notes for students with a hearing loss. Some schools incorporate the needs of one group of students with the needs of others in unique ways, such as by employing students in need of extra financial assistance to provide these services to fellow students in need of them. It is not surprising that some students with special needs become student leaders or honors winners because they are in the vanguard, a pioneer group who are proving that it can be done and that it should have been allowed to be done long ago.

In truth, the colleges need these students as much as the students need the colleges. Regrettably, most areas of the business world have not come to grips with this reality. For the noncollege young adult with a disability, as well as for the college-educated student in many cases, it is often easier to get training than it is to find employment. Our economy has had millions of surplus workers for years, and unemployment rates among minority groups and recent graduates are probably the highest. This, of course, makes it that much more difficult for a worker with a handicap, whose disability may well limit his or her choice of jobs to begin with. Even in those jobs he or she is well qualified for, discrimination can make employment unobtainable.

Disappearing Barriers in Employment

Employers often mention such concerns as high insurance rates, the costs of eliminating architectural barriers, or the possibility of frequent absenses as excuses for their not hiring more handicapped individuals. Most of these reasons are unfounded or exaggerated. But this resistance is eroding, largely because of the 1973 Vocational Rehabilitation Act, which requires companies doing business of more than $2,500 a year with the federal government to design "affirmative action" plans for hiring the handicapped or face loss of their federal contracts. More than 275,000 companies and institutions, employing more than one-third of the U.S. work force, are affected.

As a result of the law, many companies have changed former hiring practices. The giant International Telephone and Telegraph conglomerate, for example, has dropped previous rules that barred job applicants with epilepsy, cancer, and other health problems. U.S. Steel Corporation has begun to recruit at schools for the deaf. Other companies are installing ramps, lowering water fountains, and building wider restrooms for employees in wheelchairs.

Perhaps most important, the law has made many employers realize that their past arguments against hiring handicapped persons were unjustified. As one personnel executive commented: "In the past we were tempted to say, 'This girl can't type; she's blind.' We had preconceived notions." Now more and more companies are starting to explore ways that disabled employees can perform jobs with minor changes in hours or duties.

Now Americans with handicapping conditions have another potent weapon to wield in the fight against discrimination not only in employment but also in housing, transportation, and many other facets of their lives. In spring 1977 HEW Secretary Califano signed into law federal regulations that will carry out a section of the 1973 Rehabilitation Act that prohibits discrimination of any kind against handicapped individuals by anyone who receives any federal funds.

The regulations not only broaden prohibitions against job discrimination, but they require companies, schools, hospitals, and others doing business with Uncle Sam to remove physical barriers to handicapped individuals in their facilities.

At a White House Conference on Handicapped Individuals in May 1977, President Carter described the new regulations as the "Civil Rights Act" for America's disabled. "The time for discrimination against the handicapped American is over," the president declared.

Mr. Carter vowed to enforce the newly won protections vigorously. The specific regulations for Section 504 of the 1973 Rehabilitation Act can be obtained by writing the Department of Health, Education, and Welfare in Washington, D.C.

As a result of legislation the opportunities for your child to find employment or to pursue a career are improving. But the battle has not been won. More government incentives, including monetary incentives, may be necessary to encourage more businesses to hire persons with handicaps. In some areas private arrangements are helping. For example, one agency for individuals who are retarded agreed to contract for food services from a private company if that company agreed to hire some of the young adults that the agency had trained.

PREPARATION FOR ADULTHOOD: INDEPENDENCE FOR THE PERSON WITH SPECIAL NEEDS

There will come a time that you know you will never really be ready for, when your children are all grown up and leave the security of home. For some children it will be as simple as a good-bye as they settle into their own apartment and job. For others, special needs will complicate the process and present unique problems. Permanent dependence upon the family used to be expected for even the minimally handicapped person, but now more options are available and expected for a fulfilling, independent life as an adult. While very few children will need total custodial care, the majority of others will need varying degrees of assistance in order to become self-sufficient. For a child without a handicap this assistance lies in education and job preparation, among other skills. The same is true for children with handicaps, but with more dimensions, more considerations.

There often is nothing better for a young person, especially one with disabilities, than a job experience. Besides providing "pocket money" or even money to pay for special treatments or education, a job gives a growing person the experiences of independence that are so important in developing adult viewpoints and attitudes.

In addition, a job provides concrete experience in the working world. For the teen-ager, a job brings the reality of shouldering responsibilities, of being depended upon and of working hard. It provides a foundation that can be used to build a career. Hiring a person with a disability can also demonstrate that he can hold and perform a job effectively.

Perhaps most important of all for a young person with a disabling condition, a job can convince him of his own worth and help him develop self-respect. People with handicaps so often have things done for them. Parents contribute to this by "protecting" their disabled children. Such children need opportunities to try, to fail, and to succeed on their own. Helen Keller, who was both deaf and blind, put it this way: "A person who is severely impaired never knows his hidden sources of strength until he is treated like a normal human being and encouraged to shape his own life."

Part-time jobs for young people, especially the disabled, are difficult to find. If your child can't find a job, encourage her to try volunteer work in a field she is interested in. She may end up getting the same work experience that she would have had in a paid job. And the volunteer experience may help her get a paid job later.

Preparing for a Career

There are several special programs available to help prepare young people with disabilities for careers or for college.

The first place to check is the local vocational rehabilitation office in charge of job training and college preparation programs, funded in every state by the Rehabilitation Services Administration of the U.S. Department of Health, Education, and Welfare. These state offices have varying names, such as Division of Human Resources or Department of Social Services. Many of them are listed in the Directory at the end of this chapter. For further information on offices in your area, write the Rehabilitation Services Administration, Washington, D.C. 20201.

Once you have located the office in your community, make an appointment for your child to see if he qualifies for the programs. Generally, the qualifications specify that the individual must be of working age (usually sixteen), his disability must be so severe that it limits his opportunities to find work matching his potential and abilities, and the agency must be convinced that he probably will be able to get—and keep—a job for which he is trained.

When an individual is accepted into the program, he is assigned a rehabilitation counselor. He is also given a series of tests and interviews to determine in which fields his talents and abilities lie. Training courses range in subject from operating business machines to welding to academic studies. Usually, the agency provides transportation to the school, books, supplies, and living expenses. It may also provide special equipment, such as crutches, hearing aids, and Seeing Eye dogs. After the training is completed, the agency will help students find jobs or even set up their own businesses.

In addition to the federally funded programs, there may be vocational rehabilitation programs available in your community through private agencies, universities, or local governments.

How to Find Jobs

Vocational rehabilitation programs can aid only a limited number of disabled job seekers. If you are a person with disabilities who is looking for a job, there are places where you may be able to get special help beyond the usual newspaper advertisements and tips from friends and relatives.

● State employment services: Many states have special programs to help disabled citizens find jobs. The location of the nearest state employment service office is listed in the state government section of your phone book. You also might try private employment agencies, but approach them with caution. Avoid agencies that ask you to pay a fee in advance.

● The U.S. Civil Service Commission: The commission has information on job opportunities at federal agencies across the country. To qualify for such jobs, you must first pass a test and be given a civil service rating. Every federal agency has a coordinator for employment of the handicapped and a program to encourage the hiring of the disabled. For information on job opportunities and examinations, check the nearest regional office of the commission. They are listed in the Directory at the end of this chapter.

● Finally, in some areas there are nonprofit groups that specialize in finding jobs for people with handicapping conditions. One of these is an organization called Just One Break, or J.O.B., in New York City, which was started in 1949 by professionals such as Dr. Howard A. Rusk of the Institute for Rehabilitation Medicine at the New York University Medical College. J.O.B. provides free placement services for disabled individuals and prospective employers.

Chapters of J.O.B. have been started elsewhere, primarily in the eastern United States. Similar programs may be available in your community. For information on such programs, write to J.O.B. (Just One Break), 373 Park Avenue, New York, N.Y. 10016.

How to Apply for a Job

The first step toward getting that job you want is to write a letter of application. That seems simple enough, but there are some basic guidelines to follow in order to make a good impression.

The letter should be typed on good quality, standard-sized (8½ by 11½ inches) white typing paper. Send the original—no carbon or Xerox copies. It should be no longer than one page.

In clear, concise language state the position you are seeking and briefly state your qualifications. A more detailed listing of your experience, interests, and background may be included in a résumé that you can enclose with your letter.

Be sure the letter is neat, the spelling is correct, and the grammar is proper. Include your name, address, and telephone number (both your home and business numbers). Ask for a personal interview at the convenience of the prospective employer. But if there is a day or time when it is impossible for you to get to an interview, say so in your letter.

Writing a Résumé

A job résumé basically is a summary of your job experience, qualifications, interests, education, and general background. It also provides you a chance to make a positive impression with a prospective employer. The information should be concise (no more than two or three pages) and truthful. Number each page at the top and also put your name and address at the beginning of every page.

Start the résumé with a paragraph summarizing your strongest qualifications, job and educational experiences, and talents. Personnel people see a lot of résumés, many of which are simply listings of prior jobs. The goal here is to tell a prospective employer quickly why you would be a good person to hire, and to encourage him to read the rest of your résumé.

Divide the résumé into two parts—one part on general information and a second part on personal information. For clarity each part can have such categories as the following:

GENERAL INFORMATION

Occupational Objectives: State your career goals and why you want this job.

Experience: List the jobs you have held in reverse chronological order. That is, list your most recent job first and your earliest job last. State how long you held each job and briefly describe your duties.

Education: State if you have completed a high school education or a college education, or if you have attended college. Also list any vocational schooling or any skills such as typing, shorthand, or experience operating business machines. Include education in foreign languages, but only if you are really proficient in those languages.

Outside Interests: Briefly list hobbies, avocations, and affiliations with groups, professional societies, and labor unions.

PERSONAL INFORMATION

Vital Statistics:
Social security number
Date of birth
Marital status
Size of family (if you have a family)
Height and weight

General Health: Briefly describe your health and give the date of your last physical. To allay any concern because of your handicapping condition, you may want to add the weight of a statement on your health from your doctor or rehabilitation counselor.

Mention any disabilities, but don't apologize for them. Make sure there is no misunderstanding about your ability to do the job. Include a brief, clarifying statement, such as "Use wheelchair, but have full use of hands and arms" or "Legally blind, but use dog and have been able to carry out employment efficiently in the past."

Sometimes, a prospective employer will ask only for an employment vita, which is a shortened version (usually no more than one page) of a résumé. You should have a basic résumé and vita typed up before going job seeking. They can be used for more than one job application.

The Job Interview

Hopefully your letter of application and résumé will lead to a job interview. Again, there are measures you can take to make the best impression.

Before the Interview: Find out as much as you can about the company and the job you are interviewing for. This will enable you to answer questions intelligently as well as to ask intelligent questions yourself.

Find out what materials you are supposed to bring to the interview. This might include your social security card, letters of reference, school records, training certificates, or samples of previous work you may have done.

Make sure to get to the job interview on time. Arriving late for a job interview is a sure way for any job seeker to make a bad impression, but it can be especially damaging if the applicant is disabled. The tardiness raises the question of whether he frequently will be late because his disabilities make travel difficult. Before an interview check out the easiest route to the meeting during the time you will be going. Find out if there are any barriers so that you can plan ways to avoid them or deal with them.

Go to the interview well groomed and neatly dressed. Avoid flashy clothing. What you wear may not matter much to many prospective employers, but it is better to err on the side of conservatism. No cigarette smoking or gum chewing.

During the Interview: Stay alert and interested. Sit erect and face the interviewer. Answer questions directly. Don't stretch the truth, but emphasize your good points and speak with confidence and courtesy. Don't go into your personal problems, and don't criticize a former employer.

In short, sell yourself. Convince them that you can do the job. You may have to overcome any reservations that a prospective employer might have about hiring people with handicaps. You have to prove you'll be an asset and not a liability.

If you don't get the job, don't get discouraged. Young job applicants often have to go through many interviews before they finally land an offer. Each interview is practice for the next one, and each time you will learn how to be more effective.

Don't automatically assume that you are being discriminated against because of your disability; it could be that you just aren't qualified for a certain job. But if you feel that you are being discriminated against, you have powerful rights with which to fight back. Take your complaint to the local human rights department of your local or state government, or contact the Office of Human Development at the U.S. Department of Health, Education, and Welfare in Washington, D.C.

Housing

Groups such as United Cerebral Palsy have been pioneers in urging, demanding, and actually developing housing programs for people with handicaps. This assistance includes, for example, the development of housing in the Midwest and other areas of the country for adults with cerebral palsy and other physical disabilities. Such groups work closely with professionals on the design of government-sponsored housing projects that have accommodating features for senior citizens and the handicapped. The city of Minneapolis has one such project.

Such government-sponsored housing allows people who would otherwise have been confined to institutions or to similar situations of dependence upon others to function independently as adults. The apartments are designed with larger doorways and elevators, lowered sink and counter space, adapted bathrooms, and other features that help a person with limited mobility deal with his own needs. However, most areas of the country have not yet developed adequate housing for people with limited mobility. Indeed, many communities have not even realized that the lack of such housing is a problem.

Prodded by growing demands of handicapped individuals, the Carter administration is taking steps to improve housing opportunities for such persons. Patricia Roberts Harris, secretary of the Department of Housing and Urban Development, has set a new goal that 5 percent of all apartments built under the federal government's rent-subsidy and public housing programs be designed for use by the disabled. Such housing is usually built by nonprofit groups with loans insured by the federal government, which then subsidizes the tenants so that they generally pay no more than 25 percent of their incomes as rent.

Secretary Harris also created a new Office of Independent Living for the Disabled to coordinate the expanded housing programs. You can obtain information about these programs by writing the new office at the Department of Housing and Urban Development, Washington, D.C. 20410.

Transportation and Architectural Barriers

One of the major problems for the person who has physical limitations is getting from one place to another, and (once there) getting inside. Public transportation may offer reduced fares for senior citizens and others with special needs, but much public transportation remains unusable for persons with certain disabilities. For example, very few transit systems have buses that accommodate the handicapped with such features as ramps or special wheelchair lifts.

Door-to-door transportation is expensive, but it is a necessity of life for many disabled persons because without it they could not get out of their house, let alone get to work. Some people with limited mobility are able to operate their own cars, sometimes with the aid of adaptations such as hand controls or extra-long pedals. The freedom of movement this allows them extends well beyond the practical aspects to the sense of independence it affords. But beyond exorbitant insurance rates, drivers, and also passengers, with limited mobility may face the frustration of searching for a parking place close enough to where they want to go and then finding the reserved space for the handicapped taken by the nonhandicapped drivers.

Fortunately, some transportation help may be on the way. The U.S. Department of Transportation is considering requiring that municipal transit companies adapt their buses to accommodate disabled travelers. And the Interstate Commerce Commission has issued what it terms a new "bill of rights" for intercity bus travelers, which includes some special provisions for people with handicaps. The ICC rules require bus lines to transport physically disabled persons even if they are unaccompanied. The bus companies must also help such persons board the buses and must remodel their terminals to accommodate the handicapped. The rules cover all of the five hundred bus companies—such as Greyhound and Trailways—that provide intercity bus services.

Public buildings are now being constructed with increasing awareness of the need for access for all, and access to such buildings has lifted the limits imposed upon many people with handicaps. For example, in Washington, D.C., the museums and even the zoo have wheelchairs available as well as ramps and elevators. These are small considerations, but one that make the beauty of Washington accessible to so many more Americans. Perhaps the most dramatic recent example of the elimination of architectural barriers was the installation of an elevator at the Lincoln Memorial, which was previously accessible only by a steep series of stairs.

Do the public buildings in your area, particularly such service buildings as courthouses and libraries, have similar policies? There are many ways you can encourage your community to be more considerate and responsive to the needs of all citizens. Your child can only benefit from such concern, regardless of the direction it takes.

As a parent you should remember that in the long run prejudice toward any handicapped person makes it difficult for all. If you want understanding for your child, you must make sure others realize that all children and adults with special needs are people first, entitled to the same rights and freedoms, including the pursuit of happiness, as everyone else.

One way to increase public awareness about the needs of individuals with handicaps is to put increased pressure on local governments to remove barriers and to provide increased facilities for disabled citizens. As a citizen of a community, you have a say in how your local government spends its funds, including money that involves a federal program.

For example, most major cities receive federal community development block grants from the U.S. Department of Housing and Urban Development. Such cities must hold public hearings on how this money should be spent. By speaking out at such hearings, you can help make sure that disabled citizens benefit fairly from these grants. You'll have the backing of Housing and Urban Development Secretary Harris, who has initiated a program "to encourage local communities to spend a greater share" of their community development grants "for the elimination of architectural barriers and the construction of rehabilitation facilities for the handicapped."

You can also ask your local government to give greater official attention to the needs of people with disabilities. One example has been set by Westchester County, New York, which has created an Office for the Handicapped and which also provides interpreters for deaf citizens at public hearings.

Local government and business officials may simply be unaware not only of the needs of disabled citizens but also of how to go about designing, or redesigning, buildings to accommodate such persons. You can help break down this educational barrier, too. The federal government has adopted design standards for making its buildings usable by people with disabilities. Those guidelines have been published by the U.S. General Services Administration in a booklet entitled *Design Criteria: New Public Building Accessibility.*

The booklet covers all aspects of designing modern office buildings in order to avoid such architectural barriers as narrow and steep entrance ramps, furniture arranged too close together, elevator and fire alarm boxes located out of reach, and rest room facilities not adapted for use by paraplegics.

"These guidelines go a long way toward making our federal buildings more humane—more responsive to the needs of those who are blind, deaf or confined to wheelchairs," says Jay Soloman, GSA administrator. "I hope that others will carefully study these recommendations and use them to remove architectural barriers in buildings operated by private institutions and state and local government."

The publication is available for $2.60 each from General Services Administration business services offices nationwide, or from the GSA in Washington, D.C.

RETARDATION: AN EXAMPLE OF
EVOLUTION OF PERSPECTIVES

The handicap of mental retardation is a condition that most of us consider to be quite severe. People automatically assume that a mentally retarded child will always be completely dependent and faces a future without hope. Yet the progress of individuals with mental retardation provides a good example of how a handicap does not necessarily have to bring the significant limits that people envision.

Traditional Perspectives

Historically, mentally retarded children have been viewed as tragically lacking any hope for an independent future. It was not— and still is not—uncommon for parents to be told at the birth of their mentally retarded baby that she should immediately be institutionalized. The generally accepted feeling was that the child would not survive in the community or bring the family anything but heartbreak, so the best and only alternative was to "put away" the child as quickly as possible before the parents became attached to him.

Many states created institutions, sometimes called schools, to deal with these children. The institutions were usually located in less populated areas away from the communities from which the children came. Some of the institutions, which also included retarded adults, were set up as totally self-sufficient communities in which retarded persons had their own farms and businesses and where they could lead complete, if sheltered, lives.

Many of the state institutions, however, degenerated over the years from the ideal communities envisioned by their founders to virtual warehouses of people. During budget time and periods of economic hardship these institutions were an easy target for funding reductions because the residents did not vote. Most of the voting public either did not know about the institutions, didn't care about them, or assumed that the state was doing an adequate job. Frequently, the state institutions were just too large to operate adequately. For all these reasons conditions at many such institutions became deplorable, as has been revealed in newspaper exposés.

As a result of these reports as well as complaints by some families of persons in institutions many other families began keeping mildly retarded individuals within their own communities, rather than send them to state institutions. This left the state schools with the more dependent people, which in turn increased expenses. Farms became too expensive to operate. And sometimes the retarded were used inappropriately as a free source of labor. As a result many states passed laws forbidding residents of such institutions to work without pay. But very few states allotted money to pay the retarded residents for their work. Thus, more and more jobs done in the past by the residents were contracted out, performed by nonretarded state employees, or eliminated. As the expense of running the institutions mounted, the quality of care plummeted.

If you were to visit many of these older institutions today, you would be baffled by the titles *school* or *training school* that are used. In most you would not find anything faintly resembling a school, and you would see very little, if any, training. The majority of the residents are utterly idle. Not allowed to work, not allocated any money for programs—even basic recreational programs—the residents are most often left sitting with nothing to do but watch time pass or, perhaps, even hurt themselves or others in an attempt to relieve the boredom.

New Perspectives

What has brought about a change for the better is the realization that hiding away retarded people in large institutions isolated from the community just does not work. Today a growing number of the 3.6 million retarded adults in the United States are making a life on their own. Many are living and working successfully outside the institutions where they once were expected to spend their lives. And many more are bypassing institutions altogether. Over the past decade the population of public institutions for the retarded has dropped to under 142,000 from about 177,000.

People with retarded mental development, like other individuals with handicaps, cannot be lumped together into one group. Many people who are retarded are able to live independent, self-sufficient lives with jobs and with families of their own if they receive adequate preparation for society's demands. This group of persons may not need specialized housing, and they are seldom even identified as a "retarded" person by those around them.

Other retarded individuals need supervision in both housing and employment; they probably cannot manage to set up an apartment and live alone. But while they may need more assistance than the first group, they may still be able to handle major responsibilities once assistance has been provided. One alternative for such persons is supervised group living, such as small residences, halfway houses, and adult foster homes.

In some parts of the country, group homes are being established that include houseparents who can assist eight to fifteen adults in their daily living within the environment of the community. This includes such activities as getting to and from training programs or jobs on public transportation, taking responsibility for their own personal needs, and looking after their own health. Many of the residents of such a small group home can find unskilled employment in the private sector, and others will work in "sheltered workshops" that have contracts with several businesses for work such as packing small screws into boxes or putting plastic wrap on novelty items. Workers are paid either by piece or by how fast they can work, according to an average time established for the workers. After work the group home may have a social or recreational program, and household chores are shared by everyone.

A minority of retarded individuals are totally dependent for most of their needs and are able to function only in limited ways under close supervision. The totally dependent person may need an intensive care facility (ICF), which is larger than a group home or residence and is geared for total care outside a hospital setting.

The concept involved with all of these different types of facilities is that they are close to or within the community, and they are accessible to the family. An adult may return to her family's home for visits on weekends, or she may go to the movies. All of the resources of the community are available to her.

Where group homes have been established, most communities have eventually discovered that their initial fears about them were unfounded. When there have been complaints about group homes being poorly run or supervised, many communities have worked to correct conditions rather than eliminate the home.

How Segregation Breeds Stereotypes

Today a growing number of retarded individuals are living increasingly self-sufficient lives. The same is true for individuals with other types of handicapping conditions. One of the major barriers remaining in the future of your child with special needs is the need for increased understanding that people with certain limitations are not limited people.

One problem is that most adults haven't had much contact with individuals who have disabilities, especially the retarded individual. Few went to school with children who had handicaps or ever developed friendships with such children. As a result many people have stereotyped ideas about persons who have handicaps, ideas that for the most part are untrue. This is surprising because most adults do know someone within their family or circle of acquaintances who has a child with a handicapping condition. Perhaps you may have sheltered your children with special needs so well that society has forgotten about them as people. You need to make sure they do not forget.

Most of all, however, you must make sure that your children are taught to grow into self-sufficient individuals. As parents, you will probably never feel completely confident that your children will be able to face the world without you; your own parents are probably still wondering if you can make it. With a child who has special needs, the question of when that child should leave home becomes even more difficult to answer, since there are so many complicated facets. Perhaps your child will leave home before adulthood because of his needs. Other children may stay at home well into adulthood.

PREPARING A FUTURE

Leaving home starts the day your child is born. You will have to prepare yourselves and your children for that eventuality. If you truly want your children to be able to have independent and satisfying lives you will have to prepare them to lead that life, which necessitates many kinds of resources: a formal education can help a child reach full potential only when the informal education, primarily received at home, reinforces that and includes more intangible strengths.

It is not uncommon for parents to say that they want the best for their child but then not work to provide an adequate preparation for real life. You may do things for your child with special needs that she could do for herself. You may protect your child from unpleasant but necessary exposure to life, from learning experiences that could include failure or risk. It may be easier and quicker for you to do for your child now, but later it will make life slower and more difficult for both you and the child, and you will inevitably be contributing to a crippling process more insidious than the handicap itself.

When you are unsure how the child's needs can be met—perhaps because of the lack of resources to turn to, your own feelings, or controversies concerning the disability—the issues become even more involved. It becomes more important not to hesitate to find experienced professionals and get their opinions, to seek out all available resources. You need to get an idea of how much a child will be able to do, how much is normally expected. In order to make preparations for the future, all of this is essential. You cannot make decisions without information to base them on, including your own feelings and reactions.

When a child is totally dependent, decisions are more painful. You may be advised that residential settings would be best for the child. Perhaps you rejected the idea initially because you were not convinced that this was best or because you felt guilty about your own needs and feelings, your reluctance to alter your life-style so drastically. If you are now reconsidering residential placement, an evaluation by you of the child's needs, your own needs, and what is currently available to meet both is the first step. There are several guides at the end of this chapter that provide concrete information about residential placement and evaluate such programs.

The ultimate decision of whether and when a child will need residential placement is yours. You may be forced into such a decision by the lack of any other alternative services. Or you may avoid the decision because of social and other pressures to take full responsibility for your child. You can only hope for, and work for, the availability of a multiplicity of resources soon, so that such a decision need not be made as the lesser of two evils but on the basis of what is really best for all involved.

Sexuality

You may become so involved with the important issues of education, medical care, employment, and the like that you may not be aware that your child is growing toward adulthood and discovering that there are interesting differences between boys and girls. Dating will be one of the first introductions to social interaction. This is a difficult step for most adolescents, and it is even more complex for a child with special needs. One of your first problem areas will be dealing with your own attitudes and feelings. It can be quite a startling experience for many parents to discover that their child wants to establish relationships outside the home. When a child is dependent upon you for some of her needs, you may confuse this dependency with immaturity, you may treat your child as you would a child much younger.

By the time other children in the family reached the age when they could get a driver's license, or had friends who could, you probably stopped being a chauffeur for them. But it may be a much longer time, perhaps permanently, that you will have to provide this service for your child with a disability. This is one time when it is difficult to remember that even though your child may be as dependent upon you as a younger child, he is approaching adulthood or has already reached it.

It can be difficult, too, for the adolescent to accept dependence upon her parents when she is trying to establish her own sense of self and of independence. The most ordinary situations become incredibly complex. How can your son go to a party if his wheelchair doesn't fit through the door of a friend's home? How can a young couple have any privacy if one set of parents is hovering in the background waiting to drive them home?

These things can be devastating to an adolescent trying to impress a date, and it can be an excruciating period for the whole family. Fortunately, however, some young adults are able to cope with such situations with a sensitivity and confidence that you may never have had when you were teen-agers.

Eventually, you will be faced with the question of the sexual needs of your child as he or she grows into adulthood. Many people are uncomfortable with sex education for the person who has special needs. Some respond to the idea of sex for a person who is handicapped with one word: "Never." The idea is repulsive to some people, while others take it for granted that all handicapped persons are natural celibates.

You may not have even considered sex as a reality for your children in the future. But for most adults sex is a way of expressing love and of receiving warmth and approval in a personal way. To automatically exclude a person who has a disability from this experience is to deny their humanness. The Sex Information and Education Council of the U.S. (SIECUS) has developed several information programs, some of which deal specifically with issues concerning sex and the person who had a disability. Besides providing general guidance, it explodes some of the myths surrounding sex and handicaps, and it suggests that the improbable may really be very possible.

People's social lives tend to revolve around their jobs, their friends, or the churches and clubs they belong to. A person whose activities are limited by a disability may face a difficult time establishing wide-ranging social activities. These limitations can be self-imposed at times by doubts and by experiences of previous rejections. You can't force anyone to have a good time, but you can remove some of the obvious obstacles. Obstacles that are primarily psychological could possibly be overcome through professional counseling as well as just plain experience in interacting with others. Sexual love can be expressed in many ways, and many different adaptations can be made by a couple when more familiar traditional forms of sexual expression are not easily used.

Dr. Alex Comfort in *More Joy of Sex* writes:

> Virtually nobody is too disabled to have some pleasure from sexuality—with a partner if you can, without one if you must. Generations of disabled people have been hocused out of this by other people's embarrassment. . . . Everyone needs tenderness and contact, but it needn't stop there. . . . Your biggest problem, after that of getting well people to treat you as a person, will be in getting it through their heads that you have the same needs that they have . . .
>
> Above all, get rid of the idea that nobody can love, or have pleasure with, a disabled person. It simply isn't true. Thousands can and do. In fact, the need to give special help to people with impaired mobility, etc., may be the beginning of a general move in medicine to give proper sexual help to everyone who needs it.

Our Hopes for the Future

Expanding community acceptance of individuals with handicaps and expanding job markets for them at all levels seem to be producing a circular effect. Even though prejudice still exists, following the availability of jobs that in turn affect self-sufficiency and social acceptance comes opportunities for commitments to others. Marriage and a family is one opportunity for a rich fulfilling life through permanent commitments to others. Single life does not have to be unfulfilling; but perhaps because it is such a "normal" activity, people tend to think of marriage and family as the epitome of fitting into society.

Perhaps in part that is what you want most for your children, what you are willing to fight for: the chance to be normal, to belong to society as an accepted, even admired, member. The future is open to your children as long as you are willing to take an active part in preparing them for it.

DIRECTORY

Chapter References

BOOKS ON PREPARATION FOR THE FUTURE

Ayrault, Evelyn West. *Helping the Handicapped Teenager Mature.* New York: Association Press, 1971.

Siegal, Ernest, Ph.D. *The Exceptional Child Grows Up.* New York: E. P. Dutton, 1974.

Splaver, Sara. *Your Handicap: Don't Let It Handicap You.* New York: Julian Messner, 1974. (Directed at adolescents and young adults.)

PERSONAL ACCOUNTS

Blank, Joseph P. *19 Steps up the Mountain.* Philadelphia: Lippincott, 1976.

Buck, Pearl. *The Child Who Never Grew.* New York: John Day Co., 1950.

Canning, Clara and Joseph P. *The Gift of Martha.* Boston: Children's Hospital Medical Center, 1975.

Carson, Mary. *Ginny, A True Story.* Garden City, N.Y.: Doubleday & Co., 1971.

Gauchat, Dorothy. *All God's Children.* New York: Hawthorn Books, 1976.

Greenfield, Josh. *A Child Called Noah.* New York: Holt, Rinehart, and Winston, 1970.

Kaufman, Barry Neil. *Son-Rise.* New York: Harper & Row, 1976.

Kililea, Marie. *Karen.* New York: Dell, 1952 (paperback).

———. *With Love from Karen.* New York: Dell, 1963.

Kravik, P. J., ed. *Adopting Children with Special Needs.* 2d ed. Ossining, N.Y.: North American Council on Adoptable Children, 1977 (6 Madison Avenue, Ossining, N.Y. 10562). $4.

Krents, Harold. *To Race the Wind.* New York: G. P. Putnam's Sons, 1972.

Lukens, Kathleen, and Panter, Carol. *Thursday's Child Has Far to Go.* Englewood Cliffs, N.J.: Prentice-Hall, 1969.

Marx, Joseph Lawrence. *Keep Trying.* New York: Harper & Row, 1967.

Napear, Peggy. *Brain Child.* New York: Harper & Row, 1974.

Resnick, Rose. *Sun and Shadow.* New York: Atheneum, 1975.

Terese, Robert, with Owen, Corinne. *A Flock of Lambs.* Chicago: Henry Regnery Co., 1970.

Ulrich, Sharon. *Elizabeth.* Ann Arbor, Mich.: Univ. of Michigan Press, 1972.

Viscardi, Henry, Jr. *The Phoenix Child.* New York: Paul S. Eriksson, 1975.

———. *The School.* New York: Paul S. Eriksson, 1964.

Wilson, Dorothy Clark. *Handicap Race.* New York: McGraw-Hill, 1967.

BOOKS ON RESIDENTIAL FACILITIES

National Association for Retarded Citizens (NARC). *Handbook for Residential Services Committees.* 1972 (Available from: National Association for Retarded Citizens, 2709 Avenue E East, Arlington, Tex. 76011). $1.

Roos, Philip. *Current Issues in Residential Care: With Special Reference to the Problems of Institutional Care.* Arlington, Tex.: National Association for Retarded Citizens (NARC), 1969. 40¢.

Standards for Residential Facilities for the Mentally Retarded. 1971. (Available from: Program Director, Accreditation Council for Facilities for the Mentally Retarded, 875 North Michigan Avenue, Suite 2201, Chicago, Ill. 60511; Softcover, $3.50; hardcover, $6.).

BOOKS ON RESIDENTIAL ALTERNATIVES

Bergman, Joel S. and Cronin, Joan. *Community Homes for the Retarded.* Lexington: D. C. Heath, 1975.

Cherington, Carolyn, and Dybwad, Gunnar, eds. *New Neighbors: The Retarded Citizen in Quest of a Home.* President's Committee on Mental Retardation, 1974, 1976. $2.[1]

Clarke, Bill. *Enough Room for Joy: Jean Vanier's L'Arche—A Message for Our Time.* New York: Paulist Press, 1974. $4.95.

Dickman, Irving R. *No Place Like Home: Alternative Living Arrangements for Teenagers and Adults with Cerebral Palsy.* United Cerebral Palsy Association, Inc. (66 East 34 Street, New York, N.Y. 10016) 1975. $2.25.

[1] All U.S. government publications are available from the Superintendent of Documents, U.S. Government Printing Office, Washington D.C. 20402.

Fanning, John W. *A Common Sense Approach to Community Living Arrangements for the Mentally Retarded.* New York: Charles C. Thomas, 1975.

Laurie, Gini, and McQivinn, Donna. *Housing and Home Services for the Disabled.* New York: Harper & Row, 1976.

May, Elizabeth E. et al. *Independent Living for the Handicapped and the Elderly.* Boston: Houghton Mifflin, 1974.

President's Committee on Mental Retardation. *New Environments for Retarded People.* 1975. $1.15.[1]

BOOKS ON RECREATION

The Easter Seal Directory of Resident Camps for Persons with Special Needs. National Easter Seal Society, 1975 (Available from National Easter Seal Society for Crippled Children and Adults, 2023 West Ogden Avenue, Chicago, Ill. 60612). $1.50.

Kamnetz, Herman L. *Wheelchair Book: Mobility for the Disabled.* Springfield, Ill.: C. C. Thomas, 1969.

Nelson, John G. *Wheelchair Vagabond.* Santa Monica, Ca.: Project Publishing and Design, 1975. Paperback $4.95.

Sexuality and Sex Education

Organizations

National Council of Churches Committee
on Marriage and the Family
475 Riverside Drive
New York, N.Y. 10027

BOOKS ON SEXUALITY (GENERAL)

Bass, Medora S., ed. *Sexual Rights and Responsibilities of the Mentally Retarded.* 1975. 2d. ed. (Available from the editor, 216 Glenn Road, Ardmore, Pa. 19003; $2.50.)

De la Cruz, Felix F., and LaVeck, Gerald D., eds. *Human Sexuality and the Mentally Retarded.* Brunner/Mazel, 1973. $8.95. (Paperback edition from Penguin Books, $2.95.)

Gordon, Sol. *Let's Make Sex a Household Word: A Guide for Parents and Teachers.* New York: John Day Co., 1975.

---

[1] All U.S. government publications are available from the Superintendent of Documents, U.S. Government Printing Office, Washington D.C. 20402.

Pomeroy, Wardell. *Boys and Sex*. New York: Delacorte Press, 1969.
————. *Girls and Sex*. New York: Delacorte Press, 1969.

BOOKS ON SEXUALITY FOR PARENTS AND CHILDREN
Gordon, Sol. *Facts About Sex*. New York: John Day Co., 1973. (For pre-teen-agers.)
————. *Facts About Sex for Exceptional Youth*. East Orange, N.J.: New Jersey Association for Brain Injured Children, 1969.
————. *Living Fully: For Young People with a Handicap, Their Parents, Their Teachers, and Professionals*. New York: John Day Co., 1975.

Sex Information and Education Council of the U.S. (SIECUS)
1885 Broadway
New York, N.Y. 10028

Synagogue Council of America
Committee on Family
235 Fifth Avenue
New York, N.Y. 10016

U.S. Catholic Conference
Family Life Bureau
1312 Massachusetts Avenue Northwest
Washington, D.C. 20005

Bibliographies
Child Study Association
98 Ninth Street
New York, N.Y. 10028
Public Affairs Pamphlets
381 Park Avenue
New York, N.Y. 10016

Film and Workshop Training Program
"On Being Sexual"
Stanfield House
900 Euclid Avenue
P.O. Box 3208
Santa Monica, Calif. 90403

State Special Education Programs

ALABAMA: Consultant, Program for Exceptional Children and Youth, State Department of Education, Montgomery 36104.

ALASKA: Director, Instructional Services, State Department of Education, Juneau 99801.

ARIZONA: Director of Special Education, State Department of Public Instruction, Capitol Building, Phoenix 85007.

ARKANSAS: Director of Instruction and Special Education, State Department of Education, Little Rock 72201.

CALIFORNIA: Chief, Bureau of Special Education, State Department of Education, 721 Capitol Mall, Sacramento 95814.

COLORADO: Director, Division of Special Education Services, State Department of Education, State Office Building, Denver 80203.

CONNECTICUT: Chief, Bureau of Pupil Personnel and Special Education Services, State Department of Education, Hartford 06115.

DELAWARE: Director of Special Education, State Department of Public Instruction, Townsend Building, Dover 19901.

DISTRICT OF COLUMBIA: Director of Special Education, Magruder Building, 1619 M Street N.W., Washington, D.C. 20036.

FLORIDA: Administrator, Exceptional Child Education, State Department of Education, Tallahassee 32304.

GEORGIA: Director of Special Education, State Department of Education, Atlanta 30334.

HAWAII: Director of Special Education, State Department of Education, Honolulu 96813.

IDAHO: Supervisor, Special Education, State Department of Education, Boise 83707.

ILLINOIS: Director, Department for Exceptional Children, Office of the Superintendent of Public Instruction, 1020 South Spring Street, Springfield 62706.

INDIANA: Director, Division of Special Education, State Department of Public Instruction, Indianapolis 46204.

IOWA: Director, Division of Special Education, State Department of Public Instruction, Des Moines 50319.

KANSAS: Director, Division of Special Education, State Department of Education, Topeka 66612.

KENTUCKY: Director, Division of Special Education, State Department of Education, Frankfort 40601.

LOUISIANA: Supervisor, Special Education, State Department of Education, Baton Rouge 70804.

MAINE: Director of Special Education, State Department of Educational and Cultural Services, Augusta 04330.

MARYLAND: Coordinator of Office of Special Education, State Department of Education, Baltimore 21240.

MASSACHUSETTS: Director, Division of Special Education, State Department of Education, 182 Tremont Street, Boston 02111.

MICHIGAN: Director of Special Education, State Department of Public Instruction, P.O. Box 420, Lansing 48902.

MINNESOTA: Director, Division of Special Education, State Department of Education, St. Paul 55101.

MISSISSIPPI: Supervisor of Special Education, State Department of Education, P.O. Box 771, Jackson 39205.

MISSOURI: Director of Special Education, State Department of Education, Jefferson City 65101.

MONTANA: Supervisor of Special Education, State Department of Public Instruction, Helena 59601.

NEBRASKA: Director of Special Education, State Department of Education, Lincoln 68508.

NEVADA: Director, Special Education, State Department of Education, Carson City 89701.

NEW HAMPSHIRE: Director of Special Education, State Department of Education, Concord 03301.

NEW JERSEY: Director, Special Education, State Department of Education, 225 West State Street, Trenton 08625.

NEW MEXICO: Director of Special Education, State Department of Education, State Educational Building, Sante Fe 87501.

NEW YORK: Director, Division for Handicapped Children, State Education Department, Albany 12224.

NORTH CAROLINA: Director, Special Education, State Department of Public Instruction, Raleigh 27602.

NORTH DAKOTA: Director of Special Education, State Department of Public Instruction, Bismarck 58501.

OHIO: Director, Division of Special Education, State Department of Education, 933 High Street, Worthington 43085.

OKLAHOMA: Director of Special Education, State Department of Education, Oklahoma City 73105.

OREGON: Director of Special Education, State Department of Education, Salem 97310.

PENNSYLVANIA: Director, Bureau of Special Education, State Department of Education, Box 911, Harrisburg 17126.

RHODE ISLAND: Director of Special Education, State Department of Education, Providence 02908.

SOUTH CAROLINA: Director of Special Education, State Department of Education, Columbia 29201.

SOUTH DAKOTA: Director of Special Education, State Department of Public Instruction, Pierre 57501.

TENNESSEE: Director of Special Education, State Department of Education, Nashville 37219.

TEXAS: Assistant Commissioner for Special Education, Texas Education Agency, Austin 78701.

UTAH: Director of Pupil Services and Special Education, State Board of Education, 136 East South Temple, Salt Lake City 84111.

VERMONT: Director of Special Education, State Department of Education, Montpelier 05602.

VIRGINIA: Director of Special Education, State Department of Education, Richmond 23216.

WASHINGTON: Supervisor of Special Education, State Department of Public Instruction, Olympia 98504.

WEST VIRGINIA: Director of Special Education, State Department of Education, Charleston 25305.

WISCONSIN: Director, Bureau for Exceptional Children, State Department of Public Instruction, Madison 53702.

WYOMING: Director of Special Education, State Department of Education, Cheyenne 82001.

Selected, Annotated Bibliography

The following is a list of books we have found particularly helpful. Please refer to each chapter for references on specific topics.

Apgar, Virginia, and Beck, Joan. *Is My Baby Alright?* New York: Trident Press, 1974 (paperback: Pocket Books, 1974 $1.95). The world-renowned Dr. Apgar was the creator of the "APGAR" scoring system for newborn infants. This book is a guide to birth defects; it is written in clear, precise language and includes a chapter on how to prevent birth defects.

Ayrault, Evelyn West. *You Can Raise Your Handicapped Child.* New York: G. P. Putnam's Sons, 1964. Approaches to the problems of a handicapped child within the family, neighborhood, school, and community, with emphasis on the attitudes of younger children.

———. *Helping the Handicapped Teenager Mature.* New York: Association Press, 1971. The problems encountered by children with handicaps as they enter adolescence and young adulthood. Emphasis on mental retardation and learning disabilities.

Blank, Joseph P. *19 Steps up the Mountain.* Philadelphia: Lippincott, 1976. The story of the DeBolt family, who have adopted ten children, and the challenges and rewards of parenting children with special needs.

Brightman, Alan J., Ph.D. *Like Me.* Boston: Little, Brown & Co., 1976. A children's book with sensitive color photographs and text on the feelings and experiences of a retarded child.

Brutten, Milton, Ph.D.; Richardson, Sylvia O., M.D.; and Mangel, Charles. *Something's Wrong with My Child, A Parent's Book About Children with Learning Disabilities.* New York: Harcourt, Brace, Jovanovich, 1973. The source book for the Public Television special "The Puzzle Children."

Canning, Clara D. and Joseph P. *The Gift of Martha.* Boston: Children's Hospital Medical Center, 1975. A sensitive personal story, with superb photos, by the parents of Martha, a child with Down's syndrome.

Fassler, Joan, Ph.D. *Howie Helps Himself.* Chicago: Albert Whitman, 1975. A children's book about a boy with cerebral palsy learning to help himself and discovering his own value.

————. *One Little Girl.* New York: Behavioral Publications, 1968. A children's story about a "slow" child who learns about her accomplishments as well as her limitations. The author has also written several other children's books about problems of children.

Gauchat, Dorothy. *All God's Children.* New York: Hawthorn Books, 1976. Personal experiences of a family who parented many severely handicapped children through foster care.

Killilea, Marie. *Karen.* New York: Dell, 1952. A classic story written by the mother of a child with cerebral palsy.

————. *With Love from Karen.* New York: Dell, 1963. Sequel to *Karen* follows her through adolescence.

Koch, Richard, M.D., and Kathryn Jean. *Understanding the Mentally Retarded Child: A New Approach.* New York: Random House, 1974. A clear insight overview of new approaches in the field of mental retardation.

Kravik Patrica J., ed. *Adopting Children with Special Needs.* North American Council on Adoptable Children, 1977 (6 Madison Avenue, Ossining, N.Y. 10562). $4. An unusual book of personal experiences by parents, relatives, and professionals about the adoption of children with special emotional, physical, and mental needs.

Kvaraceus, William C., and Hayes, Nelson E. *If Your Child Is Handicapped.* Boston: Porter, Sargent, Inc., 1969. Personal stories of parents coping with the concerns of children with special needs.

Lasker, Joe. *He's My Brother.* Chicago: Albert Whitman, 1974. A children's story about a boy whose brother has a learning disability; a sensitive book, one to share with all children.

McDonald, Eugene T. *Understand Those Feelings.* Englewood, N.J.: Prentice-Hall, 1964. A guide for parents of special-needs children as well as for professionals.

McNamara, Joan. *Families.* 1976. (Available from North American Council on Adoptable Children, 6 Madison Avenue, Ossining, N.Y.). $1. A coloring book about different families, which includes pictures of children with physical handicaps and spaces for free drawing.

Park, Clara Clairborne, and Shapiro, Leon N., M.D. *You Are Not Alone: Understanding and Dealing with Mental Illness.* Boston: Little, Brown & Co., 1976. A guide for patients, families, and professionals.

Stein, Sara Bonnett. *About Handicaps.* New York: Walker & Co., 1974. A children's story about a friendship between two boys, one of whom has cerebral palsy, and the feelings each has about differences and about handicaps.

Viscardi, John. *The Phoenix Child.* New York: Paul S. Ericksson, 1975. A story about a handicapped foster child written by a man who has experienced a handicap and gone on to help others reach their potential. Mr. Viscardi is the author of several other books on handicaps.

Weiner, Florence. *Help for the Handicapped Child.* New York: McGraw-Hill, 1973. A resource book cataloguing a variety of handicapping conditions and resources for each.

Wentworth, Elsie H. *Listen to Your Heart: A Message to Parents of Handicapped Children.* Boston: Houghton Mifflin, 1974. A sensitive caring book about problems families face with a child with special needs, and gentle suggestions on how to cope with them.

Wolf, Bernard. *Connie's New Eyes.* Philadelphia: Lippincott, 1976. A children's story about a young teacher at a school for severely handicapped children, who is blind, and her acquisition of a Seeing Eye dog. Realistic photos.

———. *Don't Feel Sorry for Paul.* Philadelphia: Lippincott, 1974. A children's book with outstanding photographs about a little boy with artificial limbs.

Directory Accredited Private Home Study Schools. (Available from National Home Study Council, 1601 18th Street Northwest, Washington, D.C. 20009.) Free.

Smith, Clodus R. *Planning and Paying Your Way to College.* New York: Macmillan, 1968.

Splaver, Sarah. *Nontraditional College Routes to Careers.* New York: Julian Messner, 1975.

———. *Your Career if You're Not Going to College.* New York: Julian Messner, 1971.

Education

Hall, Robert E. and Lehman, Eileen F. *A Directory of Some Colleges and Universities with Special Facilities to Accommodate Handicapped Students.* 1967. (Available U.S. Department of Health, Education, and Welfare, Office of Education, Washington, D.C. 20201.) 10 pp.

Employment

A Job and Independence. A Reading List. 1962. (Available from the President's Committee on Employment of the Handicapped, Washington, D.C. 20210.) 8 pp.

Arthur, Julietta K. *Employment for the Handicapped.* Nashville, Tenn: Abingdon Press, 1967. 272 pp.

Employment of the Handicapped in Federal Service. 1966. (Available from U.S. Civil Service Commission, Washington, D.C. 20415.) 5 pp.

For the Disabled: Help through Vocational Rehabilitation. 1965. U.S. Department of Health, Education, and Welfare, Vocational Rehabilitation Administration, Washington, D.C. 20201.) 16 pp.

Gordon M. Hayes, compiler. *National Directory of Special Education Preparation Programs.* Sacramento, Calif.: California State Department of Education, 1967. 34 pp.

Some Do's & Don'ts When Applying for Work: Tips for Handicapped Job Seekers. 1962. (Available from the President's Committee on Employment of the Handicapped, Washington, D.C. 20210.) Folder.

United States Civil Service Regions

Region	Headquarters	Area Served
Atlanta	Atlanta Merchandise Mart 240 Peachtree Street Northwest Atlanta, Ga. 30303	Alabama, Florida, Georgia, Kentucky, Mississippi, North Carolina, South Carolina, Tennessee
Boston	Post Office and Courthouse Building Boston, Mass. 02109	Connecticut, Maine, Massachusetts, New Hampshire Rhode Island, Vermont
Chicago	Main Post Office Building 433 West Van Buren Street Chicago, Ill. 60607	Illinois, Indiana, Michigan, Minnesota, Ohio, Wisconsin
Dallas	1114 Commerce Street Dallas, Tex. 75202	Arkansas, Louisiana, New Mexico, Oklahoma, Texas
Denver	Building 20 Denver Federal Center Denver, Colo. 80225	Colorado, Montana, North Dakota, South Dakota, Utah, Wyoming
New York	New Federal Building 26 Federal Plaza New York, N.Y. 10007	New Jersey, New York, Puerto Rico, Virgin Islands
Philadelphia	William J. Green Jr. Federal Building 600 Arch Street Philadelphia, Pa. 19106	Delaware, Maryland, Pennsylvania, Virginia, West Virginia
Saint Louis	1256 Federal Building 1520 Market Street Saint Louis, Mo. 63103	Iowa, Kansas, Missouri, Nebraska
San Francisco	Federal Building Box 36010 450 Golden Gate Avenue San Francisco, Calif. 94102	Arizona, California, Hawaii, Nevada, Pacific overseas area
Seattle	3004 Federal Office Building First Avenue and Madison Street Seattle, Wash. 98104	Alaska, Idaho, Oregon, Washington
Washington, D.C.	U.S. Civil Service Commission Washington, D.C. 20415	Washington D.C., adjacent parts of Maryland and Virginia, overseas areas not covered in other regions

List of Agencies and Organizations, Arranged Alphabetically by States, that Help the Handicapped in the Pursuit of Employment*

The following agencies and organizations have counselors to advise disabled persons as to employment.

ALABAMA

Alabama Society for Crippled Children and Adults, Inc.
  2125 East South Blvd.,
  P.O. Box 6130,
  Montgomery, Ala. 36106
  Occupational and physical therapy.
  Write for the address of nearest
  Easter Seal Office.
Goodwill Industries of America, Inc.
  Write to the national office, 1913 N
  St., N. W., Washington, D.C. 20036
  for address of nearest local office.
  Employment of disabled persons to
  suit their limitations.
Small Business Administration
  908 South 20th St.,
  Birmingham, Ala. 35205
  Organizational advice and financial
  help for the self-employed.
State Employment Service
  See telephone directory for the
  nearest local office.
  Employment counsel and placement.
U.S. Civil Service Commission
  For employment with U.S. Government.
  Write to Georgia regional office.
U.S. Department of Commerce
  908 South 20th St.,
  Birmingham, Ala. 35205
  Marketing and commercial information.
U.S. Veterans Administration
  Aronov Building,
  474 South Court,
  Montgomery, Ala. 36104
  Veterans affairs.
Vocational Rehabilitation
  416 State Office Building,
  Montgomery, Ala. 36104

Vocational training rehabilitation
(17 local offices in the state)

ALASKA

Alaska Crippled Children's Association, Inc.
  225 "E" St.,
  Anchorage, Alaska 99501
  Occupational and physical therapy.
  Write for the address of nearest
  Easter Seal Office.
Goodwill Industries of America, Inc.
  Write to the national office, 1913 N
  St., N.W., Washington, D.C. 20036
  for address of nearest local office.
  Employment of disabled persons to
  suit their limitations.
Office of Vocational Rehabilitation
  P.O. Box 2568,
  Juneau, Alaska 99801
  Vocational training rehabilitation.
  (4 local offices in the state)
Small Business Administration
  632 Sixth Ave.,
  P.O. Box 999,
  Anchorage, Alaska 99501
  Organizational advice and financial
  help for the self-employed.
State Employment Service
  Employment counseling and placement.
  See telephone directory for the
  nearest local office.
U.S. Civil Service Commission
  Write to Washington State regional
  office.
  Employment with U.S. Government.
U.S. Department of Commerce
  306 Loussac-Sogn Building,
  Anchorage, Alaska 99501
  Marketing and commercial information.

* Juvenal L. Angel, *Employment Opportunities for the Handicapped* (New York: World Trade Press) , 1969.

U.S. Veterans Administration
Goldstein Building,
P.O. Box 2629,
Juneau, Alaska 99801
Veterans affairs.

ARIZONA

Department of Public Welfare
State Office Building,
1624 West Adams,
Phoenix, Arizona 85007

Division of Vocational Rehabilitation
7 North 15th Ave.,
Phoenix, Arizona 85007
Vocational training rehabilitation.

Easter Seal Society for Crippled
Children and Adults of Arizona, Inc.
550 West Indian School Road,
Phoenix, Arizona 85013
Write for the address of nearest
Easter Seal Office.

Goodwill Industries of America, Inc.
Write to the national office, 1913 N
St., N.W., Washington, D.C. 20036
for address of nearest local office.
Employment of disabled persons to
suit their limitations.

Small Business Administration
2727 N. Central Ave.,
Phoenix, Arizona 85004
Organizational advice and financial
help for the self-employed.

State Employment Service
See telephone directory for the
nearest local office.
Employment counseling and placement.

U.S. Civil Service Commission
Write to Colorado Regional office.
Employment with U.S. Government.

U.S. Department of Commerce
5413 New Federal Building,
230 North First Ave.,
Phoenix, Arizona 85025
Marketing and commercial information.

U.S. Veterans Administration
230 N. First Ave.,
Phoenix, Arizona 85025
Veterans affairs.

ARKANSAS

Arkansas Association for the Crippled, Inc.
2081 Lee Ave.,
Little Rock, Ark. 72205
Occupational and physical therapy.
Write for the address of nearest
Easter Seal office.

Arkansas Rehabilitation Service
211 Broadway,
Little Rock, Ark. 72201
Vocational training rehabilitation.
(20 local offices in the state)

Goodwill Industries of America, Inc.,
Write to the national office, 1913 N
St., N.W., Washington, D.C. 20036
for address of nearest local office.
Employment of disabled persons to
suit their limitations.

Rehabilitation Services for the Blind
900 West 4th St.,
Little Rock, Ark. 72201
Vocational training rehabilitation.

Small Business Administration
600 W. Capital Ave.,
Little Rock, Ark. 72201
Organizational advice and financial
help for the self-employed.

State Employment Service
Employment counseling and placement.
See telephone directory for the
nearest local office.

U.S. Veterans Administration
700 West Capitol Ave.,
Little Rock, Ark. 72201
Veterans affairs.

CALIFORNIA

Bureau of Vocational Rehabilitation
721 Capitol Ave.,
Sacramento, Calif. 95814
Vocational training rehabilitation.
(26 local offices in the state)

Easter Seal Society for Crippled Children
and Adults of California
228 McAllister St.,
San Francisco, Calif. 94102
Occupational and physical therapy.
Write for the address of nearest
Easter Seal office.

Goodwill Industries of America, Inc.
Write to the national office, 1913 N
St., N.W., Washington, D.C. 20036
for address of nearest local office.
Employment of disabled persons to
suit their limitations.
Small Business Administration
Organizational advice and financial
help for the self-employed.
312 W. 5th St.,
Los Angeles, Calif. 90013
110 W. C. St.,
San Diego, Calif. 92101
450 Golden Gate Ave.,
San Francisco, Calif. 94102
State Department of Rehabilitation
and Div. of Rehabilitation of the Blind
1500 Fifth St.,
Sacramento, Calif. 95814
Vocational training rehabilitation.
U.S. Civil Service Commission
450 Golden Gate Ave.,
San Francisco, Calif. 94102
Employment with U.S. Government.
U.S. Department of Commerce
Marketing and commercial information.
1031 South Broadway,
Los Angeles, Calif. 90015
450 Golden Gate Ave.,
San Francisco, Calif. 94102
U.S. Veterans Administration
Veterans affairs.
49 Fourth St.,
San Francisco, Calif. 94103
1380 South Sepulveda Blvd.,
Los Angeles, Calif. 90073

COLORADO

Colorado Society for Crippled Children
and Adults, Inc.
110 Sixteenth St.,
Denver, Colo. 80202
Write for the address of nearest
Easter Seal office.
Department of Rehabilitation
705 State Services Building,
Denver, Colo. 80203
Vocational training rehabilitation.
Goodwill Industries of America, Inc.
Write to the national office, 1913 N

St., N.W., Washington, D.C. 20036
for address of nearest local office.
Employment of disabled persons to
suit their limitations.
Small Business Administration
1961 Stout St.,
Denver, Colo. 80202
Organizational advice and financial
help for the self-employed.
State Employment Service
Employment counseling and placement.
See telephone directory for the
nearest local office.
U.S. Civil Service Commission
Building 20,
Denver Federal Center,
Denver, Colo. 80225
Employment with the U.S. Government.
U.S. Department of Commerce
16419 Federal Building,
20th and Stout St.,
Denver, Colo. 80202
Marketing and commercial information.
U.S. Veterans Administration
Denver Federal Center,
Denver, Colo. 80225
Veterans affairs.

CONNECTICUT

Board of Education and Services for
the Blind
State Office Building,
165 Capitol Avenue,
Hartford, Conn. 06115
Vocational rehabilitation for the blind.
Connecticut Society for Crippled
Children and Adults, Inc.
682 Prospect Ave.,
Hartford, Conn. 06105
Occupational and physical therapy.
Write for the address of nearest
Easter Seal office.
Connecticut Bureau of Vocational
Rehabilitation
33 Garden St.,
Hartford, Conn. 06105
Vocational training rehabilitation.
Goodwill Industries of America, Inc.
Write to the national office, 1913 N
St., N.W., Washington, D.C. 20036

for address of nearest local office.
Employment of disabled persons to
suit their limitations.

Small Business Administration
450 Main St.,
Hartford, Conn. 06103
Organizational advice and financial
help for the self-employed.

Connecticut State Employment Service
Employment counseling and placement.
See telephone directory for the
nearest local office.

U.S. Civil Service Commission
Employment with U.S. Government
Write to Massachusetts regional office.

U.S. Department of Commerce
18 Asylum St.,
Hartford, Conn. 06103
Marketing and commercial information.

U.S. Veterans Administration
450 Main St.,
Hartford, Conn. 06103
Veterans affairs.

DELAWARE

Delaware Commission for the Blind
305 West 8th St.,
Wilmington, Del. 19801
Vocational rehabilitation of the blind.

Delaware Society for Crippled Children
and Adults, Inc.
1324 Market St.,
Wilmington, Del. 19801
Occupational and physical therapy.

Delaware State Employment Service
Employment counseling and placement.
See telephone directory for the
nearest local office.

Goodwill Industries of America, Inc.
Write to the national office, 1913 N
St., N.W., Washington, D.C. 20036
for address of nearest local office.
Employment of disabled persons to
suit their limitations.

JOB (Just-One-Break, Inc.)
Wilmington, Del.
Free employment service for
the handicapped.

Rehabilitation Division
1300 Shallcross Ave.,

P.O. Box 1190,
Wilmington, Del. 19899
Vocational training rehabilitation.

U.S. Civil Service Commission
Employment with U.S. Government.
Write to Pennsylvania regional office.

U.S. Veterans Administration
1601 Kirkwood Highway,
Wilmington, Del. 19899
Veterans affairs.

DISTRICT OF COLUMBIA

Department of Vocational Rehabilitation
1331 H St., N.W.,
Washington, D.C.
Vocational training rehabilitation

District of Columbia Employment Service
Employment counseling and placement.
See telephone directory for the nearest
local office.

District of Columbia Society for the
Crippled Children, Inc.
2800 Thirteenth St., N.W.,
Washington, D.C. 20009
Occupational and physical therapy.

Davis Memorial Goodwill Industries
1218 New Hampshire Ave., N.W.,
Washington, D.C. 20036
Employment of disabled persons to
suit their limitations.

Small Business Administration
1321 N St., N.W.,
Washington, D.C. 20417
Organizational advice and financial
help for the self-employed.

U.S. Civil Service Commission
Washington, D.C. 20415
Employment with U.S. Government.
(The Washington, D.C. metropolitan
area and overseas areas, except the
Pacific, are under jurisdiction of the
U.S. Civil Service Commission.)

U.S. Civil Service Commission
Medical Division
1900 E St., N.W.,
Washington, D.C. 20415
Employment with U.S. Government.
(The handicapped should address the
Medical Division of the Commission.)

U.S. Veterans Administration
810 Vermont Ave., N.W.,
Washington, D.C. 20420
Veterans affairs.
Vocational Rehabilitation Administration
Washington, D.C. 20201
Supervise the federal programs for
the vocational rehabilitation of the
handicapped.

FLORIDA

Division of Vocational Rehabilitation
725 South Bronough St.,
Tallahassee, Fla. 32304
Vocational training rehabilitation.
Florida Council for the Blind
108 W. Pensacola St.,
Tallahassee, Fla. 32301
Vocational rehabilitation for the
blind.
Florida Society for Crippled Children
and Adults, Inc.
1712 Le Road,
Orlando, Fla. 32801
Occupational and physical therapy.
Write for the address of nearest
Easter Seal Office.
Florida State Employment Service
Employment counseling and placement.
See telephone directory for the
nearest local office.
Goodwill Industries of America, Inc.
Write to the national office, 1913 N
St., N.W., Washington, D.C. 20036
for address of nearest local office.
Employment of disabled persons
to suit their limitations.
Small Business Administration
Organizational advice and financial
help for the self-employed.
47 W. Forsyth, Jacksonville, Fla. 32202
51 S.W. 1st Ave.,
Miami, Fla. 33130
U.S. Civil Service Commission
Employment with U.S. Government.
Write to Georgia regional office.
U.S. Department of Commerce
Marketing and commercial information.
201 Laura St.,
Jacksonville, Fla. 32202

51 S.W. First Ave.,
Miami, Fla. 33130
U.S. Veterans Administration
P.O. Box 1437,
St. Petersburg, Fla. 33731
Veterans affairs.

GEORGIA

Georgia Division of Vocational
Rehabilitation
129 State Office Building
Atlanta, Ga. 30334
Vocational training rehabilitation.
(23 local offices in the state)
Georgia Society for Crippled Children
and Adults, Inc.
1211 Spring St., N.W.,
Atlanta, Ga. 30309
Occupational and physical therapy.
Write for the address of nearest
Easter Seal office.
Georgia State Employment Service
Employment counseling and placement.
See telephone directory for the
nearest local office.
Goodwill Industries of America, Inc.
Write to the national office, 1913 N
St., N.W., Washington, D.C. 20036
for address of nearest local office.
Employment of disabled persons to
suit their limitations.
Small Business Administration
52 Fairie St., N.W.,
Atlanta, Ga. 30303
Organizational advice and financial
help for the self-employed.
U.S. Civil Service Commission
Atlanta Merchandise Mart,
240 Peachtree St., N.W.,
Atlanta, Ga. 30303
Employment with U.S. Government.
U.S. Department of Commerce
Marketing and commercial information.
4th Floor, Homes Savings Building,
75 Forsyth St., N.W.,
Atlanta, Ga. 30303
125-29 Bull St.,
Savannah, Ga. 31402

U.S. Veterans Administration
441-449 West Peachtree St., N.E.,
Atlanta, Ga. 30308
Veterans affairs.

HAWAII

Goodwill Industries of America, Inc.
Write to the national office, 1913 N
St., N.W., Washington, D.C. 20036
for address of nearest local office.
Employment of disabled persons to
suit their limitations.
Hawaii Chapter, National Society for
Crippled Children and Adults, Inc.
1018 Lunalilo St., P.O. Box 2318,
Honolulu, Hawaii 96822
Occupational and physical therapy.
Hawaii Division of Vocational
Rehabilitation
Department of Education,
Queen Liliukalani Building,
P.O. Box 2360,
Honolulu, Hawaii 96804
Vocational training rehabilitation.
Hawaii State Employment Service
Employment counseling and placement.
See telephone directory for the
nearest local office.
Rehabilitation Services Branch for the
Blind and Visually Handicapped
Department of Social Services,
P.O. Box 339,
Honolulu, Hawaii 96809
Vocational rehabilitation for the blind.
Small Business Administration
1149 Bethel St.,
Honolulu, Hawaii 96813
Organizational advice and financial
help for the self-employed.
U.S. Civil Service Commission
Employment with U.S. Government.
Write to the regional office in
California.
U.S. Department of Commerce
202 International Savings Building,
1022 Bethel St.,
Honolulu, Hawaii 96813
Marketing and commercial information.
U.S. Veterans Administration
680 Ala Moana Blvd.,

P.O. Box 3198,
Honolulu, Hawaii 96801
Veterans affairs.

IDAHO

Goodwill Industries of America, Inc.
Write to the national office, 1913 N
St., N.W., Washington, D.C. 20036
for address of nearest local office.
Employment of disabled persons to
suit their limitations.
Idaho Department of Public Assistance
Continental Building, Box 1189,
Boise, Idaho 83701
Vocational training rehabilitation.
Idaho Society for Crippled Children
and Adults, Inc.
128 S. Fifth St.,
Boise, Idaho 83702
Occupational and physical therapy.
Write for the address of nearest
Easter Seal office.
Idaho State Employment Service
Employment counseling and placement.
See telephone directory for the
nearest local office.
Small Business Administration
216 N. 8th St.,
Boise, Idaho 83702
Organizational advice and financial
help for the self-employed.
U.S. Veterans Administration
Fifth and Fort St.,
Boise, Idaho 83701
Veterans affairs.
Vocational Rehabilitation Service
210 Eastman Building,
Boise, Idaho 83702
Vocational training rehabilitation.

ILLINOIS

Goodwill Industries of America, Inc.
Write to the national office, 1913 N
St., N.W., Washington, D.C. 20036
for address of nearest local office.
Employment of disabled persons to
suit their limitations.
Illinois Association for the Crippled, Inc.
2715 S. 4th St., P.O. Box 1767,
Springfield, Ill. 62705

Occupational and physical therapy.
Write for the address of nearest
Easter Seal office.

Illinois Division of Vocational
Rehabilitation
623 East Adams St.,
Springfield, Ill. 62706
Vocational training rehabilitation.
(23 local offices in the state)

Illinois State Employment Service
Employment counseling and placement.
See telephone directory for the
nearest local office.

Small Business Administration
219 S. Dearborn St.,
Chicago, Ill. 60604
Organizational advice and financial
help for the self-employed.

U.S. Civil Service Commission
Main Post Office Building,
433 W. Van Buren St.,
Chicago, Ill. 60607
Employment with the U.S. Government.

U.S. Department of Commerce
210 South Dearborn St.,
Chicago, Ill. 60604
Commercial and marketing information.

U.S. Veterans Administration
2030 West Taylor St.,
Chicago, Ill. 60612
Veterans affairs.

INDIANA

Goodwill Industries of America, Inc.
Write to the national office, 1913 N
St., N.W., Washington, D.C. 20036
for address of nearest local office.
Employment of disabled persons to
suit their limitations.

Indiana Agency for the Blind
536 West 30th St.,
Indianapolis, Ind. 46223
Vocational training rehabilitation.

Indiana Board of Industrial Aid and
Vocational Rehabilitation for the Blind
536 West 30th St.,
Indianapolis, Ind. 46223
Vocational rehabilitation for the blind.

Indiana Division of Vocational
Rehabilitation
401 State House,
Indianapolis, Ind. 46204
Vocational training rehabilitation.

Indiana Society for Crippled Children
and Adults, Inc.
3616 Sherman Drive,
Indianapolis, Ind. 46218
Occupational and physical therapy.
Write for the address of nearest
Easter Seal Office.

Indiana State Employment Service
Employment counseling and placement.
See telephone directory for the
nearest local office.

Small Business Administration
911 S. Pennsylvania St.,
Indianapolis, Ind. 46202
Organizational advice and financial
help for the self-employed.

U.S. Civil Service Commission
Employment with the U.S. Government.
Write to the regional office in Chicago.

U.S. Veterans Administration
36 South Pennsylvania St.,
Indianapolis, Ind. 46209
Veterans affairs.

IOWA

Goodwill Industries of America, Inc.
Write to the national office, 1913 N
St., N.W., Washington, D.C. 20036
for address of nearest local office.
Employment of disabled persons to
suit their limitations.

Iowa Commission for the Blind
Fourth and Keosauqua,
Des Moines, Iowa 50309
Vocational rehabilitation for the blind.

Iowa Division of Vocational
Rehabilitation
415 Bankers Trust Building,
Des Moines, Iowa 50309
Vocational training rehabilitation.

Iowa Society for Crippled Children
and Adults, Inc.
P.O. Box 911,
Des Moines, Iowa 50309

Occupational and physical therapy.
Write for the address of nearest
Easter Seal office.

Iowa State Employment Service
Employment counseling and placement.
See telephone directory for the
nearest local office.

Small Business Administration
5th St. and Grand Ave.,
Des Moines, Iowa 50309
Organizational advice and financial
help for the self-employed.

U.S. Civil Service Commission
Employment with U.S. Government.
See telephone directory for the
nearest regional office.

U.S. Department of Commerce
1216 Paramount Building,
509 Grand Ave.,
Des Moines, Iowa 50309
Marketing and commercial information.

U.S. Veterans Administration
Veterans Administration Hospital,
Des Moines, Iowa 50308
Veterans affairs.

KANSAS

Division of Vocational Rehabilitation
State Board for Vocational Education,
State Office Building,
Topeka, Kans. 66612
Vocational training rehabilitation.

Goodwill Industries of America, Inc.
Write to the national office, 1913 N
St., N.W., Washington, D.C. 20036
for address of nearest local office.
Employment of disabled persons to
suit their limitations.

Kansas Society for Crippled Children
801 First National Bank Building
Wichita, Kans. 67202
Occupational and physical therapy.
Write for the address of nearest
Easter Seal office.

Kansas State Employment Service
Employment counseling and placement.
See telephone directory for the
nearest local office.

Services for the Blind
State Department of Social Welfare,
State Office Building,
Topeka, Kans, 66612
Vocational training rehabilitation.

Small Business Administration
120 S. Market St.,
Wichita, Kans. 67202
Organizational advice and financial
help for the self-employed.

U.S. Civil Service Commission
Employment with the U.S. Government.
Write to the regional office in Missouri.

U.S. Department of Commerce
911 Walnut St.,
Kansas City, Mo. 64106
Marketing and commercial information.

U.S. Veterans Administration
5500 East Kellogg,
Wichita, Kans. 67218
Veterans affairs.

KENTUCKY

Bureau of Rehabilitation Services
State Office Bulding,
High St.,
Frankfort, Ky. 40601
Vocational training rehabilitation.
(12 local offices in the state)

Goodwill Industries of America, Inc.
Write to the national office, 1913 N
St., N.W., Washington, D.C. 20036
for address of nearest local office.
Employment of disabled persons to
suit their limitations.

Kentucky Society for Crippled Children
233 E. Broadway,
Louisville, Ky. 40202
Occupational and physical therapy.
Write for the address of nearest
Easter Seal Office.

Kentucky State Employment Service
Employment counseling and placement.
See telephone directory for the
nearest local office.

Small Business Administration
4th and Broadway,
Louisville, Ky. 40202

Organizational advice and financial
help for the self-employed.

U.S. Civil Service Commission
Employment with the U.S. Government.
Write to the regional office in Illinois.

U.S. Veterans Administration
1405 West Broadway,
Louisville, Ky. 40201
Veterans affairs.

LOUISIANA

Goodwill Industries of America, Inc.
Write to the national office, 1913 N
St., N.W., Washington, D.C. 20036
for address of nearest local office.
Employment of disabled persons to
suit their limitations.

Louisiana Chapter, National Society for
Crippled Children and Adults, Inc.
843 Carondelet St.,
New Orleans, La. 70130
Write for address of nearest
local office.

Louisiana State Employment Service
Employment counseling and placement.
See telephone directory for the
nearest local office.

Small Business Administration
610 South St.,
New Orleans, La. 70130
Organizational advice and financial
help for the self-employed.

State Department of Public Welfare
Division for the Blind.
P.O. Box 4065
Baton Rouge, La. 70804
Vocational training rehabilitation.
(4 local offices)

U.S. Civil Service Commission
Employment with U.S. Government.
Write to the regional office in Texas.

U.S. Department of Commerce
610 South St.,
New Orleans, La. 70130
Marketing and commercial information.

U.S. Veterans Administration
701 Layola Ave.,
New Orleans, La. 70113
Veterans affairs.

Vocational Rehabilitation Division
2655 Plank Road,
Baton Rouge, La. 70805
Vocational training rehabilitation.

MAINE

Goodwill Industries of America, Inc.
Write to the national office, 1913 N
St., N.W., Washington, D.C. 20036
for address of nearest local office.
Employment of disabled persons to
suit their limitations.

Division of Eye Care and Special Services
Department of Health and Welfare,
Augusta, Maine 04330
Vocational training rehabilitation.
(2 local offices)

Maine Employment State Service
Employment counseling and placement.
See telephone directory for the
nearest local office.

Pine Tree Society for Crippled Children
and Adults, Inc.
616 High St.,
Bath, Maine 04530
Occupational and physical therapy.
Write for the address of nearest
Easter Seal office.

Small Business Administration
20 Willow St.,
Augusta, Maine 04330
Organizational advice and financial
help for the self-employed.

U.S. Civil Service Commission
Employment with the U.S. Government.
Write to the regional office in
Massachusetts.

U.S. Veterans Administration
Veterans Administration Hospital,
Togue, Maine 04333
Veterans affairs.

Vocational Rehabilitation Division
32 Winthrop St.,
Augusta, Maine 04330
Vocational training rehabilitation.

MARYLAND

Goodwill Industries of America, Inc.
Write to the national office, 1913 N
St., N.W., Washington, D.C. 20036

for address of nearest local office.
Employment of disabled persons to
suit their limitations.

Maryland Division of Vocational
Rehabilitation
  2 West Redwood St.,
  Baltimore, Md. 21201
  Vocational training rehabilitation.
  (13 local offices)

Maryland Division of Vocational
Rehabilitation
  301 Preston St.,
  Baltimore, Md. 21201
  Vocational training rehabilitation.

Maryland Society for Crippled Children
and Adults, Inc.
  3700 Fourth St.
  Baltimore, Md. 21225
  Occupational and physical therapy.
  Write for address of nearest
  local office.

Maryland State Employment Service
  Employment counseling and placement.
  See telephone directory for the
  nearest local office.

Small Business Administration
  Fayette and St. Paul Sts.,
  Baltimore, Md. 21202
  Organizational advice and financial
  help for the self-employed.

U.S. Civil Service Commission
  Employment with U.S. Government.
  Write to the regional office in
  Pennsylvania.

U.S. Department of Commerce
  305 U.S. Customhouse,
  Gay and Lombard Sts.,
  Baltimore, Md. 21202
  Marketing and commercial information.

U.S. Veterans Administration
  Fayette and St. Paul Sts.,
  Baltimore, Md. 21202
  Veterans affairs.

MASSACHUSETTS

Easter Seal Society for Crippled Children
and Adults of Massachusetts, Inc.
  30 Highland St.,
  Worcester, Mass. 01608

Occupational and physical therapy.
Write for address of nearest
local office.

Goodwill Industries of America, Inc.
  Write to the national office, 1913 N
  St., N.W., Washington, D.C. 20036
  for address of nearest local office.
  Employment of disabled persons to
  suit their limitations.

JOB (Just-One-Break, Inc.)
  927 Washington St.,
  Boston, Mass. 02111
  Free employment service.

Massachusetts Division of the Blind
  13 Court Square,
  Boston, Mass. 02108
  Vocational rehabilitation for the blind.

Massachusetts Rehabilitation Commission
  296 Boylston St.,
  Boston, Mass. 02116
  Vocational training rehabilitation.

Massachusetts State Employment Service
  Employment counseling and placement.
  See telephone directory for the
  nearest local office.

Small Business Administration
  470 Atlantic Ave.,
  Boston, Mass. 02210
  Organizational advice and financial
  help for the self-employed.

U.S. Civil Service Commission
  Post Office and Courthouse Building,
  Boston, Mass. 02203
  Employment with U.S. Government.

U.S. Department of Commerce
  J. F. Kennedy Federal Building,
  Boston, Mass. 02203
  Marketing and commercial information.

U.S. Veterans Administration
  1 Beacon St.,
  Boston, Mass. 02108
  Veterans affairs.

MICHIGAN

Department of Social Welfare
  P.O. Box 1016,
  Lansing, Mich. 48904
  Vocational training rehabilitation.
  (4 local offices)

Goodwill Industries of America, Inc.
  Write to the national office, 1913 N
  St., N.W., Washington, D.C. 20036
  for address of nearest local office.
  Employment of disabled persons to
  suit their limitations.
Michigan Society for Crippled Children
and Adults, Inc.
  10601 Puritan Ave.,
  Detroit, Mich. 48238
  Occupational and physical therapy.
  Write for address of nearest local
  office.
Michigan State Employment Service
  Employment counseling and placement.
  See telephone directory for the
  nearest local office.
Office of Services for the Blind
  Department of Social Services,
  520 Hollister Building,
  Lansing, Mich. 48933
  Vocational rehabilitation for the blind.
Small Business Administration
  Organizational advice and financial
  help for the self-employed.
  1249 Washington Blvd.,
  Marquette, Mich. 49855
  502 West Kay Ave.,
  Marquette, Mich. 49855
U.S. Civil Service Commission
  Employment with U.S. Government.
  Write to the regional office in Illinois.
U.S. Department of Commerce
  455 Federal Building,
  Detroit, Mich. 48226
  Marketing and commercial information.
U.S. Veterans Administration
  210 Gratiot Ave.,
  Detroit, Mich. 48231
  Veterans affairs.

MINNESOTA

Goodwill Industries of America, Inc.
  Write to the national office, 1913 N
  St., N.W., Washington, D.C. 20036
  for address of nearest local office.
  Employment of disabled persons to
  suit their limitations.

Division of Vocational Rehabilitation
  4th Floor, Centennial Building,
  St. Paul, Minn. 55101
  Vocational training rehabilitation.
Minnesota Easter Seal Society
  1821 University Ave.,
  St. Paul, Minn. 55104
  Occupational and physical therapy.
  Write for address of nearest
  Easter Seal office.
Minnesota State Employment Service
  Employment counseling and placement.
  See telephone directory for the
  nearest local office.
Small Business Administration
  603 2nd Ave., S.
  Minneapolis, Minn. 55402
  Organizational advice and financial
  help for the self-employed.
State Services for the Blind
  Department of Public Welfare,
  Centennial Building,
  St. Paul, Minn. 55101
  Vocational rehabilitation for the blind.
U.S. Civil Service Commission
  Employment with U.S. Government.
  Write to the regional office in
  Missouri.
U.S. Department of Commerce
  306 Federal Building,
  110 South Fourth St.,
  Minneapolis, Minn. 55401
  Marketing and commercial information.
U.S. Veterans Administration
  Fort Snelling,
  St. Paul, Minn. 55111
  Veterans affairs.

MISSISSIPPI

Goodwill Industries of America, Inc.
  Write to the national office, 1913 N
  St., N.W., Washington, D.C. 20036
  for address of nearest local office.
  Employment of disabled persons to
  suit their limitations.
Mississippi Easter Seal Society
  P.O. Box 2776,
  Jackson, Miss. 39207

Occupational and physical therapy.
Write for address of nearest local
office.

Mississippi State Employment Service
Employment counseling and placement.
See telephone directory for the
nearest local office.

Small Business Administration
Capital and West Sts.,
Jackson, Miss. 39201
Organizational advice and financial
help for the self-employed.

U.S. Civil Service Commission
Employment with U.S. Government.
Write to the regional office in Georgia.

U.S. Veterans Administration
1500 East Woodrow Wilson Drive,
Jackson, Miss. 39216
Veterans affairs.

Vocational Rehabilitation for the Blind
528 N. State St.,
P.O. Box 1669,
Jackson, Miss. 39205
Vocational rehabilitation of the blind.
(10 local offices)

Vocational Rehabilitation Division
State Office Building,
P.O. Box 1698,
Jackson, Miss. 39205
Vocational training rehabilitation.
(22 local offices)

MISSOURI

Bureau of the Blind
Division of Welfare,
State Office Building,
Jefferson City, Mo. 65102
Vocational training rehabilitation.
(5 local offices)

Goodwill Industries of America, Inc.
Write to the national office, 1913 N
St., N.W., Washington, D.C. 20036
for address of nearest local office.
Employment of disabled persons
according to their limitations.

Missouri Society for Crippled Children
and Adults, Inc.
1530 Big Bend Blvd.,
St. Louis, Mo. 63117

Occupational and physical therapy.
Write for address of nearest
local office.

Missouri State Employment Service
Employment counseling and placement.
See telephone directory for the
nearest local office.

Small Business Administration
911 Walnut St.,
Kansas City, Mo. 64106
208 N. Broadway,
St. Louis, Mo. 63102
Organizational advice and financial
help for the self-employed.

U.S. Civil Service Commission
1256 Federal Building,
1520 Market St.,
St. Louis, Mo. 63103
Employment with U.S. Government.

U.S. Department of Commerce
2511 Federal Building,
1520 Market St.,
St. Louis, Mo. 63103
Marketing and commercial information.

U.S. Veterans Administration
911 East Linwood Blvd.,
Kansas City, Mo. 64109
Rm. 4705 Federal Building,
St. Louis, Mo. 63103
Veterans affairs.

Vocational Rehabilitation Department
1448 W. Kunklin,
Jefferson City, Mo. 65102
Vocational training rehabilitation.
(9 local offices)

MONTANA

Division of Vocational Rehabilitation
508 Power Block,
Helena, Mont. 59601
Vocational training rehabilitation.

Goodwill Industries of America, Inc.
Write to the national office, 1913 N
St., N.W., Washington, D.C. 20036
for address of nearest local office.
Employment of disabled persons
according to their limitations.

Montana Society for Crippled Children
and Adults, Inc.
    4400 Central Ave., P.O. Box 805,
    Great Falls, Mont. 59401
    Occupational and physical therapy.
    Write for address of nearest
    local office.
Montana State Employment Service
    Employment counseling and placement.
    See telephone directory for the
    nearest local office.
Small Business Administration
    Main St. and 6th Ave.,
    Helena, Mont. 59601
    Organizational advice and financial
    help for the self-employed.
U.S. Civil Service Commission
    Employment with U.S. Government.
    Write to the regional office in
    Washington State.
U.S. Veterans Administration
    Veterans Administration Hospital,
    Fort Harrison, Mont. 59636
    Veterans affairs.
Vocational Rehabilitation for the Blind
    Department of Public Welfare,
    10th and North Ewing Sts.,
    Helena, Mont. 59601
    Vocational rehabilitation of the blind.

NEBRASKA

Division of Rehabilitation Services
    Room 1518, State Capitol Building,
    Lincoln, Neb. 68509
    Vocational training rehabilitation.
Goodwill Industries of America, Inc.
    Write to the national office, 1913 N
    St., N.W., Washington, D.C. 20036
    for address of nearest local office.
    Employment of disabled persons
    according to their limitations.
Nebraska Society for Crippled Children
and Adults, Inc.
    402 S. 17th St.,
    Omaha, Neb. 68102
    Occupational and physical therapy.
    Write for address of nearest
    local office.
Nebraska State Employment Service
    Employment with U.S. Government.

    See telephone directory for the
    nearest local office.
Services for the Visually Impaired
    State Capitol Building,
    Lincoln, Neb. 68509
    Vocational training rehabilitation.
    (2 local offices)
Small Business Administration
    215 N. 17th St.,
    Omaha, Neb. 68102
    Organizational advice and financial
    help for the self-employed.
U.S. Veterans Administration
    220 South 17th St.,
    Lincoln, Neb. 68508
    Veterans affairs.

NEVADA

Bureau of Service to the Blind
    515 East Musser St.,
    Carson City, Nev. 89701
    Vocational rehabilitation of the blind.
Goodwill Industries of America, Inc.
    Write to the national office, 1913 N
    St., N.W., Washington, D.C. 20036
    for address of nearest local office.
    Employment of disabled persons
    according to their limitations.
Nevada Society for Crippled Children
and Adults, Inc.
    235 Chism St.,
    Reno, Nev. 89503
    Occupational and physical therapy.
    Write for address of nearest
    local office.
Nevada State Employment Service
    Employment counseling and placement.
    See the telephone directory for the
    nearest local office.
Small Business Administration
    1721 E. Charleston St.,
    Las Vegas, Nev. 89104
    Organizational advice and financial
    help for the self-employed.
U.S. Civil Service Commission
    Employment with U.S. Government.
    Write to the regional office in
    California.
U.S. Department of Commerce
    300 Booth St.,

Reno, Nev. 89502
Marketing and commercial information.
Vocational Rehabilitation Division
Heroes Memorial Building,
Carson City, Nev. 89701
Vocational training rehabilitation.

NEW HAMPSHIRE

The Easter Seal Agency of
New Hampshire
  80 Tarrytown Road,
  Manchester, N.H. 03103
  Occupational and physical therapy.
  Write for address of nearest
  local office.
Goodwill Industries of America, Inc.
  Write to the national office, 1913 N
  St., N.W., Washington, D.C. 20036
  for address of nearest local office.
  Employment of disabled persons
  according to their limitations.
New Hampshire State Employment
Service
  Employment counseling and placement.
  See telephone directory for the
  nearest local office.
Service to the Blind, New Hampshire
Department of Health and Welfare
  State House Annex,
  Concord, N.H. 03301
  Vocational training rehabilitation.
Small Business Administration
  18 School St.,
  Concord, N.H. 03310
  Organization advice and financial
  help for the self-employed.
U.S. Civil Service Commission
  Employment with U.S. Government.
  Write the regional office in
  Massachusetts.
U.S. Veterans Administration
  State House Annex,
  Concord, N.H. 03301
  Vocational training rehabilitation.

NEW JERSEY

Commission for the Blind
  1100 Raymond Blvd.,
  Newark, N.J. 07102

Vocational training rehabilitation.
  (3 local offices)
Goodwill Industries of America, Inc.
  Write to the national office, 1913 N
  St., N.W., Washington, D.C. 20036
  for address of nearest local office.
  Employment of disabled persons
  according to their limitations.
JOB (Just-One-Break, Inc.)
  369 Union St.,
  Hackensack, N.J.
  Kessler Institute,
  Pleasant Valley-Way,
  West Orange, N.J.
  Free employment service for
  the disabled.
New Jersey Rehabilitation Commission
  Labor and Industry Building,
  John Fitch Plaza,
  Trenton, N.J. 08625
  Vocational training rehabilitation.
  (13 local offices)
New Jersey Society for Crippled Children
and Adults, Inc.
  799 Main St.,
  Hackensack, N.J. 07601
  Occupational and physical therapy.
  Write for address of nearest
  local office.
New Jersey State Employment Service
  Employment counseling and placement.
  See telephone directory for the
  nearest local office.
Small Business Administration
  10 Commerce Court,
  Newark, N.J. 07102
  Organizational advice and financial
  help for the self-employed.
U.S. Civil Service Commission
  Employment with U.S. Government.
  Write to the regional office of
  New York City.
U.S. Veterans Administration
  20 Washington Place,
  Newark, N.J. 07102
  Veterans affairs.

NEW MEXICO

Division of Services for the Blind
  New Mexico Department of

Public Welfare,
408 Galisteo Street,
P.O. Box 2348,
Santa Fe, N.M. 87501
Vocational rehabilitation of the blind
Division of Vocational Rehabilitation
P.O. Box 2406,
Santa Fe, N.M. 87501
Vocational training rehabilitation.
Goodwill Industries of America, Inc.
Write to the national office, 1913 N
St., N.W., Washington, D.C. 20036
for address of nearest local office.
Employment of disabled persons
according to their limitations.
New Mexico Society for Crippled Children and Adults, Inc.
1802 Central Ave., S.E.,
Albuquerque, N.M. 87106
Occupational and physical therapy.
Write for address of nearest
local office.
New Mexico State Employment Service
Employment counseling and placement.
See telephone directory for the
nearest local office.
Small Business Administration
500 Gold Ave., S.W.,
Albuquerque, N.M. 87101
Organizational advice and financial
help for the self-employed.
U.S. Civil Service Commission
Employment with U.S. Government.
Write the regional office in Colorado.
U.S. Department of Commerce
U.S. Courthouse,
Albuquerque, N.M. 87101
Marketing and commercial information.
U.S. Veterans Administration
517 Gold Avenue, S.W.,
Albuquerque, N.M. 87101
Veterans affairs.

New York

Association for Crippled Children
and Adults of N.Y.
239 Park Avenue South,
New York, N.Y. 10003
Occupational and physical therapy.

Commission for the Blind and
Visually Handicapped
15 Park Row,
New York, N.Y. 10038
Vocational training rehabilitation.
Goodwill Industries of America, Inc.
Write to the national office, 1913 N
St., N.W., Washington, D.C. 20036
for address of nearest local office.
Employment of disabled persons
according to their limitations.
JOB (Just-One-Break, Inc.)
79-01 Broadway,
Elmhurst, N.Y. 11373
717 First Ave.,
New York, N.Y. 10017
Free employment service for
the disabled.
New York State Employment Service
Employment counseling and placement.
See telephone directory for the
nearest local office.
Small Business Administration
121 Ellicott St.,
Buffalo, N.Y. 12403
42 Broadway,
New York, N.Y. 10004
500 S. Salina St.,
Syracuse, N.Y. 13202
Organizational advice and financial
help for the self-employed.
State Department of Social Welfare
Commission for the Blind,
Vocational Rehabilitation Service,
112 State St.,
Albany, N.Y. 12707
(7 local offices)
State Education Department, Division of
Vocational Rehabilitation
162 Washington Ave.,
Albany, N.Y. 12210
Vocational training rehabilitation.
U.S. Civil Service Commission
220 E. 42nd St.,
New York, N.Y. 10017
Employment with U.S. Government.
U.S. Department of Commerce
117 Ellicott St.,
Buffalo, N.Y. 14203

350 Fifth Ave.,
New York, N.Y. 10001
Marketing and commercial information.
U.S. Veterans Administration
12-16 Russell Rd.,
Albany, N.Y. 12201
250 Livingston St.,
Brooklyn, N.Y. 11201
1021 Main St.,
Buffalo, N.Y. 14203
252 7th Ave.,
New York, N.Y. 10001
500 So. Salina St.,
Syracuse, N.Y. 13202
Veterans affairs.

North Carolina
Commission for the Blind
Mansion Park Building,
P.O. Box 2658,
Raleigh, N.C. 27602
Vocational rehabilitation of the blind.
Division of Vocational Rehabilitation
Department of Public Instruction,
Raleigh, N.C. 27602
Vocational training rehabilitation.
Goodwill Industries of America, Inc.
Write to the national office, 1913 N
St., N.W., Washington, D.C. 20036
for address of nearest local office.
Employment of disabled persons
according to their limitations.
North Carolina Society for Crippled
Children and Adults, Inc.
311 W. Rosemay St.,
P.O. Box 839,
Chapel Hill, N.C. 27514
Occupational and physical therapy.
Write for address of nearest
local office.
North Carolina State Employment Service
Employment counseling and placement.
See telephone directory for the
nearest local office.
Small Business Administration
201 S. Tryon St
Charlotte, N.C. 28202
Organizational advice and financial
help for the self-employed.

U.S. Civil Service Commission
Employment with U.S. Government.
Write to the regional office in Georgia.
U.S. Department of Commerce
412 U.S. Post Office Building,
Greensboro, N.C. 47402
Marketing and commercial information.
U.S. Veterans Administration
310 West 4th St.,
Winston-Salem, N.C. 27102
Veterans affairs.

North Dakota
Division of Vocational Rehabilitation
418 East Rosser,
P.O. Box 758,
Bismarck, N.D. 58501
Vocational training rehabilitation.
(5 local offices)
Goodwill Industries of America, Inc.
Write to the national office, 1913 N
St., N.W., Washington, D.C. 20036
for address of nearest local office.
Employment of disabled persons
according to their limitations.
North Dakota Society for Crippled
Children and Adults, Inc.
422 Second Ave., N.W.,
Jamestown, N.D. 58401
Occupational and physical therapy.
Write for address of nearest
local office.
Small Business Administration
207 N. 5th St.,
Fargo, N.D. 58102
Organizational advice and financial
help for the self-employed.
U.S. Civil Service Commission
Employment with U.S. Government.
Write the regional office in Missouri.
U.S. Veterans Administration
Veterans Administration Hospital,
Fargo, N.D. 58102
Veterans affairs.

Ohio
Bureau of Vocational Rehabilitation
240 S. Parson Ave.,

Columbus, Ohio 43215
Vocational training rehabilitation.

Department of Public Welfare
Division of Services for the Blind.
83 S. Washington Ave.,
Columbus, Ohio 43215
Vocational rehabilitation for the blind.

Goodwill Industries of America, Inc.
Write to the national office, 1913 N
St., N.W., Washington, D.C. 20036
for address of nearest local office.
Employment of disabled persons
according to their limitations.

Ohio Society for Crippled Children
and Adults, Inc.
311 Kendall Place,
Columbus, Ohio 43205
Occupational and physical therapy.
Write for address of nearest
local office.

Ohio State Employment Service
Employment counseling and placement.
See telephone directory for the
nearest local office.

Small Business Administration
4515 Federal Building,
Cincinnati, Ohio
1370 Ontario St.,
Cleveland, Ohio 44113
50 W. Gay St.,
Columbus, Ohio 43215
234 Summit St.,
Toledo, Ohio 43602
Organizational advice and financial
help for the self-employed.

U.S. Civil Service Commission
Employment with U.S. Government.
Write the regional office in Illinois.

U.S. Department of Commerce
8028 Federal Office Building,
550 Main St.,
Cincinnati, Ohio 45202
Federal Reserve Bank Building,
East 6th St. and Superior Ave.,
Cleveland, Ohio 44101
Marketing and commercial information.

U.S. Veterans Administration
Federal Office Building,
550 Main St.,

Cincinnati, Ohio 42202
Veterans affairs.

U.S. Veterans Administration
Cuyahoga Building,
216 Superior Ave.,
Cleveland, Ohio 44114
Veterans affairs.

OKLAHOMA

Goodwill Industries of America, Inc.
Write to the national office, 1913 N
St., N.W., Washington, D.C. 20036
for address of nearest local office.
Employment of disabled persons
according to their limitations.

Oklahoma Society for Crippled Children,
Inc.
722 N.W. Thirtieth St.,
Oklahoma City, Okla. 73118
Occupational and physical therapy.
Write for the address of nearest
local office.

Oklahoma State Employment Service
Employment counseling and placement.
See telephone directory for the
nearest local office.

Small Business Administration
3rd and Robinson,
Oklahoma City, Okla. 73102
Organizational advice and financial
help for the self-employed.

U.S. Civil Service Commission
Employment with U.S. Government.
Write the regional office in Texas.

U.S. Veterans Administration
Second and Court Sts.,
Muskogee, Okla. 74401
Veterans affairs.

Vocational Rehabilitation Division
307 Will Rogers Memorial
Office Building,
State Capitol Complex,
Oklahoma City, Okla. 73105
Vocational training rehabilitation.
(21 local offices)

OREGON

Division of Vocational Rehabilitation
507 Public Service Building,

Salem, Ore. 97310
Vocational training rehabilitation.
Goodwill Industries of America, Inc.
Write to the national office, 1913 N
St., N.W., Washington, D.C. 20036
for address of nearest local office.
Employment of disabled persons
according to their limitations.
Oregon Society for Crippled Children
and Adults, Inc.
200 Orton Building,
1135 S.W. Yamhill St.,
Portland, Ore. 97205
Occupational and physical therapy.
Write for address of nearest
local office.
Oregon State Commission for the Blind
535 S.E. 12th Ave.,
Portland, Ore. 97214
Vocational rehabilitation for the blind.
Oregon State Employment Service
Employment counseling and placement.
See telephone directory for the
nearest local office.
Oregon State Commission for the Blind
535 S.E. 12th Ave.,
Portland, Ore. 97214
Vocational training rehabilitation.
Small Business Administration
921 S. Washington St.,
Portland, Ore. 97205
Organizational advice and financial
help for the self-employed.
U.S. Civil Service Commission
Employment with U.S. Government.
Write the regional office in
Washington State.
U.S. Department of Commerce
217 Old U.S. Courthouse,
520 S.W. Morrison St.,
Portland, Ore. 97204
Marketing and commercial information.
U.S. Veterans Administration
208 Southwest Fifth Ave.,
Portland, Ore. 97204
Veterans affairs.

PENNSYLVANIA

Bureau of Vocational Rehabilitation
Labor and Industry Building,

7th and Forester Sts.,
Harrisburg, Pa. 17120
Vocational training rehabilitation.
(12 local offices)
Goodwill Industries of America, Inc.
Write to the national office, 1913 N
St., N.W., Washington, D.C. 20036
for address of nearest local office.
Employment of disabled persons
according to their limitations.
Office for the Blind, Department of
Public Welfare
R. 102, Health and Welfare Building,
Harrisburg, Pa. 17120
Vocational rehabilitation for the blind.
(6 local offices)
Pennsylvania Society for Crippled
Children and Adults, Inc.
1107 No. Front St.,
P.O. Box 290,
Harrisburg, Pa. 17108
Occupational and physical therapy.
Write for the address of
nearest local office.
Pennsylvania State Employment Service
Employment counseling and placement.
See the telephone directory for the
nearest local office.
Small Business Administration
1015 Chestnut St.,
Philadelphia, Pa. 19107
Organizational advice and financial
help for the self-employed.
Small Business Administration
100 Liberty Ave.,
Pittsburgh, Pa. 15222
Organizational advice and financial
help for the self-employed.
U.S. Civil Service Commission
Customhouse,
Second and Chestnut Sts.,
Philadelphia, Pa. 19106
Employment with U.S. Government.
U.S. Department of Commerce
Jefferson Building,
1015 Chestnut St.,
Philadelphia, Pa. 19107
Marketing and commercial information.
U.S. Department of Commerce
2201 Federal Building

1000 Liberty Ave.,
Pittsburgh, Pa. 15222
Marketing and commercial
information.
U.S. Veterans Administration
107 Sixth St.,
Pittsburgh, Pa. 15222
Veterans affairs.

PUERTO RICO

Goodwill Industries of America, Inc.
Write to the national office, 1913 N
St., N.W., Washington, D.C. 20036
for address of nearest local office.
Employment of disabled persons
according to their limitations.
National Society for Crippled Children
and Adults, Inc.
P.O. Box 325,
Hato Rey, P.R. 00917
Occupational and physical therapy.
Write for the address of nearest
local office.
Puerto Rico Employment Service
Employment counseling and placement.
See telephone directory for the
nearest local office.
Small Business Administration
1200 Ponce de Leon Ave.,
Santurce, P.R. 00908
Organizational advice and financial
help for the self-employed.
U.S. Civil Service Commission
Employment opportunities with U.S.
Government.
Write the regional office in Georgia.
U.S. Department of Commerce
605 Condado Ave.,
Santurce, P.R. 00907
Marketing and commercial information.
U.S. Veterans Administration
520 Ponce de Leon Ave.,
San Juan, P.R. 00910
Veterans affairs. (Including the
Virgin Islands)
Vocational Rehabilitation Division
Oksio Building, Stop 31
417 Ponce de Leon Ave.,
Hato Rey, P.R. 00910

Vocational training rehabilitation.
(12 local offices)

RHODE ISLAND

Crippled Children and Adults of
Rhode Island, Inc.
333 Grotto Ave.,
Providence, R.I. 02906
Occupational and physical therapy.
Write for the address of nearest
local office.
Division of Vocational Rehabilitation
40 Fountain St.,
Providence, R.I. 02903
Vocational training rehabilitation.
Goodwill Industries of America, Inc.
Write to the national office, 1913 N
St., N.W., Washington, D.C. 20036
for address of nearest local office.
Employment of disabled persons
according to their limitations.
Rhode Island Division of Services for
the Blind
Harborside Park,
1 Washington Ave.,
Providence, R.I. 02905
Vocational training rehabilitation.
Rhode Island State Employment Service
Employment counseling and placement.
See the telephone directory for the
nearest local office.
Small Business Administration
57 Eddy St.,
Providence, R.I. 02903
Organizational advice and financial
help for the self-employed.
U.S. Civil Service Commission
Employment with U.S. Government.
Write the regional office in
Massachusetts.
U.S. Veterans Administration
Federal Building,
Kennedy Plaza,
Providence, R.I. 02903
Veterans affairs.

SOUTH CAROLINA

Goodwill Industries of America, Inc.
Write to the national office, 1913 N

St., N.W., Washington, D.C. 20036
for address of nearest local office.
Employment of disabled persons
according to their limitations.
Small Business Administration
1801 Assembly St.,
Columbia, S.C. 29201
Organizational advice and financial
help for the self-employed.
South Carolina Society for Crippled
Children and Adults, Inc.
1517 Laurel St.,
Columbia, S.C. 29201
Occupational and physical therapy.
Write for the address of nearest
local office.
South Carolina State Employment Service
Employment counseling and placement.
See telephone directory for the
nearest local office.
State Department of Public Welfare
P.O. Box 1108
Columbia, S.C. 29202
Vocational training rehabilitation.
U.S. Civil Service Commission
Employment with U.S. Government.
Write to the regional office in Georgia.
U.S. Department of Commerce
Federal Building, Suite 631,
334 Meeting St.,
Charleston, S.C. 29403
Marketing and commercial information.
U.S. Veterans Administration
1801 Assembly Road,
Columbia, S.C. 29201
Veterans affairs.
Vocational Rehabilitation Department
State Office Building,
400 Wade Hampton,
Columbia, S.C. 29201
Vocational training rehabilitation.

SOUTH DAKOTA

Division of Vocational Rehabilitation
State Capitol Building,
Pierre, S.D. 57501
Vocational training rehabilitation.
Goodwill Industries of America, Inc.
Write to the national office, 1913 N

St., N.W., Washington, D.C. 20036
for address of nearest local office.
Employment of disabled persons
according to their limitations.
Small Business Administration
402 8th and Main Ave.,
Sioux Falls, S.D. 57102
Organizational advice and financial
help for the self-employed.
South Dakota Service to the Blind
and Visually Handicapped
802 N. Euclid Ave.,
Pierre, S.D. 57501
Vocational rehabilitation of the blind.
South Dakota Society for Crippled
Children and Adults, Inc.
201 E. Capital Ave.,
P.O. Box 252,
Pierre, S.D. 57501
Occupational and physical therapy.
Write for the address of nearest
local office.
South Dakota State Employment Service
Employment counseling and placement.
See telephone directory for the
nearest local office.
U.S. Civil Service Commission
Employment with U.S. Government.
Write the regional office in Missouri.
U.S. Veterans Administration
Veterans Administraton Hospital,
Sioux Falls, S.D. 57101
Veterans affairs.

TENNESSEE

Blind Service Section, Department of
Public Welfare
303 State Office Building,
Nashville, Tenn. 37219
Vocational rehabilitation for the blind.
(7 local offices)
Division of Vocational Rehabilitation
Room 615, 1717 West End Building,
Nashville, Tenn. 37203
Vocational training rehabilitation.
Goodwill Industries of America, Inc.
Write to the national office, 1913 N
St., N.W., Washington, D.C. 20036
for address of nearest local office.

Employment of disabled persons according to their limitations.

Small Business Administration
301 S. Cumberland Ave.,
Knoxville, Tenn. 37902
Organizational advice and financial help for the self-employed.

Small Business Administration
500 Union St.,
Nashville, Tenn. 37219
Organizational advice and financial help for the self-employed.

Tennessee Society for Crippled Children and Adults, Inc.
119 Seventeenth Ave., So.,
Nashville, Tenn. 37203
Occupational and physical therapy. Write for the address of nearest local office.

Tennessee State Employment Service
Employment counseling and placement. See telephone directory for the nearest local office.

U.S. Civil Service Commission
Employment with U.S. Government. Write to the regional office in Georgia.

U.S. Department of Commerce
345 Federal Office Building,
167 North Main St.,
Memphis, Tenn. 38103
Marketing and commercial information.

U.S. Veterans Administration
U.S. Courthouse,
807 Broadway,
Nashville, Tenn. 37203
Veterans affairs.

TEXAS

Goodwill Industries of America, Inc.
Write to the national office, 1913 N St., N.W., Washington, D.C. 20036 for address of nearest local office. Employment of disabled persons according to their limitations.

Small Business Administration
Organizational advice and financial help for the self-employed.

1025 Elm St.,
Dallas, Tex. 75202
201 Fannin St.,
Houston, Tex. 77002
1616 19th St.,
Lubbock, Tex. 79401
101 E. Austin St.,
Marshall, Tex. 75671
410 S. Main St.,
San Antonio, Tex. 78204

State Commission for the Blind
State Office Building,
318 Sam Houston,
Austin, Tex. 78710
Vocational rehabilitation for the blind. (8 local offices)

Texas Society for Crippled Children and Adults, Inc.
4429 No. Central Expressway,
Dallas, Tex. 75205
Occupational and physical therapy. Write for the address of the nearest local office.

U.S. Civil Service Commission
1114 Commerce St.,
Dallas, Tex. 75202
Employment with U.S. Government.

U.S. Department of Commerce
Marketing and commercial information.
1114 Commerce Street,
Dallas, Tex. 75202
515 Rusk Ave.,
Houston, Tex. 77002

U.S. Veterans Administration
Veterans affairs.
515 Rusk Ave.,
Houston, Tex. 77061
1612 19th St.,
Lubbock, Tex. 79401
307 Dwyer Ave.,
San Antonio, Tex. 78204
121 So. Sixth St.,
Waco, Tex. 76703

Vocational Rehabilitation Division
Texas Education Agency
Capitol Station,
Austin, Tex. 78711
Vocational training rehabilitation. (37 local offices)

UTAH

Division of Vocational Rehabilitation
   136 E. South Temple,
   Salt Lake City, Utah 84111
   Vocational training rehabilitation.
   (3 local offices)
Goodwill Industries of America, Inc.
   Write to the national office, 1913 N
   St., N.W., Washington, D.C. 20036
   for address of nearest local office.
   Employment of disabled persons
   according to their limitations.
Small Business Administration
   125 State St., South,
   Salt Lake City, Utah 84111
   Organizational advice and financial
   help to the self-employed.
U.S. Civil Service Commission
   Employment with U.S. Government.
   Write to the regional office in Colorado.
U.S. Department of Commerce
   3235 Federal Building,
   125 South State St.,
   Salt Lake City, Utah 84111
   Marketing and commercial information.
U.S. Veterans Administration
   125 South State St.,
   Salt Lake City, Utah 84111
   Veterans affairs.
Utah Society for Crippled Children
and Adults, Inc.
   560 So. West Temple,
   Salt Lake City, Utah 84101
   Occupational and physical therapy.
   Write for the address of nearest
   local office.
Utah State Employment Service
   Employment counseling and placement.
   See telephone directory for the
   nearest local office.

VERMONT

Division of Services for the Blind
   Department of Social Welfare,
   128 State St.,
   Montpelier, Vt. 05602
   Vocational rehabilitation for the blind.
Small Business Administration
   State St.,
   Montpelier, Vt. 05601
   Organizational advice and financial
   help for the self-employed.
U.S. Civil Service Commission
   Employment with U.S. Government.
   Write to the regional office in
   Massachusetts.
U.S. Veterans Administration
   Veterans Administration Hospital,
   White River Junction, Vt. 05001
   Veterans affairs.
Vermont Association for the Crippled,
Inc.
   88 Park St.,
   Rutland, Vt. 05701
   Occupational and physical therapy.
   Write for the address of nearest
   local office.
Vermont State Employment Service
   Employment counseling and placement.
   See telephone directory for the
   nearest local office.
Vocational Rehabilitation Division
   State Office Building,
   Montpelier, Vt. 05602
   Vocational training rehabilitation.
   (4 local offices)

VIRGINIA

Goodwill Industries of America, Inc.
   Write to the national office, 1913 N
   St., N.W., Washington, D.C. 20036
   for address of nearest local office.
   Employment of disabled persons
   according to their limitations.
Small Business Administration
   1904 Byrd Ave.,
   Richmond, Va. 23226
   Ogranizational advice and financial
   help for the self-employed.
State Department of Vocational
Rehabilitation
   P.O. Box 11045,
   4615 West Broad St.,
   Richmond, Va. 23230
   Vocational training rehabilitation.
U.S. Civil Service Commission
   Employment with U.S. Government.

Write to the regional office of
Pennsylvania.
U.S. Department of Commerce
400 North 8th St.,
Richmond, Va. 23240
Marketing and commercial information.
U.S. Veterans Administration
211 West Campbell Ave.,
Roanoke, Va. 24011
Veterans affairs.
Virginia Commission for the Visually
Handicapped
3003 Parkwood Ave.,
Richmond, Va. 23221
Vocational training rehabilitation.
Virginia Society for Crippled Children
and Adults, Inc.
4841 Williamson Rd.,
P.O. Box 5496
Roanoke, Va. 24008
Occupational and physical therapy.
Write for the address of nearest
local office.
Virginia State Employment Service
Employment counseling and placement.
See telephone directory for the
nearest local office.

WASHINGTON

Division of Vocational Rehabilitation
P.O. Box 528,
Olympia, Wash. 98501
Vocational training rehabilitation.
(13 local offices)
Goodwill Industries of America, Inc.
Write to the national office, 1913 N
St., N.W., Washington, D.C. 20036
for address of your nearest local office.
Employment of disabled persons
according to their limitations.
Department of Public Assistance, Office
of Program Development, Services for
the Blind
P.O. Box 1162,
Olympia, Wash. 98501
Vocational training rehabilitation.
Services for the Blind
3411 S. Alaska St.,
Seattle, Wash. 98118
Vocational rehabilitation for the blind.

Small Business Administration
506 2nd Ave.,
Seattle, Wash. 98140
Organizational advice and financial
help for the self-employed.
Small Business Administration
N. 108 Washington St.,
Spokane, Wash. 99201
Organizational advice and financial
help for the self-employed.
U.S. Civil Service Commission
302 Federal Office Building,
First Ave. and Madison St.,
Seattle, Wash. 98104
Employment with U.S. Government.
U.S. Veterans Administration
Sixth and Lenora Building,
Seattle, Wash. 98121
Washington Society for Crippled
Children and Adults, Inc.
2233 Fifth Ave.,
Seattle, Wash. 98121
Occupational and physical therapy.
Write for the address of the
nearest local office.
Washington State Employment Service
Employment counseling and placement.
See telephone directory for the
nearest local office.

WEST VIRGINIA

Division of Vocational Rehabilitation
Service
West Wing, State Capitol Building,
Charleston, W.Va. 25305
Vocational training rehabilitation.
(18 local offices)
Goodwill Industries of America, Inc.
Write to the national office, 1913 N
St., N.W., Washington, D.C. 20036
for address of nearest local office.
Employment of disabled persons
according to their limitations.
Small Business Administration
227 W. Pike St.,
Clarksburg, W.Va. 26301
500 Quarrier St.,
Charleston, W.Va. 25301
Organizational advice and financial
help for the self-employed.

U.S. Department of Commerce
3002 New Federal Office Building,
500 Quarrier St.,
Charleston, W.Va. 25301
Marketing and commercial information.

U.S. Civil Service Commission
Employment with U.S. Government.
Write to the regional office in
Pennsylvania.

U.S. Veterans Administration
502 West Eighth St.,
Huntington, W.Va. 25701
Veterans affairs.

West Virginia Society for Crippled
Children and Adults, Inc.
612 Virginia St., E-Room 200,
Charleston, W.Va. 25301
Occupational and physical therapy.
Write for the address of nearest
local office.

West Virginia State Employment Service
Employment counseling and placement.
See telephone directory for the
nearest local office.

WISCONSIN

Division of Public Assistance
State Department of Public Welfare
1 W. Wilson St.,
Madison, Wis. 53702
Vocational training rehabilitation.
(8 local offices)
Vocational rehabilitation for the blind.
(9 local offices)

Goodwill Industries of America, Inc.
Write to the national office, 1913 N
St., N.W., Washington, D.C. 20036
for address of nearest local office.
Employment of disabled persons
according to their limitations.

Small Business Administration
Organizational advice and financial
help for the self-employed.
25 W. Main St.,
Madison, Wis. 53703
238 W. Wisconsin Ave.,
Milwaukee, Wis. 53202

U.S. Civil Service Commission
Employment with the U.S. Government.

See the telephone directory for the
nearest local office.

U.S. Department of Commerce
Strauss Building,
238 W. Wisconsin Ave.,
Milwaukee, Wis. 53203
Marketing and commercial information.

U.S. Veterans Administration
342 North Water,
Milwaukee, Wis. 53202
Veterans affairs.

Rehabilitation Division
State Board of Vocational,
Technical and Adult Education,
1 W. Wilson St.,
Madison, Wis. 53702
Vocational training rehabilitation.

Wisconsin Easter Seal Society for
Crippled Children and Adults, Inc.
21 E. Gorham St.,
Madison, Wis. 53703
Occupational and physical therapy.
Write for the address of the
nearest local office.

Wisconsin State Employment Service
Employment counseling and placement.
See telephone directory for the
nearest local office.

WYOMING

Division of Vocational Rehabilitation
Special Education,
123 Capitol Building,
Cheyenne, Wyo. 82001
Vocational training rehabilitation.
(7 local offices)

Goodwill Industries of America, Inc.
Write to the national office, 1913 N
St., N.W., Washington, D.C. 20036
for address of nearest local office.
Employment of disabled persons
according to their limitations.

Small Business Administration
300 N. Center,
Casper, Wyo. 82601
Organizational advice and financial
help for the self-employed.

U.S. Civil Service Commission
Employment with U.S. Government.
Write to the regional office in Colorado.

U.S. Department of Commerce
6022 Federal Building,
2120 Capitol Ave.,
Cheyenne, Wyo. 82001
Marketing and commercial information.

U.S. Veterans Administration
2360 East Pershing Blvd.
Cheyenne, Wyo. 82001
Veterans affairs.

Wyoming Easter Seal Society for Crippled
Children and Adults, Inc.
1613 Evans St., P.O. Box 7,
Cheyenne, Wyo, 82443
Occupational and physical therapy.
Write for the address of the
nearest local office.

Wyoming State Employment Service
Employment counseling and placement.
See telephone directory for the
nearest local office.

Index